The Inspired Body

THE Inspired Body

Paul, the Corinthians, and Divine Inspiration

by
Allen Rhea Hunt

MERCER UNIVERSITY PRESS
Macon, Georgia

ISBN 0-86554-528-6

The Inspired Body: Paul, the Corinthians, and Divine Inspiration
by Allen Rhea Hunt

Copyright 1996
Mercer University Press
6316 Peake Road
Macon, Georgia 31210-3960

Library of Congress Cataloging-in-Publication Data

Hunt, Allen Rhea, 1964–
    The inspired body : Paul, the Corinthians, and divine inspiration
/ by Allen Rhea Hunt.
    viii + 168 pp.   6 x 9" (15 x 23 cm.)
    Includes bibliographical references and index.
    ISBN 0-86554-528-6 (alk. paper)
    1. Bible. N. T. Corinthians, 1st. II, 6–16—Criticism,
interpretation, etc. 2. Inspiration—Biblical teaching. 3. Inspiration
in literature—History and criticism. 4. Paul, the Apostle, Saint.
I. Title.
BS2675.2.H76 1996
227'.206—dc20   96–36074
                                                        CIP

Contents

Part II: A New Reading of I Corinthians 2:6-16 and Its Implications

Preface

Investment in its variety of forms fuels the world, including one's ability to pursue a graduate degree. The most important of the many investments represented in this work has been the complete personal investment of my wife, Anita, and our two daughters, Sarah Ann and Griffin Elizabeth. Their love and support has been not only vital but also unwavering. The commitment of Fr. Steven Boguslawski, O.P., has approached that of an intimate family member as well.

Financial investment is often an unsung hero in scholarship, but a neglect to mention its value does not lessen its critical role. I am most grateful for the financial support of Ray and Jerry Ann Griffin, Brunner and Pat Hunt, A Foundation for Theological Education, and Yale University, all of whose support clearly represents an investment in my own potential as a scholar, teacher, and minister.

The paedogogical investment of countless teachers has contributed to my own intellectual development. For this, too, I am grateful. Professor Wayne Meeks has been a faithful guide and director for my work and the dissertation on which this book is based. Yale Professors Abraham Malherbe, Susan Garrett, and David Bartlett also provided critical viewpoints that have proven invaluable. Teachers from Candler, like Fred Craddock, Carl Holladay, and Carol Newsom, have all had significant influences on my professional growth in New Testament scholarship. Education is a cumulative process; thus, it is important to recognize also the investments of particularly good earlier teachers like Wayne Mixon at Mercer University, Clara Hirschfield at Lakeland (FL) High School, and Sonia Lyda at Brevard (NC) Middle School.

Also, my gratitude for the personal friendships of a variety of colleagues merits specific mention. Charles E. Hoover, Fr. Dean Béchard, SJ, Craig Wansink, Rebecca Krawiec, Ferrell Drummond, the Dominican Sisters at The Monastery of Our Lady of Grace, and the saints at Hamden Plains United Methodist Church and Chapel Hill United Methodist have all given to this effort far more than they have received. Thank you.

ταῖς ἐπὶ 'Ορᾶνγ καὶ Κάννερ

Abbreviations and Citations

Abbreviations for biblical, apocryphal, intertestamental, rabbinic books, early patristic writings, and periodicals and series may be found in the instructions for contributors for *Journal of Biblical Literature* 107 (1988): 579-96, and in Liddell-Scott-Jones, *A Greek-English Lexicon with Supplement* (Oxford: Clarendon, 1968) xvi-xlv. References to other classical texts and to some periodicals and series follow the abbreviations listed in the *Oxford Classical Dictionary*.

Classical texts are cited according to the text and translation of the Loeb Classical Library editions where available, all of which are listed in the bibliography.

Introduction

The Problem

Divine inspiration is an attribute often ascribed to the New Testament but rarely considered from a historical viewpoint. At the same time, the New Testament seems a reasonable place to look for such a historical viewpoint since it is usually the body of texts being described as inspired in the first place. Moreover, given the data we possess regarding the historical realia of the Pauline churches and the literary correspondence between these churches and their founder, the letters of Paul appear to offer a particularly rich mine in which to search for clues regarding early Christian views of divine inspiration. Would Paul have considered himself or, more specifically, his writings to be divinely inspired?[1] If so, how would he define and describe this phenomenon? Most importantly, are there any clues in the Pauline letters we now possess regarding this issue of inspiration?

Texts that immediately come to mind when one considers the concept of divine inspiration in the New Testament are 1 Cor 2:6-16 and 1 Corinthians 7.[2] The discussion in 1 Corinthians 7 mixes a variety of

---

[1]Works that were particularly instrumental in the beginning of my formulation of questions such as these are Leander Keck, "Images of Paul in the New Testament," *Interpretation* 43 (1989): 341-51; and George Lyons, *Pauline Autobiography: Toward a New Understanding*, SBLDS (Atlanta: Scholars, 1985). Keck looks briefly at several key images used by Paul to describe his own activity while Lyons focuses on the Pauline use of autobiography in Galatians and 1 Thessalonians. These two works raised questions regarding how Paul portrays himself in his letters, and more specifically, how he might understand any possibility of his own inspiration.

[2]For example, in the biblical theology of Peter Stuhlmacher, these texts prove central to his discussion regarding the divine inspiration of scripture. Cf. his *Biblische Theologie des Neuen Testaments* (Göttingen: Vandenhoeck und Ruprecht, 1: 1992–2: forthcoming). However, I wonder if he does not collapse the notions of inspiration, scripture, and authority into a single category. Such a category would identify scripture that is deemed as authoritative in a particular religious community as also inspired by definition. Such

issues as Paul provides ethical directives regarding sexual relations and
marriage, directives that he bases on various authorities such as possible
sayings of, or traditions about, Jesus, Paul's own authority as the
church's founder, as well as Paul's own authority as an apostle.[3] At 7:10,
he says, "To the married I command, not I but the Lord." At 7:12, Paul
reverses that statement when he says, "To the rest I say, not the Lord."
At 7:25, Paul then states that he has no command of the Lord but gives
his own trustworthy opinion, and finally, at 7:40, Paul says, "I think that
I too have the spirit of God." A reading of claims to divine inspiration
in these statements or this chapter, however, seems erroneous. More
likely, Paul eschews specific claims for himself and appeals instead to
other sources and traditions for his directives because of the uncertain
position he now occupies in the Corinthian church. Moreover, at 7:32-35,
Paul makes his objectives known. He is concerned with the Corinthians'
benefit and with their single-minded devotion to the Lord. Even reading
1 Cor 7:40 as a claim to inspiration will not hold up to careful exegetical
scrutiny.[4] Probably then, Paul uses these claims more to locate the
authority of his statements than to say anything in particular about divine
inspiration.[5]

---

a definition, however, does not seem particularly helpful for a historical investigation of
Paul's own self-references and claims to authority in letters not originally viewed as
canonical scripture by Christians. Nor is such a definition helpful for viewing Paul's
comments on inspiration, a phenomenon that may have also extended, as I intend to
demonstrate, beyond his preaching and writing to the activities of other Christians in
forms such as prophecy, teaching, speaking in tongues, and prayer.

[3]For an important and thorough discussion of the nature of Paul's authority, see John
Howard Schütz, *Paul and the Anatomy of Apostolic Authority* (Cambridge: University
Press, 1975). For possible Jesus sayings in 1 Corinthians 7, see Peter Richardson and
Peter Gooch, "Logia of Jesus in 1 Corinthians," *Gospel Perspectives: The Jesus Tradition
Outside the Gospel*, 5, ed. David Wenham (Sheffield: JSOT Press, 1985) 39-62. Cf. also
Dale Allison, "The Pauline Epistles and the Synoptic Gospels: The Pattern of the
Parallels," *NTS* 28 (1982): 1-32; and David L. Dungan, *The Sayings in the Churches of
Paul: The Use of the Synoptic Tradition in the Regulation of Early Church Life*
(Philadelphia: Fortress, 1971).

[4]1 Cor 7:40b is discussed in more detail in later chapters of this investigation.

[5]It is a peculiarly modern notion that claims to inspiration are to be equated by
necessity with claims to authority. For a discussion of various modern theological
positions regarding inspiration, cf. Donald K. McKim, ed. *The Authoritative Word: Essays
on the Nature of Scripture* (Grand Rapids: Eerdmans, 1983).

On the other hand, 1 Cor 2:6-16, traditionally vexing to interpreters because of its rather opaque language, is especially attractive for an investigation of Paul's view of inspiration because there Paul says: "We do speak a wisdom among the perfect" (2:6a); "We speak God's wisdom, secret and hidden" (2:7a); "We speak of these things in words not taught by human wisdom but taught by the Spirit" (2:13a); and "We have the mind of Christ" (2:16b).[6] These statements seem less interested in establishing the authority of Paul's directives and more interested in staking some kind of claim to inspiration. In other words, unlike in chapter 7, here in chapter 2 Paul focuses on the notion of the divine communication of knowledge to humans and the possible articulation of that knowledge to others. Moreover, this particular passage has played an important role in subsequent discussions of inspiration.[7]

What exactly does Paul mean here by speaking "wisdom" and having the "mind of Christ?" In addition, to whom does he refer as "we?" Are the wisdom speakers here simply an editorial "we" applying only to Paul, or to himself and some select group of preachers or prophets, or to a wider body of specially designated recipients and proclaimers of wisdom, or even to all Christians? Finally, why does Paul talk here of a secret and hidden wisdom immediately after seemingly having denigrated wisdom immediately prior in 1:18–2:5? Questions like these merit considerably more attention than has been awarded to this often-discussed but rarely elucidated passage.[8] In an effort to understand better Paul's conception

---

[6]Citations from scripture come from the RSV. If a citation varies from the RSV, the translation is my own unless otherwise noted.

[7]Christian thinkers as diverse as Clement of Alexandria, Origen, Augustine, Luther, and Bultmann all have made this text important for various reasons, often in their discussions of Christian inspiration and communication. For an introduction to such uses, see Peter Stuhlmacher, "The Hermeneutical Significance of 1 Cor. 2:6-16," trans. Colin Brown, *Tradition and Interpretation in the New Testament: Essays in Honor of E. E. Ellis*, ed. Gerald F. Hawthorne and Hans Dieter Betz (Grand Rapids: Eerdmans, 1987) 328-43.

[8]The citation of an unknown text in 2:9 has also generated much interest. I will not give much attention to the nature of this citation, especially its origin. For such information, see Pierre Prigent, "Ce que l'oeil n'a pas vu, 1 Cor 2.9," *ThZ* 14 (1958): 416-29; Ottfried Hofius, "Das Zitat 1 Kor 2:9 und das koptische Testament des Jakobs," *ZNW* 66 (1975): 140-42; H. Ponsot, "D'Isaie 64:3 a la 1 Corinthiens 2:9," *RB* 90 (1983): 229-42; E. Von Nordheim, "Das Zitat des Paulus in 1 Kor 2:9 und seine Beziehung zum koptischen Testament Jakobs," *ZNW* 65 (1974): 112-20; and Klaus Berger, "Zur

of inspiration, my investigation therefore begins with a focus on 1 Cor 2:6-16.

Previous Scholarship

Several potential exegetical and theological benefits can emerge by seeking to understand these issues surrounding 1 Cor 2:6-16. First, of course, this passage can provide important information about one early Christian view of inspiration. Second, I hope to produce a better comprehension of the original context of this language as well as the function of this passage within 1 Corinthians. This understanding includes not only garnering information about what Paul is seeking to achieve here but also how the language might have been heard by the first-century Corinthian Christians. Third, it is important to investigate the prominent role of the Spirit (πνεῦμα) in 1 Cor 2:6-16 since the claims to inspiration from and possession of the Spirit in this passage have produced various interpretations throughout the history of interpretation. By doing so, I hope to read this esoteric passage in a new light that will illumine a passage that heretofore has escaped a consensus of scholarly interpretation.

Crucial to these areas of inquiry is the need for understanding this passage's relatively uncommon language and its background. For example, unique to this passage is the Pauline claim to speak a wisdom (σοφία: 2:6) hidden in mystery (ἐν μυστηρίῳ: 2:7) among the perfect (τέλειος: 2:6). Interesting also is the concentration of forms and cognates of κρίνω and γινώσκω as well as the use of relatively uncommon words like ἐραυνάω and βάθος. The unique character of these ideas and this language, along with their presence in this letter, has led many interpreters to assume that these necessarily are terms and ideas of the Corinthians themselves or of some subset of the congregation.[9] By

Diskussion über die Herkunft von 1 Kor 2:9," *NTS* 24 (1978): 270-83. Given this citation's presence in Pseudo-Philo's *Biblical Antiquities* 26.13, it seems likely that Paul did not compose it. In later Christian literature, this quotation gains broad coverage in texts such as 1 Clement 34:8 and Clement *Protrept.* 10:76 and 12:91.

[9]Variations on this theme occur in most of the scholarly literature on this passage. Ulrich Wilckens represents one end of the spectrum with his position that the passage reflects only the theology of Paul's opponents in Corinth, a theology which Paul refutes

seeking a broader understanding of this language's use in antiquity and of Paul's selection of such words in this context, however, I think that a sharper reading of this passage can be gained.

The history of scholarly interpretation of this passage is frequently marked by misconception. The language of this passage has been linked to the milieu of the mystery religions;[10] it has been used to posit a Pauline bifurcation of Christians into rigid strata of the mature and the infantile;[11] it has been understood as a digression from the topic at hand in chapters 1–4;[12] and it has even been deemed an anti-Pauline interpolation.[13] Much of this problem has been due to a tendency to insist on locating the background of this passage either solely in the mystery religions or in Judaism; however, an either/or categorization is not necessary and ultimately only obfuscates interpretation.

Not surprisingly, Wilhelm Bousset and Richard Reitzenstein claim that the language of 1 Cor 2:6-16 simply originates in the mysteries. For Bousset and Reitzenstein, the means for locating this text exclusively in the realm of the mysteries begins with Paul's use of τέλειος in 2:6 and μυστήριον in 2:7, two key terms that Reitzenstein claims are part of a fixed sacral formula in "most Oriental religions and Gnosticism."[14] Using

---

in 3:1ff. Cf. his *Weisheit und Torheit: Eine exegetische-religionsgeschichtliche Untersuchung zu 1 Kor. 1 und 2*, BHTh 26 (Tübingen: JCB Mohr, 1959) 52-96. Robin Scroggs, "Paul: Σοφός καὶ πνευματικός," *NTS* 14 (1967–1968): 33-55, represents the other end of the spectrum with the claim that this passage says almost nothing about Paul's Corinthian opponents. Dieter Lührmann, *Das Offenbarungsverständnis bei Paulus und in paulinischen Gemeinden*, WMANT 16 (Neukirchen-Vluyn: Neukirchener Verlag des Erziehungsvereins, 1965) 114ff., represents a middle position that claims that Paul takes over a portion of his opponents' preaching and modifies it.

[10]*E.g.*, Wilhelm Bousset, *Der Erste Brief an die Korinther*, Die Schrifte des Neuen Testaments 2, 3rd ed. (Göttingen: Vandenhoeck und Ruprecht, 1917) 84. See also Richard Reitzenstein, *Hellenistic Mystery Religions*, trans. J. E. Steely, Pittsburgh Theological Monographs 15 (Pittsburgh: Pickwick, 1978) 358.

[11]*E.g.*, Rudolf Bultmann, *Faith and Understanding*, vol. 1, trans. L. P. Smith (New York: Harper and Row, 1969).

[12]*E.g.*, Hans Conzelmann, *1 Corinthians*, Hermeneia, trans. J. W. Leitch (Philadelphia: Fortress, 1975) 57, who sees this passage as counteracting the preceding section of the letter.

[13]Martin Widmann, "1 Kor. 2: 6-16: Ein Einspruch gegen Paulus," *ZNW* 70 (1979): 44-53.

[14]Reitzenstein, 432.

The Inspired Body

evidence from Plato and Apuleius, Reitzenstein consistently reads τέλειος throughout ancient literature as the "perfect" or the "initiated." He also takes this term to represent the reception of the consummating vision of God in the mysteries.[15] Moreover, Reitzenstein deepens his claim of Hellenistic mystery influences in Paul by interpreting this term, τέλειος, as a technical designation for the person who has the capacity to νοεῖν and who has full γνῶσις, terms that also appear in 1 Cor 2:6-16.[16] In doing so, Reitzenstein and Bousset aim to mark the parallels between Pauline Christianity and the Hellenistic mystery cults and to posit lines of influence between the two. In fact, Reitzenstein makes this passage central to his investigation and claims that it provides decisive proof for his theory that "Paul is a pneumatic."[17] Thus, Reitzenstein sees Hellenistic formulaic language as the key for the interpretation of 1 Cor 2:6-16, and he also sees Paul as standing in the early stages of a Gnostic dualism that would develop in earnest over subsequent centuries.[18]

Bultmann uses the work of Reitzenstein and Bousset to bolster the case for the existence of a full-fledged pre-Christian Gnosticism, so Bultmann also interprets this passage in light of the language of the mystery cults. In fact, he sees all of 1 Cor 2:6–3:2 as the amalgamation of Paul's ideas and those ideas peculiar to the mysteries. He bases this interpretation on the presence of πνεῦμα, τέλειος, and ψυχικός in

---

[15]Cf. Birger Pearson, *The Pneumatikos-Psychikos Terminology in 1 Corinthians: A Study in the Theology of the Corinthian Opponents of Paul and Its Relation to Gnosticism*, SBLDS 12 (Missoula MT: Scholars Press, 1973). Pearson rightly rejects this position by showing that the mere presence of a word is not enough to locate this language exclusively in the mysteries. Instead, Pearson, 28, proposes a broader background of Stoicism and Hellenistic Judaism as reflected in Philo, who enlarges the philosophical usage of τέλειος to include the highest religious attainments as well as the achievement of σοφία. Later, I will build on such a position and enlarge it still further.

[16]Reitzenstein bases this claim on Philo but cites no texts in support. He also routinely refers to the "mysteries" throughout the work, yet such a term seems so broad as to elude usefulness in comparison with a text like 1 Cor 2:6-16. For example, see his 433.

[17]Reitzenstein, 426ff.

[18]Herein lies a major problem with Reitzenstein's interpretation. Most, if not all, the textual evidence cited is from much later periods, particularly the *PGM* and the *Corpus Hermeticum*. Moreover, his penchant for generalizations about "Gnosticism" and "Mysteries" often leads to the appearance of a fully developed and documented gnostic thought system that simply is not supported by the textual evidence.

2:6-3:2. Bultmann's deeper theological interest here lies in an existential understanding of the content of wisdom and knowledge of God in order to modify Barth's materialist reading of this same passage in *The Resurrection of the Dead*. To achieve this end, Bultmann interprets 1 Cor 2:6-16 by focusing on the apparent contradictions that it holds. In this way, Bultmann exploits his conception of the pre- Christian Gnostic dualism. The contradiction is not that the Christian has the Spirit yet does not possess/own it but rather that Paul simultaneously claims that all baptized Christians have the Spirit and yet separates a certain elite class of Christian πνευματικοί or τέλειοι. Thus, Bultmann interprets these classifications quite literally and sees the ethical immaturity of the Corinthians as precluding their receiving Paul's wisdom about God and the cross.[19]

In developing further the history-of-religions work of Bultmann, Walter Schmithals and Ulrich Wilckens have posited that the language of 1 Cor 2:6-16 specifically reflects the theology of Paul's gnostic opponents in Corinth.[20] This position emphasizes the cosmological dualism evidenced in the antithetical structure of statements such as 1 Cor 2:7 and 2:12 where God stands opposite to the world. Here, the language appears to draw a radical and polar distinction between the material world and the spiritual realm, a common gnostic construction of reality. In this way, Schmithals sees this passage as Paul's apologetic defense against charges that he withheld σοφία from the Corinthians. Thus, Schmithals and Wilckens agree that 2:6-16 reproduces the understanding of the σοφία of false teachers in Corinth.[21] This passage therefore reflects the Gnostic

---

[19]See Bultmann, 70-72, for his main discussion of this passage.

[20]Ulrich Wilckens, *Weisheit*, 52-96, sees this pericope as an anti-Gnostic polemic in which Paul seeks to correct what Wilckens views as Gnostic opponents in Corinth. Wilckens later changes his position somewhat in his article, "Zu 1 Kor 2: 6-16," in *Theologia Crucis—Signum Crucis, Festschrift für Erich Dinkler zum 70. Geburtstag,* ed. Carl Andresen and Günter Klein (Tübingen: Mohr, 1979) 501-37. See also Walter Schmithals, *Gnosticism in Corinth: An Investigation of the Letter to the Corinthians,* trans. John Steely (Nashville: Abingdon, 1971). Pearson, *Pneumatikos-Psychikos Terminology,* 1-9, has provided a good refutation of such a position. He sees οἱ πνευματικοί in 1 Corinthians as those who are ἐν Χριστῷ, who therefore have received God's eschatological gift of the Spirit.

[21]Schmithals is careful to point out the minor differences between his vantage point and that of Wilckens although both insist on interpreting this passage, as well as the

Christology of the Corinthian opponents to Paul.[22] As such, Schmithals develops an entire monograph elaborating on the details of the Corinthians' gnostic positions and their specific opposition to Paul.

In moves away from a rigidly history-of-religions interpretation, Hans Conzelmann interprets the entire passage of 1 Cor 2:6-16 as a digression from the topic at hand in 1 Cor 1:10–4:21, and Martin Widmann goes still further in viewing 2:6-16 as an anti-Pauline interpolation.[23] Conzelmann fails to see any thematic or linguistic link between 2:6-16 and that which precedes it. He bases this reading largely on the seeming disparity between the views of σοφία in 1:18–2:5 and in 2:6-16. Widmann, on the other hand, takes the same evidence as Conzelmann and interprets it even more radically by proposing that the view of σοφία in 2:6-16 is so disparate from that in 1:18-2:5 that it could not possibly have been authored by Paul and therefore must have been inserted later. Moreover, Widmann claims this interpretation is anti-Pauline in character, a reading that does not differ too much from that of Wilckens who sees this passage as reflecting anti-Pauline sentiments in Corinth rather than in later interpolators of Paul's writings. Conzelmann's and Widmann's readings represent efforts to look at possibilities not admitted by earlier history-of-religions interpreters.

Birger Pearson, in his incisive and thorough dissertation seeks to broaden the background against which one reads 1 Corinthians, and

---

entire letter, through the hermeneutical overlay of "Gnosticism." However, Schmithals disagrees with Wilckens when he asserts that Paul was already familiar with the concepts of this passage. Wilckens, by contrast, sees here only the details from the preaching of Corinthian gnostics. See Schmithals, 151-54, and Wilckens, *Weisheit*, 60ff. Cf. Dieter Georgi, *The Opponents of Paul in 2nd Corinthians* (Philadelphia: Fortress, 1986). Georgi accepts the proposition that 1 Corinthians deals with gnostic opponents, but Georgi contends that 2 Corinthians presents Paul's adversaries as espousing a Christianity steeped in Hellenistic-Jewish apologetics.

[22]Little attention is given here to such a position. I reject Schmithals' viewpoint as untenable. He uses his conclusions as criteria for the initial evaluation of evidence and then posits a grand schema of ancient pre-Christian gnosticism, for which there simply is little or no textual evidence. Moreover, he overgeneralizes gnosticism by conflating the sources and their data so that the category becomes so broad that it defies any usefulness whatsoever. His version of "Gnosticism" has few if any distinctions. However, for an example of early Christian gnostic usage of 1 Cor 2:6-16, see Irenaeus *Adv. Haer.* 1.8.3.

[23]See notes 11-12 above for references.

2:6-16 in particular. By looking at Hellenistic Jewish literature in addition to gnostic texts, Pearson can contend that Paul uses his opponents' terminology but radically reinterprets it with an apocalyptic twist. In doing so, Pearson proposes that Paul holds Christian existence in his typical eschatological tension of the already and the not yet. Pearson therefore sees this passage reflecting Paul's reinterpretation of his opponents' language in an apocalyptic fashion that allows him to substitute his own concept of wisdom for that of his opponents.[24] Thus, Paul does not inherit the terms but puts his own indelible stamp on the character of Christian σοφία.

More recently, Karl Sandnes has sought to prove that Paul saw himself as standing in the succession of Old Testament prophets, a group distinct from other early Christian prophets.[25] In his study, Sandnes investigates 1 Cor 2:6-16 as one of the key texts in his effort to prove such a prophetic status for Paul. Thus, Sandnes seeks to read 2:6-16 alongside other Pauline texts that he considers to be utterances of prophetic oracles, such as 1 Cor 15:51ff and 1 Thessalonians 4:15-17. At the same time, however, Sandnes never seeks to understand or explain the language of this passage. He recognizes the "prophetic frame of reference" for 2:6-16 but fails to draw out the implications of such a frame of reference regarding what this passage is actually doing in its literary and cultural settings.

Likewise, Thomas Gillespie has also sought to demonstrate that the unstated subject of this pericope is early Christian prophecy, but he bases his argument solely on internal evidence within 1 Corinthians by linking this pericope linguistically and lexicographically to the discussions of

---

[24]See Pearson, *Pneumatikos-Psychikos Terminology*, especially chap. 4. However, a careful reading of Pearson's synthesis of his conclusions regarding this notion of reinterpretaton reveals a thoroughly Lutheran reading of the passage. *E.g.*, "Paul thus affirms the radical break between God and natural man, a break which can be bridged only from God's side" (41). Nevertheless, I do think that Pearson is fundamentally correct in his conclusion and in his rejection of Schmithals and Wilckens. Pearson overturns both the need for a theory of gnostic opponents and the need to look exclusively at gnostic literature in order to understand 1 Cor 2:6-16.

[25]See Karl Olav Sandnes, *Paul–One of the Prophets?: A Contribution to the Apostle's Self-Understanding*, Wissenschaftliche Untersuchungen zum Neuen Testament: 2 Reihe 43 (Tübingen: Mohr, 1991).

prophecy in 1 Corinthians 12 and 14.[26] Although more or less correct, his conclusion is only partially helpful because of its limited look at the evidence. Moreover, Gillespie, like Sandnes, does not move to draw out the implications of prophecy as the unstated subject here. Broadening the basis for reaching such a conclusion is important because looking at the larger phenomenon of inquiry into the divine mind in antiquity sheds light not only on this pericope and chapters 12 and 14, but also on the entire letter. More is taking place here than a simple linkage with chapters 12 and 14. Important to that view is examining how Paul adopts common cultural language but adapts it to his own purposes in a way not previously done in antiquity.

The Present Study

A number of these scholarly interpretations provide a starting point for my own investigation of the language found in 1 Cor 2:6-16. In particular, the work of Pearson, Sandnes, and Gillespie serve as building blocks for this study. Pearson rightly looks to Jewish sources, including Philo, for assistance in interpreting this passage and also seeks, like Sandnes and Gillespie, to connect 2:6-16 with Christian prophecy as it is found in 1 Corinthians 12 and 14. There is still more work to be done here, however. The background from which this passage's language and ideas develop requires more study.

Important questions for my investigation are: (1) From where does this language derive, and (2) To what purpose is it used in 2:6-16? Moreover, what does this information reveal about Paul's understanding of inspiration? My thesis first of all is that Paul draws on a common pool of language used in antiquity to describe the human search for knowledge of and from the divine. Classical authors such as Pindar, Aeschylus, and Plato, and Greco-Roman writers such as Philo, Julian, and Plutarch all utilize language like that employed by Paul in this passage. As I will discuss later in more detail, within the New Testament, the same notion

---

[26]See Thomas W. Gillespie, "Interpreting the Kerygma: Early Christian Prophecy According to 1 Corinthians 2:6-16," in *Gospel Origins and Christian Beginnings: Essays in Honor of James M. Robinson*, ed. J. Goehring, et al. (Sonoma CA: Polebridge Press, 1990) 151-66. Gillespie goes further to claim that such prophecy functioned solely to interpret the apostolic kerygma, a conclusion of which I am less convinced.

and terminology for such a search also occur at 1 Peter 1:10-12, Romans 11:33ff, and Revelation 2:23-24. For example, terms like ἐραυνάω and βάθος (1 Cor 2:10) frequent ancient discussions of the human search for divine knowledge. An emphasis on the need for divine initiative because of human inadequacy to attain such knowledge without assistance (1 Cor 2:10-12) is common to such discussions. So too is the prominent role of σοφία as the object and result of such a search (cf. 1 Cor 2:5, 6, 7, and 13). In other words, Paul seeks to describe the human search for the divine mind.

Secondly, my thesis also contends that 1 Cor 2:6-16 applies to all Christians rather than only to Paul himself. Therefore, in using this language from the larger context, Paul transforms the language from its traditionally highly individualistic frame of reference into a communal one whereby the notion of inspiration applies also to the entire Corinthian *community*. All interests and gifts are thereby subordinated to the edification and needs of the believing community. Paul's focus here is communal unity, so he aims at disarming the claims of those who would elevate themselves. He uses the language not to distinguish himself but rather to build up the community. Hence, "*We* have the mind of Christ" (2:16b: emphasis mine).

Thus, 1 Cor 2:6-16 functions in a previously unrecognized way to assist in reading the rest of 1 Corinthians. Therefore, this investigation will seek to demonstrate this new interpretation of 1 Cor 2:6-16, as it articulates the notion of communal inspiration and as it functions in 1 Corinthians to modify behavior and attitudes in the Corinthian community.

In chapter 1, I will look at some other notable ancient Greek discussions of inspiration, such as those of Plato and Plutarch. I will particularly seek to identify places where the language used or ideas expressed closely resemble those of Paul in 1 Cor 2:6-16. Chapter 2 will then move to survey similar texts from ancient Judaism as well as from some early Christian texts.

First, it will be important to corroborate that such language did indeed frequent such ancient discussions of inspiration and the human search for ultimate knowledge. For this, I will turn chiefly to several key authors: Plato, Philo, Josephus, Plutarch, and Julian.[27] A variety of other ancient texts, including the LXX, the New Testament, and other early Christian texts, will lend still more evidence here. The key authors have been chosen for the broad spectrum of viewpoints (geographical, chronological, political, philosophical, and social) that they represent[28] but also for the fact that they provide developed statements regarding inspiration. They all parallel Paul in important ways. Careful attention will be paid to the variety of contexts in which such language appears. Key questions will include: Who is inspired and how? Who is seeking divine knowledge and for whom will such knowledge be appropriated?

When investigating these texts, the method will first be descriptive and historical-critical as the texts and writers are presented and interpreted on their own terms. I will emphasize what these texts say about inspiration and how they express it. Then, in chapter 3, I will identify preliminarily in 1 Cor 2:6-16 parallels with ideas and language found in other ancient discussions of inspiration and inquiry into the divine mind. In this way, I seek to demonstrate in chapter 4 the origins and meanings of Paul's language and ideas in 1 Cor 2:6-16. I will also seek to answer questions regarding what this text is doing rhetorically not only here but also how it helps the reader to understand later passages in 1 Corinthians as well. For example, questions of a social-historical character emerge. How might the original audience have heard such language and claims? How might this passage have modified their behavior?

Chapter 4 is where I will also move to note how the language of inspiration, along with the related human search for the divine mind in 2:6-16, takes on a communal dimension and how this language functions in its setting within the broadly paraenetic section of 1:10–4:21. My

---

[27]Of course, other views of inspiration abound in ancient writers. For two examples, cf. Aristotle *Rhet.* 1408 and Iamblichus *De Myst.* 3.8; 7.4.

[28]For example, Plato and several ancient dramatists provide classical examples of such discussions that were still in the background of the first century. In literature more contemporaneous with Paul, Philo, a Hellenistic Jewish philosopher, writes in Alexandria while Josephus, also a Jew, hails from Palestine but writes in Rome. Plutarch, who writes in Chaironeia, represents a unique figure because of his clear access both to Greek intellectual life at the Platonic Academy and to Hellenistic religious practice at Delphi. Several centuries later, Julian provides an example of a thoroughly Hellenized ruler trying to reclaim a prominent role for his own synthesis of Hellenistic beliefs and practices, which were waning in influence in the culture of his time.

thesis here is that, because of the situation in Corinth, Paul eschews explicit inspiration claims for himself in order to counter the claims of superior knowledge of some members within the Corinthian community. Hence, in this chapter I will examine how Paul uses this notion of the inspired community to locate all Christians on the same spiritual plane, an idea that will be developed in more detail in the remainder of the book.

At 1 Cor 3:1-4, Paul moves to employ this notion of communal inspiration in order to modify the Corinthians' behavior and actions, particularly in relation to the problem of dissension. In chapter 5, I will examine 1 Cor 3:1-4 in an effort to elucidate how the preceding discussion of 2:6-16 serves Paul's rhetorical argument in 3:1-4. Here again Paul draws on language common to the larger cultural context when he expresses that the Corinthians were unable to receive all of the teaching that he had to offer. Further, the imagery of feeding children and babes was not uncommon to the time either. Such language, combined with terms like ζῆλος and ἔρις of 3:3 (cf. also 1:11), demonstrates Paul's concern in this passage for the Corinthians' behavior as a community and the fostering of an ethic of reciprocity and communal responsibility.

Later in the same letter, 2:6-16 also shows significant parallels with the larger discussions of Christian prophecy in 1 Corinthians 12 and 14. There Paul argues that it is possible, at least potentially, for all Christians to prophesy by virtue of their receipt of the Holy Spirit at baptism. Such a claim, working in tandem with the image of the inspired body of Christ, also serves to modify Corinthian behavior and attitudes in corporate worship activity. In chapter 6, I will move to draw connections between the communal understanding of inspiration in 2:6-16 and the discussion of similar ideas in 1 Corinthians 12. In particular, the body of Christ, with its various inward workings of the same Spirit (cf. 12:11, 13), will serve as the governing notion in an effort to demonstrate how the message of 2:6-16 underlies the discussion in 1 Corinthians 12.

In chapter 7, I will then examine 1 Corinthians 14, where corporate worship and the role of inspiration and prophecy figure in a prominent way. The linguistic parallels with this passage and the texts that already will have been examined are striking. Once more, the issue of reciprocity in communal behavior is of paramount importance, as are the issues of the role of the Spirit, the authority of the community, and the community's upbuilding.

I will then draw some conclusions from the investigation. In particular, my conclusions will focus on how 2:6-16 should be interpreted and what it reveals about a Pauline view of inspiration. It will be important here to note how Paul's views differ from those other witnesses investigated earlier in the study. Such an interpretation also has significant implications for our reading of the rest of 1 Corinthians. In the end, I plan to generate a better interpretation of 2:6-16 in order to clarify our understanding of the idea of inspiration in antiquity and to demonstrate some of Paul's primary concerns and methods in writing the Christians at Corinth. Such an understanding will have much to say not only to the historian and biblical scholar but also to the modern reader and to the church.

Chapter 1
Ancient Inquiry into the Divine Mind
The Greek Tradition

In this chapter, I examine descriptions of inspiration in several key ancient secular writers and note especially those places where the idea of the search for the divine mind occurs. This broad survey includes classical Greek dramatists and poets, Plato, Plutarch, and Julian, and it seeks to locate 1 Cor 2:6-16 against a larger cultural backdrop than has previously been done. Crucial to considering these texts is discovering how each text depicts *who* is inspired and *how* that person(s) is inspired.

Greek Drama and Poetry

A rapid and broad survey demonstrates the breadth of literature in which this notion of the human search for the divine mind can be found. On a few occasions, prominent Greek dramatists describe inspiration as well as this search for the divine mind. For example, in *Oedipus the King (OT)*, Sophocles records a conversation in which Oedipus interrogates Creon, seeking to determine whether he himself is the murderer of Laius. Creon recommends consulting the priest from Delphi who had failed to identify Oedipus earlier. Trying to understand why that priest had failed to identify him, Oedipus then asks, "Did this same prophet (μάντις) then pursue his craft? . . . But was no search (ἐρευνάω) and inquisition made? . . . Why failed the seer (ὁ σοφός) to tell his story then? (562-68)."[1] Here, the search (ἐρευνάω)[2] resembles that for a

---

[1] All citations from classical literature come from the version found in the Loeb Classical Library unless otherwise specified. When the translation varies from the Loeb edition, the translation is my own.

[2] For Paul, the form is ἐραυνάω rather than ἐρευνάω. Paul's usage reflects the later form, which had changed by Paul's time although some later users still preferred ἐρευνάω. Nearly all Christian literature uses the later form while most earlier literature uses the earlier form. The distinction is solely morphological and can be noted

criminal, yet it is used in regard to the activity of a priest at the oracle of Delphi.

Later in the same work, however, Jocasta exhibits no faith in the oracular predictions regarding her husband and says, "Such was the prophet's (μαντικαί) horoscope, O King, regard it not. Whatever the god (θεός) deems fit to search (ἐρευνάω), himself unaided will reveal" (*OT* 725). In other words, Jocasta contends that the gods need no oracles to do their revealing. Rather, the gods will simply reveal directly if they so choose and thereby eliminate the need for an intermediary.

Sophocles' language in these two texts links the prophet, the μάντις, with a search or inquiry that includes the themes of wisdom (σοφία) and the divine role. However, in the first instance (*OT* 562-568), the search by a priest resembles that of a physical search for a criminal while the latter example (*OT* 725) locates the agency of the search not in a human but in the god. Thus, Sophocles does use the language of the search for divine knowledge, particularly in the latter example, but his usage differs from that which we will see in the other writers to be considered.[3]

Sophocles is not the only dramatist to be interested in the human capacity to discover and know the divine mind. Euripides also produces scenes where similar language occurs. Like Sophocles, Euripides can also depict the raving frenzy of the divinely possessed man.[4] Likewise, Euripides can utilize the idea of inspiration in the search for the divine mind. For example, in *Medea*, Euripides provides a dialogue between Aegeus and Medea that links the prophet and the search for knowledge. In this example, Medea, a sorceress renowned for her wisdom, asks Aegeus why he has gone to the oracle of Phoebus.

> Medea: Why did you fare to earth's *prophetic* navel?
> Aegeus: To *ask* (ἐρευνάω) how seed of children might be mine.
> (669: emphasis mine)

---

chronologically. It does not indicate a change in meaning or substance. For more on this, consult Gerhard Delling, "ἐρευνάω," *TDNT* 2:655-57.

[3]Sophocles also describes an instance where Oedipus raves under the power of a daimon. Cf. *OT* 1258.

[4]Cf. *Bacc.* 299 where Euripides discusses the frenzies that Dionysus, or Bacchus, could send. Those frenzies often occurred at Delphi.

Thus, "earth's prophetic navel" in this case is an oracular site, and one searches and inquires (ἐρευνάω) when one goes there.

Furthermore, in *Helen*, Euripides identifies the divine role in this search in a conversation between Helen and Menelaus where Menelaus attempts to get Helen to disclose how and why she was removed from her home.

> Helen: Woe's me for the bitter tale you *seek* (ἐρευνάω) to know.
> Menelaus: From *God*'s hand all things come.
>
> (*Hel.* 662: emphasis mine)

Helen emphasizes that knowledge of her past as well as her fate can be sought, but only the god can reveal it.

In *Prometheus Bound*, Aeschylus also links the deities with the search for wisdom as he places these words in the mouth of the chorus:

> To us at least Hermes seems not to speak untimely; for he bids thee lay aside thy stubbornness and *seek* (ἐρευνάω) the good counsel of *wisdom*. Be advised! 'Tis shameful for the *wise* (σοφός) to persist in error (ἐξαμαρτάνω).   (*Prom.* 1038: emphasis mine)

Here, the chorus exhorts Prometheus to listen to Hermes at the very moment that Prometheus is about to be cast into Tartarus at the end of the play. Moreover, Hermes says that Prometheus is raving and frenzied. Prometheus is exhorted by the chorus to seek but is characterized by Hermes as being under the influence of μανία. In this case, μανία prevents, rather than enhances, the ability to search for wisdom.

This cluster of ideas and terms surrounding inspiration and the search for the divine mind can also be found in classical Greek literature outside drama in a writer like Pindar, the sixth-century BCE lyrical poet. For example, in *Fragment 61*, Pindar, often known for his athletic imagery and his religious language, utilizes this same cluster and adds other terms associated with obtaining knowledge of the divine.

> Why do you deem that to be *wisdom* (σοφία), in which one man in small measure excelleth another? For man is *not able with his human mind* to *search out* (ἐρευνάω) the counsels of the *gods* (τὰ θεῶν βουλεύματα), but he was born of a mortal mother.

Here, Pindar employs terms similar to those highlighted above as he also notes the human inability to discern the divine will without assistance and emphasizes human mortality in contrast to divinity.[5] Pindar is explicit that the agent of the search for the divine mind is the human, yet the human is ultimately incapable of a successful search. This emphasis on human mortality recurs throughout all of the texts under consideration here. The mere human simply cannot search the thoughts of the gods.

These few early examples from classical Greek literature illustrate the presence of a cluster of terms and ideas that often frequent ancient descriptions of the human search for the divine mind. In addition, several of these authors also provide discussions of divine inspiration that emphasize frenzied possession as well. These ideas receive considerably more attention in the writings of Plato.

Plato

An important example from classical Greek literature is the philosophical vantage point of Plato who provides several discussions of the phenomenon of inspiration. Likewise, Plato can speak of the search for ultimate knowledge. For example, in his *Apology*, he mentions such a search on two different occasions.[6] First, at 23b, as the σοφός, Plato describes the search by Socrates for knowledge. "I am . . . searching (ἐρευνάω) and investigating at the god's behest (κατὰ τὸν θεόν) anyone . . . who I think is wise (σοφός)." Later at 41b, when Plato has Socrates contemplate death and the after-life, he says, "The greatest pleasure would be to pass my time in examining and investigating (ἐρευνάω) the people there, as I do here, to find out who . . . is wise (σοφός)." In

---

[5]It is interesting that Clement of Alexandria at *Strom.* 5.14.129.3 quotes this same passage from Pindar and also refers to Pindar at 5.14.98.8. Both of these instances occur when Clement emphasizes the human need for divine assistance. In fact, at 5.14.129.3, Clement adds to Pindar's statement a quote nearly identical to the Isa 40:13 citation used by Paul at 1 Cor 2:16.

[6]In addition to these two examples, Plato also has other interesting discussions in *Theaet.* 155E and 200E, in which these same search terms appear. Cf. also *Phaed.* 63A where the σοφός again searches for truth. Plato often uses the verb ἐρευνάω to describe the close scrutiny of ideas, words, and meaning. Cf. *Soph.* 241B; 243D; 260E; *Leg.* 821A.

these two instances, of course, Plato's σοφός is investigating other humans in his pursuit of wisdom rather than searching for the divine mind. Thus, the search is more horizontal than vertical, and consequently, the search here is not accompanied by any mention of inspiration. However, at *Theaet.* 174B, Socrates ponders how the philosopher's mind disdains and ignores the things of the world in order to be borne in other directions so as to investigate (ἐρευνάω) the universal nature of all existence.[7] Only here does Plato approach a vertical sense of the search, yet he makes no mention of the divine. Plato's real interest is the purely human philosophical search for truth and knowledge.

When he describes the idea of divine inspiration, Plato usually uses means other than the notion of a search for the divine mind. On a number of occasions, Plato points out how humans can, and often must, be taken over by superhuman, supernatural, or even divine forces in order to produce higher thoughts or expresssions. One such place occurs at *Leg.* 682A where Homer's verse is reckoned to be divinely inspired (θεῖον) in unison with the voices of god and nature. At *Apol.* 21C-22C, Plato describes a gadfly's seeking answers to various philosophical questions from various groups of people. One such group is the poets. Plato muses that the poets are unable to comment intelligently on their own poems, and he concludes that they composed these great works not by wisdom (σοφία) but by nature (φύσις) and because they were inspired (ἐνθουσιάζομαι) like "the prophets and givers of the oracles."[8] As E. R. Dodds has noted, the inspired gift of the Muses to the poets is the power of true speech.[9] Here, inspiration is obviously only temporary since the poets fail to understand what they themselves have written.[10] Moreover, this inspiration has either replaced the mind or

---

[7]In fact, Plato here quotes Pindar to bolster the case for the philosopher's lack of attention to worldly matters.

[8]For similar expressions of the inspiration of poets, cf. Pindar *Frag.* 150; Longinus, *On the Sublime* 8.1,4; 9.7-9; 13.2; and 15.1-2, 8. Cf. also Democritus' *On Poetry*, a work that is lost but accessible via several sources: Clem. *Strom.* 6.168.2; Dio Chrys. *Or.* 36.1; Cicero *De Div.* 1.80.

[9]E. R. Dodds, *The Greeks and the Irrational* (Berkeley CA: University of California Press, 1951) 81.

[10]Cf. Plato *Crat.* 396D where Socrates describes an instance of his own temporary inspiration when a fellow seeker with "superhuman wisdom" takes possession of Socrates' soul.

heightened it since the poet's mind in an ordinary state cannot understand the poem.[11]

Two other examples from Plato demonstrate his consistent emphasis on inspiration from without and inspiration that displaces the human νοῦς. At *Tim.* 71E–72A, it is noted that "no man achieves true and inspired divination" (μαντικὴ ἔνθεος καὶ ἀληθής) when in his "rational mind" (ἔννους) but only when his intelligence is fettered. Moreover, Plato notes that a frenzied visionary or seer cannot judge the apparitions or voices that he himself has seen or uttered as long as he is still in a frenzy.

This idea of the fettered rational intelligence is expressed in considerably more detail in *Phaedr.* 244-53 where Plato provides something like an "ascending scale of inspiration."[12] Here Socrates remarks that "the greatest of blessings come to us through madness (διὰ

---

[11]Cf. *Phaedr.* 245 where nonmad poets are seen as useless. Without μανία, they "vanish into nothing." Throughout this investigation, I use "irrational" to signify places where the human νοῦς or understanding is displaced, taken over, possessed, inactive, or thwarted. Dale Martin, "Tongues of Angels and Other Status Indicators," *JAAR* 59 (1991): 547-89 rightly notes how "rationality" is often used by scholars to denote modern rather than ancient ideas and concepts. However, I seek to avoid such anachronism by using the above definition and adhering to it through the reading of the texts under consideration.

[12]This is the phrase of Robert Grant, *The Letter and Spirit* (London: SPCK, 1957) 6. The phrase is also used by Christopher Forbes, "Early Christian Inspired Speech and Hellenistic Popular Religion," *NovTest* 28 (1986): 257-70. Related to the varieties of inspiration described by Plato is the work of Dodds, *Greeks and Irrational*, who seeks to trace the general development of ancient Greek religious experience. In his chapter 3, Dodds contends that Plato emphasized four kinds of divine madness: prophetic madness from Apollo, ritual madness from Dionysus, poetic madness from the Muses, and erotic madness from Aphrodite. Dodds notes that the earliest attestations of ecstatic prophecy date from the eleventh century BCE and agrees with philologists who think that the Greeks connected the μάντις and μαίνομαι. Cf. Plato *Phaedr.* 244C; Eur. *Bacc.* 299; and 1 Cor 14:23. Dodds, 74, also notes the rarity of open skepticism about Delphi before the Roman period. However, Dodds is interested primarily in understanding the anthropology and psychology of inspiration in modern terms rather than ancient ones. For example, Dodds seeks to bridge the centuries between Plato and modern pentecostalism with concepts like psychic experience, guilt feelings, and shame. I, on the other hand, am seeking an understanding of the various ways in which inspiration is depicted in antiquity in an effort to understand Paul. For another critique of Dodds' propensity to impose modern categories on Plato and other ancient texts, cf. Dale Martin, "Tongues of Angels," 569 n46.

μανίας) when it is sent as a gift of the gods" (244A). In this way, the prophetess at Delphi and others generate beneficial results only when they are not in their right minds (σωφρονέω); in other words, divine madness (μανία) is superior to sanity, which is of human origin.[13]

In *Phaedr.* 249C-E, however, Plato tempers that view somewhat when he discusses the ideal philosopher, whose mind communes with the god in order to separate himself from human interests, to focus on the divine, and to receive inspiration (ἐνθουσιάσμος).[14] This is the pinnacle on the ascending scale of inspiration, so Plato notes that this is the best of all kinds of inspiration since it allows the human mind to attain wings and ponder the realm of the absolute.[15] In this way, the followers of various gods search within themselves to imitate god, to be inspired (ἐνθουσιάζομαι), to receive character from god, and to have a part in god (253A).[16]

In his study of Hermas and Christian prophecy, Jannes Reiling has proposed that there are three specific kinds of prophetic inspiration.[17] However, with some modification, those three categories can illumine our understanding of nonprophetic inspiration as well. In the first type, the human will and consciousness are both eliminated so that the human is a passive instrument. In the second type, the will is eliminated while the

---

[13]The priestess at Delphi here is a προφήτης whereas at *Tim.* 72B, the προφήτης interprets and evaluates the utterances of the priestess, who is called a μάντις.

[14]Here I disagree with Dodds. He, 218, thinks that Plato only begrudgingly accepted the "irrational" channels of poetic and prophetic inspiration but deeply valued the activities of the rational self. Dodds too hastily dichotomizes the ideas here. Plato clearly has these forms of inspiration related to one another as the whole of the *Phaedrus* shows. Of course, the philosopher's communings with the gods are of a higher sort; after all, Plato himself says that this is the best of all kinds of inspiration. However, Plato recognizes varieties of inspiration and by no means makes the philosopher wholly rational on a non-divine basis. It is a higher inspiration, but nevertheless it is a divine inspiration. Cf. *Phaedr.* 253A.

[15]Plato here also provides very τέλος-dominated language including some mentioning of the "perfect" (τέλεος). The philosopher can be initiated into "perfect mysteries" and become truly "perfect" (τέλεος). Cf. 1 Cor 2:6 and the discussion to follow in my chapter 4.

[16]Cf. *Theat.* 176A where true σοφία is defined as becoming like god in righteousness.

[17]For these three categories, cf. Jannes Reiling, *Hermas and Christian Prophecy: A Study of the 11th Mandate*, NovTSup 37 (Leiden: Brill, 1973) 19.

consciousness is simply passive but aware enough that there is clear recollection after the inspiration. Finally, the third type of inspiration allows the will and the consciousness to remain intact so that the receiver speaks what is revealed to him/her as a divine message.

These categories can be helpful in reading Plato and the other writers under consideration here because, in the case of the oracles and the Sibyl, the will and consciousness seem temporarily to be eliminated. However, Plato's view of the exact nature of poetic inspiration seems not to fit Reiling's categories, for clearly the will and the consciousness are in some measure intact. The poets do compose poems, an action that hardly seems possible with no will or consciousness. Yet the manner of inspiration clearly varies from the more mystical ascent of the philosopher's mind as it attains the mystical wings of the highest form of inspiration while considering the realm of the absolute.

Thus, Plato allows for various modes and types of inspiration.[18] The poet's mind can be taken over, as can the Delphic priestess's mind. The highest inspiration occurs when the philosopher's mind attains wings in order to consider the absolute and to seek perfection. Madness is often seen as validating true inspiration, particularly in the case of the oracles and the Sibyl. Moreover, Plato even provides for one human, albeit with superhuman wisdom, to take possession of another human in order to inspire. Grant and Forbes are right: Plato does seem to have an ascending scale of inspiration. Forbes is too quick to move directly from Plato to Paul,[19] however, and he incorrectly reads Plato at *Tim.* 71-72 as suggesting that the rational interpretation of visions and utterances is superior to the visions and utterances themselves. Rather, Plato simply

---

[18]Here I disagree with Martin, "Tongues of Angels." Martin makes both Plato and Philo one-dimensional and ignores the other evidence in these two writers of varieties of inspiration. Martin's focus is different from my own. He is interested in a category he defines as "esoteric speech" (548) in an effort to understand speaking in tongues in 1 Corinthians. However, a broader and more nuanced reading of Philo (Martin focuses only on *Who is the Heir*) and of Plato (Martin fails to mention *Phaedr.* 249) is needed. Nevertheless, Martin's article is both provocative and helpful, particularly as it seeks a background for possible ancient understandings of the phenomenon of speaking in tongues.

[19]For a more complete critique of Forbes, see Martin, "Tongues of Angels," 548 n4 and 558 n22. Forbes's work is weakened by his zealous insistence on the absolute uniqueness of ancient Christian speaking in tongues.

emphasizes that the frenzied seer cannot recollect and ponder while (s)he is *still* in an ecstatic state.

Plato clearly sees inspiration as from without, but his details regarding that inspiration vary in significant ways. The Delphic priestess is inspired as her mind is displaced. The poet seems to acquire inspiration as the mind is heightened, or perhaps displaced. The philosopher, however, appears to be inspired in a more mystical ascension of the mind.[20] This process seems more rational than that which is applied to the priestess and the poet. In addition, Plato does depict a human search for truth, but that search is usually wholly human rather than divinely initiated or centered. Thus, Plato does not define in any substantive way inspiration as the search for the divine mind.

Plutarch

More than five centuries after Plato, Paul's near contemporary, Plutarch, in his *The E at Delphi (Apud)*, *The Oracles at Delphi (Pyth.)*, and *The Obsolescence of the Oracles (Defectu)*, provides famous apologetic discussions of the phenomena of ancient prophecy and oracles.[21] In these discussions, Plutarch examines in detail the idea of inspiration, particularly as it relates to the oracular activity at Delphi. Writing these persuasive essays in Chaironeia in Boeotia, Plutarch extensively employs the language of ecstatic utterance, which played such an important role in cultural beliefs about the oracles, and he utilizes some of the same kinds of language that have been illustrated above.[22] Furthermore, Plutarch

---

[20]This theme, which is but a slight nuance in Plato's writings, will pervade Philo's writings. See my chapter 3 below.

[21]Plutarch is unique because of his exposure to both Greek intellectual life (via his time at the Platonic Academy) and Hellenistic religion (via his time at Delphi). For overviews of Plutarch's life, see R. H. Barrow, *Plutarch and His Times* (Bloomington IN: Indiana University Press, 1967); and Simon Swain, "Plutarch: Chance, Providence, and History," *American Journal of Philology* 110 (1989): 272-302. Swain's interest is to show that Plutarch believed that the course of history was predetermined and that in particular, the rise of Rome was due to providence. Thus, Swain reads Plutarch's *Moralia* with an eye for those things that happen by chance.

[22]*E.g.*, cf. the search in *Pyth.* 399A. For the issue of the necessity of ecstasy and irrational behavior in order to authenticate or vindicate the oracular utterance, see *Defectu* 435. Cf. again the language in Plato's *Phaedr.* 244; also Julian 215 B.

often displays a diverse accumulation of influences and backgrounds in his writing.[23]

The irrational element of inspiration is both important and prominent in Plutarch's writings. For him, the mind is clearly removed or disengaged when the divine spirit takes over, as evidenced by his extensive use of terms like ἔνθους, ἐνθουσιασμός, μάντις, and φαντασ- τικός. For example, in *Defectu* 432A-D, he says:

> Even so the soul (ψυχή) does not acquire the prophetic power (μαντικὴ δύναμις) when it goes forth from the body as from a cloud; it possesses that power even now but is blinded by being combined and commingled with the mortal nature (θνητός) . . . a temperament through which the reasoning (λογιστικός) and thinking faculty (φροντιστικός) of the souls is relaxed from their present state as they range amid the irrational (ἄλογος) and imaginative (φαντασιαστικός) realms of the future. . . . But that which foretells the future (μαντικός) . . . is both irrational (ἄλογος) and indeterminate (ἀόριστος) in itself but receptive of impressions and presentiments through what may be done to it. . . . It is subjected to a change we call inspiration (ἐνθουσιασμός). . . . Moreover the earth sends forth for men streams of many other potencies. But the prophetic current and breath is most divine and holy.

In this essay, Plutarch seeks to explain why many oracles have ceased to function, but he expands on a variety of other topics as well.

---

[23]*E.g.*, cf. Frederick E. Brenk, "From Mysticism to Mysticism: The Religious Development of Plutarch of Chaironeia," *SBL Seminar Papers, 1975*, vol. 1, ed. George MacRae (Missoula MT: Scholars, 1975) 193-98. Brenk seeks to show some of the Pythagorean, Stoic, and Platonic influences at work in Plutarch. Brenk labels this accumulation of principles "exotic"—as Plutarch endeavors to modify Platonism along with various syncretistic concepts of God. For Plutarch's parallels with contemporary Christianity and his possible influences on later Christianity, a good starting point is Hans Dieter Betz, ed., *Plutarch's Theological Writings and Early Christian Literature* (Leiden: Brill, 1975). Betz's volume attempts to list all the parallels of Plutarch's writings found in Christian literature. For a comparison of Plutarch's view of moral virtue as compared to Paul's in 1 Corinthians 5-6, see Benjamin J. Fiore, SJ, "Passion in Paul and Plutarch: 1 Corinthians 5-6 and the Polemic Against Epicureans," *Greeks, Romans, and Christians: Essays in Honor of Abraham J. Malherbe*, ed. David Balch, Everett Ferguson, and Wayne Meeks (Philadelphia: Fortress, 1991) 135-43.

In this particular case, he mentions the prophetic power present in some souls, a power that is released in dreams or at the time of death. Only on rare occasions is the soul cleansed of its impurities so that it may attain the temperament necessary to withdraw from the material realm (432CD). Integral to this ecstatic understanding is the idea that the divine grants humans knowledge.[24] A human learns via divine appropriation of the soul when the soul is enabled to gain release from its mortal nature in order to attain prophetic awareness and knowledge. Only through this irrational release from the mortal nature can the human soul acquire the sight that its mortal nature prevents. Upon its release, the human soul becomes aware of divine breaths and movements that emanate from a variety of sources in order to inspire.[25] Again, the active role of the νοῦς diminishes since it is disengaged so that the soul (ψυχή) can ascend to new heights. Terms like ἔνθους, ἐνθουσιασμός, μάντις, ἄλογος, ἀόριστος, and φανταστικός communicate this disengagement.[26]

Like Plato, Plutarch understands this process as purely individualistic with little or no corporate dimension. A lone human soul seeks to learn the divine mind. However, through the vehicle of the oracles, Plutarch does provide for some measure of the communication of that knowledge of the divine mind to other humans. For example, at *Apud* 384F–85C, Plutarch says

---

[24]Cf. *Apud* 391E; *Pyth.* 397C.

[25]It was commonly held that the divine spirit emanated from beneath the shrine at Delphi and that such breath served as the source of the Delphic priestess's inspiration. Cf. Strabo, *Geog.* 9.3.5. For more on the Delphic oracle, see Joseph Fontenrose, *The Delphic Oracle, Its Responses, and Operations* (Berkeley: University of California Press, 1978) and his article "Oracle" in *Oxford Classical Dictionary*, ed. H. H. Scullard and N. Hammond (Oxford: Clarendon, 1970) 754. For another view, see H. W. Parke and D. E. W. Wormell, *The Delphic Oracle* (Oxford: Blackwell, 1956).

[26]The view of Martin, "Tongues of Angels," could be broadened with the inclusion of the perspective of Plutarch, for Plutarch clearly does not fit Martin's model of dichotomy. Martin proposes that Plato operates with a hierarchy of νοῦς over δόξα and νοῦς over σῶμα, while Philo has a hierarchy of νοῦς over σῶμα but πνεῦμα over νοῦς. Moreover, these models are too rigidly applied so that the nuanced varieties of inspiration in the writings of Plato and Philo are lost.

It seems that our beloved Apollo finds a remedy and a solution for the problems connected with our life by the oracular responses which he gives to those who consult him; but the problems connected with our power to reason (λόγος) it seems that he himself launches and propounds to him who is by nature (φύσις) inclined to the love of knowledge (φιλόσοφος), thus creating in the soul (ψυχή) a craving that leads onward to the truth. . . . I began to seek some answer (ζητέω) myself and to put questions (ἐρωτάω) to them. . . . That the god (θεός) is no less a philosopher (φιλόσοφος) than a prophet (μάντις) Ammonius seemed to all to postulate and prove correctly, . . . "Since," he went on to say, "inquiry (ζητέω) is the beginning of philosophy, and wonder and uncertainty (τὸ θαυμάζειν καὶ ἀπορεῖν) the beginning of inquiry, it seems only natural that the greater of what concerns the god should be concealed in riddles (αἴνιγμα)."

In this essay, Plutarch endeavors to explain the representation of the letter "E" beside the inscriptions at Delphi. The passage cited above comes at the outset of the essay and opens the investigation into the meaning of the mysterious "E." The divine Apollo addresses human needs through the oracles. Thus, the center of this discussion is the human seeker who confronts the unknowable. Such a curious person inquires (ζητέω) of a god and receives the oracle, which often is itself enigmatic.

The god most frequently mentioned in Plutarch is, of course, Apollo, the god usually associated with the oracles.[27] Here Apollo is proactive in the world, providing in the oracles a means for the solution of human ills and problems.[28] Although his vocabulary differs slightly from Paul's, Plutarch seeks to describe the human search for the divine mind. Here, the agent of the search is human in the form of the priestess at Delphi who mediates between ordinary inquirers and the gods. In a sense, then, there are two inquirers: the priestess and her client. Only the priestess is

---

[27]Note the other names given to Apollo here in 385C: " 'Pythian' (Inquirer)"; " 'Delian' (Clear)"; " 'Phanaean' (Disclosing)"; " 'Ismenian' (Knowing)"; and " 'Leschenorian' (Conversationalist)."

[28]Cf. also *PGM* V.410-21 where the spell invokes Hermes as the "prophet of events and dream divine . . . who send forth oracles by day and night." In this spell, the user asks Hermes to "prophesy" to him/her so that the user may comprehend the divine nature.

described as inspired, however. Furthermore, Plutarch utilizes an important concept of irrationality to explain his understanding of inspiration. In *Defectu* 432, the soul is clouded by the human's mortal nature. What is needed is the ἄλογος, ἀόριστος, and φανταστικός. Only then is the reasoning element relaxed enough to ponder the divine mind.

Plutarch, unlike Paul and others we will see later in this investigation, only uses forms of ἐρευνάω to describe a military search or ransacking, or its equivalent; however, he clearly portrays a prophetic search for the divine mind and inspiration using the similar theme of the search.[29] To describe that search, Plutarch, like Plato, prefers the terms σκοπέω and ζητέω, a preference that this passage demonstrates with its emphasis on inquiry (ζητέω).[30] However, Plato only utilizes the search when considering a human seeking knowledge and wisdom from other humans rather than from the divine. Moreover, Plato's "search" is uniquely philosophical in character.

Obviously, Plutarch emphasizes the irrational element in the oracular and prophetic search. With lesser frequency and intensity than other writers such as Julian, Plutarch nevertheless mentions the enigmatic character of the information available to humans seeking ultimate knowledge. Plutarch is more concerned with the oracles than with the mysteries and ancestral myths that captivate Julian, but Plutarch is careful to show that much of the data in this world about the divine is concealed in riddles and paradoxes. Plutarch often—particularly when he glamorizes preceding eras when the oracles were "really" prolific and valued— emphasizes that the oracular utterances required translation, interpretation, or expansion because of the priestess's irrationality and unintelligibility. In other words, the divine message was often too cryptic for human comprehension without other assistance.[31]

Plutarch provides still more detail regarding the oracles and this process of seeking the divine mind at *Pyth.* 404B-E.

---

[29]Plutarch uses forms and cognates of ἐρευνάω about twenty times, none of which comes in a clearly prophetic context or in a setting to describe the quest for the divine mind.

[30]Cf. Plut. *Apud* 385D and *Pyth.* 399A. Cf. also Plato *Apol.* 21C-22E for σκοπέω and ζητέω.

[31]This fits well with Plato's insistence that the frenzied one is unable to interpret or understand while still in a frenzy. Cf. *Tim.* 71E-72A.

However, neither of these, my young friend, goes counter to reason if
only we hold correct and uncontaminated opinions about the god, and
do not believe that it was he himself who used to compose the verses
in earlier times, while now he suggests the oracles (χρησμός) to the
prophetic priestess (Πυθία) as if he were prompting an actor in a play
(ἐκ προσωπείων φθεγγόμενον) to speak his words. . . . [L]et us
recall what we have learned in brief: that the body (σῶμα) makes use
of many instruments (ὀργάνοι) and that the soul (ψυχή) makes use
of this very body and its members (μέρος); moreover, the soul is
created to be the instrument of God, and the virtue of an instrument is
to conform (μιμέομαι) as exactly as possible to the purpose of the
agent that employs it by using all the powers which Nature has
bestowed upon it. . . . I imagine that you are familiar with the saying
found in Heracleitus to the effect that the Lord whose prophetic shrine
(μαντεῖον) is at Delphi neither tells nor conceals (κρύπτω) but
indicates (σημαίνω). Add to these words, which are so well said, the
thought that the god of this place employs the prophetic priestess for
men's ears just as the sun employs the moon for men's eyes. For he
makes known and reveals his own thoughts, but he makes them known
through the associated medium of a mortal body and a soul that is
unable to keep quiet.

Again, Plutarch's digressions are as frequent as his attention to his
main topic in *The Oracles at Delphi*. Plutarch here discusses the custom
of the giving of oracles in verse form, a form that had varied over time.
Plutarch emphasizes how important it is to note that the voice, the
utterance, the diction, and the meter are not divine. Rather the god puts
visions into the woman's mind and creates a light in her soul. The god
plays her like an instrument. The priestess is a mere vessel. This,
Plutarch says, "is inspiration (ἐνθουσιασμός)."[32]

Plutarch invokes the language of the theater and drama in addition to
images from the natural order. He possibly also hints at an analogy from
music with his use of ὄργανον, something developed more fully, and
also with a more social character, in both Philo and Paul.[33] It is

---

[32]Cf. *Pyth.* 397C.
[33]See my chapters 3 and 7 below. Cf. also *Defectu* 418D; 431A; 436F; 437D. In
Christian literature, cf. Athenagoras *Leg.* 7.2; 9.1; 25.1-3.

important, too, that Plutarch claims that at Delphi, and probably at all the oracles, the god only "indicates" rather than "tells." In other words, a sign is given, but it is not unambiguous; rather, vagueness is the norm.[34] Ironically, it is just this ambiguity that is used by writers like Lucian and Philostratus to ridicule what they consider to be prophetic quackery.[35]

Thus, the verbal communication by one human to others regarding what is learned about the divine mind, a communication that is missing

---

[34]A great deal of scholarly attention has been devoted to the relationship of Paul's understanding of interpreted tongues and prophecy and the parallel phenomena at the Delphic oracle. James D. G. Dunn, *Jesus and the Spirit* (London: SCM Press, 1975) contends that Paul's understanding mirrored the oracular phenomena. This position is often assumed in some form by other scholars. Cf. also Terrence Callan, "Prophecy and Ecstasy in Greco-Roman Religion and in 1 Corinthians," *NovT* 27 (1985): 125-40. Luke Johnson, "Norms for True and False Prophecy," *American Benedictine Review* 22 (1971): 29-45, also contends for a close equivalence between glossolalic and Hellenistic phenomena. For another view, see Christopher Forbes, "Early Christian Inspired Speech and Hellenistic Popular Religion." Forbes dissects Dunn's view and argues that there are considerable differences between (1) Paul's understanding of interpreted tongues and prophecy and (2) the oracular utterances and their interpretations. First, the inspired speaker at Delphi is usually called the μάντις while the interpreter, never explicitly said to be inspired, is called the προφήτης. Forbes relies on Plato who says the προφήτης uses his rational faculties rather than divine inspiration (cf. *Tim.* 71E-72B) although in the *Phaedrus*, the προφήτης can be inspired. For example, as we have already seen, at *Phaedr.* 244ff, there is an ascending scale of inspiration. However, Forbes seems to collapse Paul's understandings of prophecy and tongues into a single unit. As I will discuss in chapter 7 below, tongues and prophecy are two very different phenomena. However, it is important that Forbes does point out that the evidence for the meanings of ancient terms like μάντις and ἔκστασις is far less clear than modern scholarship often assumes. This final point urges valuable caution in this and other such investigations. For example, both Parke and Fontenrose cite Plutarch as crucial evidence for their own views of Delphic events. However, Parke and Wormell, *The Delphic Oracle*, 33, claim that the priestess spoke in linguistically unintelligible babble while Fontenrose, *The Delphic Oracle*, 204-12, finds no reliable evidence for a frenzied or raving priestess nor for such babble. What is of value for my point here is the fact that vagueness, albeit of debatable form, typified the oracular utterances. Martin, "Tongues of Angels," 558, draws the boundaries more carefully by allowing his category of "esoteric speech" to include only cases where the language, not its interpretation, is uncertain.

[35]*E.g.*, cf. Lucian *Alex.* 22 where Alexander "gave responses that were sometimes obscure and ambiguous, sometimes downright unintelligible, for this seemed to him in the oracular manner." Cf. also *Alex.* 13; 27-28.

in many other writers, is by no means a clear and forthright process in Plutarch. The priestess is irrationally inspired; the priestess then provides some kind of sign of the knowledge derived in her inspired search to other humans. Even then that sign may be ambiguous, debatable, or in need of interpretation; in fact, it nearly always is.[36]

Like the other writers under consideration, Plutarch also emphasizes the role of the divine entity in making accessible the divine mind. Humans are wholly dependent upon the willingness of the divine to provide that access; without such access, no inspiration is possible. The "Lord" in this passage makes use of a soul that is "unable to keep quiet." Unlike many other writers, however, Plutarch does not develop and emphasize the role of the human νοῦς; rather the emphasis is solely on the ψυχή, which is the human's means of interaction with the divine and the spiritual. In fact, for Plutarch, it is important that the νοῦς is actually disengaged and inactive so that the ψυχή can assume a temporary sovereignty and freedom.

Julian

Julian, writing in the middle of the fourth century CE, also provides several unique descriptions of the search for divine knowledge, adds his own interpretations to the topic, and still illustrates the common pool of language from which so many such descriptions in antiquity, including Paul's, drew. Unlike Plutarch's essays, Julian's writings have a sharp polemical edge. Julian is not explicating a particular text, although he does express interest in the ancestral myths. Instead, Julian writes to advocate a position based on his own rather general synthesis of Hellenistic beliefs and practices. Julian is obvious in his attempt to

---

[36]There is also debate as to the role of priests as interpreters at the oracular sites. The evidence is ambiguous. For example, Strabo, *Geog.* 9.3.5 says that poets or priests, not the μάντις, put the oracles into verse. For a detailed analysis of possible parallels between Christian prophecy and that in the Hellenistic world, see Theodore M. Crone, *Early Christian Prophecy: A Study of its Origin and Function* (Baltimore: St. Mary's University Press, 1973). Cf. also Erich Fascher, Προφήτης: *Eine sprach- und religionsgeschichtliche Untersuchung* (1927), who collects and catalogs evidence for the use of the word προφήτης.

supplant the Constantinian place of Christianity as the state cult in favor of his preference for Hellenism.[37]

Julian's *Hymn to the Mother of the Gods* illustrates this Hellenistic position with its two broad themes of the defense of Hellenism and the importance of the preservation of ancient traditions. At 170AB, Julian demonstrates some of his concerns regarding the human search for divine knowledge.

> But let no one suppose my meaning to be that this was ever done or happened in a way that implies that the gods (θεοί) themselves are ignorant of what they intend to do, or that they have to correct their own errors (ἀμαρτήματα). But our ancestors in every case tried to trace (διερευνάω) the original meanings of things, whether with the guidance of the gods or independently—though perhaps it would be better to say that they sought (ζητέω) for them under the leadership of the gods—then when they had discovered (εὑρίσκω) those meanings they clothed them in paradoxical myths (μῦθοι παραδόξοι). This was in order that, by means of the paradox and the incongruity, the fiction might be detected and we might be induced to search out the truth. Now I think ordinary men derive benefit enough from the irrational myth. . . . But those who are more highly endowed with wisdom will find the truth about the gods helpful; though only on condition that such a man examine and discover (εὑρίσκω) and comprehend (λαμβάνω) it under the leadership of the gods, and if by such riddles as these he is reminded that he must search out (ζητέω)

---

[37]For this broader perspective on Julian's agenda, I am indebted to Polymnia Athanassiadi-Fowden, *Julian and Hellenism: An Intellectual Biography* (Oxford: Clarendon, 1981), who provides a less tendentious overview of Julian's life and writings than do the earlier works of Glen Warren Bowersock, *Julian the Apostate* (Cambridge MA: Harvard University Press, 1978) and Robert Browning, *The Emperor Julian* (London: Weidenfeld and Nicolson, 1975). Athanassiadi-Fowden shows how Julian was influenced by Iamblichan Neoplatonism and how he became frustrated when the popular response to his efforts at cultural reform was tepid. Bowersock portrays Julian as a reclusive fanatic, while Browning tends to romanticize Julian into a tragic figure victimized psychologically by the murder of his relatives. For the long-term effect on Christianity of Julian's anti-Christian polemic and policy, see Robert L. Wilken, "The Jews and Christian Apologetics after Theodosius I *Cunctos populos*," *HTR* 73 (1980): 451-71. Cf. also Richard Klein, ed., *Julian Apostata*, Wege der Forschung; Bd 509 (Darmstadt: Wissenschaftliche Buchgesellschaft, 1978).

their meaning and so attains to the goal (τέλος) and summit of his quest through his own researches, he must not be modest and put faith in the opinions of others rather than in his own mental powers (νοῦς ἐνέργεια).

Julian uses a cognate of ἐρευνάω, in this case διερευνάω, to describe the ancestral quest for ultimate meaning, and he repeatedly describes this effort as a search. Julian also uses ζητέω and εὑρίσκω to depict the action of acquiring knowledge about the gods. In particular, Julian encourages the one "more highly endowed with wisdom" to seek, research, discover, and comprehend, as well as to trust his "own mental powers," in order to reach the τέλος. Unlike Plutarch, Julian locates much of this activity in the human νοῦς and emphasizes that this process occurs "under the leadership of the gods." In other words, the human mind requires divine assistance in the effort to comprehend ultimate truths, an idea common to all of the writers discussed here.[38] Unlike Plutarch, however, Julian stresses that the seeker should trust in the power of his νοῦς.

When the ancestors discovered divine truths, they then clothed such truths in irrational myths, which benefit "ordinary men." Julian here approaches altruism, with a touch of condescension, as he expresses an interest in the common, ordinary citizenry. It is important to remember that this text is chiefly addressed to a highly literate and educated circle of pagan clergy whom Julian hoped to organize into a formidable social force.[39] How familiar this text and its concepts may have been to the lesser educated is unclear.

As in other texts that we will see later in this investigation, there are different levels of understanding or human abilities. Whereas Plato provides an ascending scale of inspiration, Julian describes "ordinary men" and "those more highly endowed with wisdom." Elsewhere, Julian declares that myths or tales are needed to train children (παιδία), whose childhood may be defined either in years or in intelligence.[40] The

---

[38]Cf. also *PGM* III.594-605 where the divine "grants (χαρίζομαι) intellect (νοῦς), [speech] (λόγος), and knowledge (γνῶσις)." Cf. 1 Cor 2:12, 16.

[39]*E.g.*, cf. 177CD.

[40]223A. At 216C, nature does not want the hidden truth about the "essential nature of the gods to be flung in naked words" to the profane.

presence of these levels of comprehension in Julian should come as no surprise since he held in such high regard the mysteries, which were rituals predicated on the notion of levels and progression through them. In fact, Julian himself was initiated first into the Neoplatonic mysteries around 351 and later into the Mithraic cult. Moreover, Julian claimed to be the sole earthly representative and spokesman for Helios-Mithra, who had chosen him to show humanity the pathway to true *paideia*.[41] It is Helios who frees the soul from the body so that it may ascend to the region of the subtances of god (152B). This ascending soul (ψυχή) sounds remarkably like those described in Plato and Plutarch.[42]

Julian demonstrates his valuing of the mysteries, for example, at *To the Cynic Heracleios* 222A–23A, in a text that also illustrates Julian's belief in the fundamental unity of all Hellenistic philosophy. This address responds to a speech by Heracleios in the royal court, a speech that Julian found to be far-fetched and littered with inanity. From this fundamental unity of philosophy, however, Julian excludes the Epicureans as well as the contemporary version of the Cynics, whom he specifically refutes here. This text also provides a second important example of how Julian viewed the search for the divine mind.

> However, let Dionysus himself decide about these things, though I do indeed implore him to inspire (ἐκβακχεύω) my mind and yours with his own sacred frenzy for the true knowledge (γνῶσις) of the gods, . . . For he in whom the abundance of life has not been perfected (τελεσιουργέω) by the essential nature of Dionysus, . . . he I say who has not been perfected by means of the Bacchic and divine frenzy (ἔνθεος) for the god, . . . since he will be forever deprived of that knowledge of the gods which I hold to be more precious than to rule over the whole world. . . . Whenever myths on sacred subjects are incongruous in thought, by that very fact they cry aloud, as it were, and

---

[41]Cf. Athanassiadi-Fowden, p. 124 and see also A. H. Armstrong, "The Way and the Ways: Religious Tolerance and Intolerance in the 4th Century A.D.," *Vigiliae Christianae* 38 (1984): 1-17. For a discussion of Julian's relationship to the oracles, and Delphi in particular, see Timothy E. Gregory, "Julian and the Last Oracle at Delphi," *Greek, Roman, and Byzantine Studies* 24 (1983): 355-66. He confirms, against recent scholarship, that the so-called last oracle at Delphi was delivered to Julian. Gregory thinks that it was probably given by pagan priests hoping to influence Julian to restore the oracle's fortunes.

[42]Cf. Plato *Phaedr.* 244-45; 253; Plutarch *Defectu* 432.

summon us not to believe (πιστεύω) them literally but to study (σκοπέω) and track down (διερευνάω) their hidden meaning. And in such myths the incongruous element is even more valuable than the serious and straightforward . . . that pure intelligence may rise to the comprehension of the distinctive nature of the gods that transcends all existing things. These then are the reasons why that branch of philosophy which is connected with initiation and the doctrines of the Mysteries (μυσταγωγός) ought by all means to be expressed in devout and serious language, while as regards the thought, the narrative may be expounded in a style that has stranger qualities.

Clearly many of the elements in the earlier examples are present in this passage from Julian but with some important modifications and innovations. The cognitive element (e.g., νοῦς), the search (e.g., ἐρευνάω, εὑρίσκω, and ζητέω), the divine entity (e.g., θεός), error (e.g., ἁμαρτία), and the goal (e.g., τέλος) all cluster in this discussion about knowledge of and from the divine.[43] Julian clearly seeks to describe human inquiry into the divine mind.

In this passage, however, Julian introduces ideas regarding the irrational inspiration of humans. He uses the common term ἔνθεος, to describe the divine frenzy, and the less common term ἐκβακχεύω to refer to inspiration.[44] Clearly the work of the divine is crucial here as the god actually enters the philosopher's mind to inspire and infuse knowledge; it is the essential nature of Dionysus that does the perfecting.[45]

---

[43]In other places, Julian presents variations on this same topic, incorporating again this common pool of inspiration language. It is interesting to note also that he adds still more terms and phrases that are present in Paul's discussion, particularly the concept of "hidden" (ἀποκεκρυμμένος) knowledge. Cf. 222C–23A for another comprehensive example of Julian's use of this kind of language; 152B for the use of σοφία; and 216B–17C for the use of διαμαρτύρομαι, πιστεύω, and ἀποκεκρυμμένος. The hidden meaning in scripture also appears in Christian literature at Clem. *Dives* 5.2.

[44]Again, cf. Plato *Phaedr.* 245; also Clem. *Strom.* 5.14.129.3.

[45]This notion of perfecting the inquirer appears not only here and in Paul but also in later Christian literature. Cf. Origen's *Philocalia* 1.14.9 where the aim of the Spirit is directed at an unspeakable mystery (μυστήριον) and those who "search the scriptures" (ἐρευνάω) to fathom their "depths" (βάθος) hope to "reach perfection" (τελειό-τητος). Cf. also Clem. *Strom.* 7.2.5.6, which provides a lengthy and eloquent example of Clement's Christology. Here, the Son "scrutinizes" (ἐρευνάω) powers and His nature is "most perfect" (τελειοτάτη). This Son then trains the Gnostic by or in

Again, it is important to note that Julian does not move to consider the articulation and communication to others of that inspired knowledge. It is solely an individualistic affair.

Like Paul, Julian recognizes the precondition of ethics as necessary for the reception of divine knowledge. Julian, however, wants to despise the body in order to focus the νοῦς on divine, pure thoughts (226C). To do so is "to come out of oneself" (ἐξίστημι: 226C). In doing so, one realizes one's divinity (θεῖος). The seeker's mind is inspired, he receives some precious knowledge of the gods, and he progresses in initiation in the mysteries. In fact, one can hope to have one's νοῦς "perfected" (τελειόω: 217D). Moreover, there is an admixture of philosophy, religion, and mysticism all occurring as part of Julian's Hellenizing agenda. He urges the embrace of all things Hellenic in their unified variety. In fact, he blends Hellenism with Mithraism and traditionalism in his effort to bring together all the main god-logoi of Hellenism (cf. 144A).

Not surprisingly, then, the terms referring to the divine in Julian differ from those found in writers like Philo or Paul. The god is not the God of Abraham, but a variety of gods, as was usual in the mysteries. For example, Julian here names Bacchus and Dionysus, using the two names synonymously while elsewhere Julian prefers Helios, or Mithras. Hence, it becomes more clear how Julian can refer to the "perfecting" of individuals.[46] This language is not particularly common in many forums of antiquity, but it does occur in ancient discussions of the mysteries, as demonstrated by Reitzenstein, and in broader Hellenistic literature such as Philo's, as shown by Pearson.[47] Plato also provided for the enlightened philosopher to be initiated into perfect mysteries and to become "truly perfect."[48] Given Julian's particular interest in Mithraism and in Hellenistic philosophy, it seems reasonable to locate this element of his thought in those circles of influence.

Julian's vocabulary to describe inspiration can also include other terms as well. For example, Julian uses the verb σκοπέω, a particular

---

"mysteries" (μυστήριον).

[46]Note the forms and cognates of τέλος here and elsewhere to describe not only the goal or end of the search for knowledge but also the process itself.

[47]See section B of my Introduction for more detail on these scholars' positions.

[48]*Phaedr.* 249C-E.

favorite of Plutarch. In doing so, Julian parallels the work of the seeker
in discovering the divine mind with the work of a scout who scours the
world for relevant information that informs and elucidates a particular
situation.[49] So too Julian's seeker studies and tracks down the hidden
meanings of the incongruous myths on sacred subjects.[50] Moreover, such
a seeker is probably not a Cynic nor an Epicurean; rather, the inspired
seeker in Julian's writings is more likely to be an inclusive embracer of
Hellenistic ways and practices, a lover of the mysteries, philosophy, and
truth.

Furthermore, Julian emphasizes irrationality in his own way. As we
will see, Philo employs a mystical, supernatural transcendence of the
material realm by the divinely appropriated soul. Julian, on the other
hand, uses the idea of the incongruous, paradoxical myth as the crucial
avenue to divine knowledge. Such myths can be taken at face value by
the common person. Indeed, myths are designed to "insinuate" divine
knowledge into the ears of the multitude "who cannot receive divine
truths in their purest form" (216D). The true seeker, however, finds the
irrationality of the myth's enigmas and riddles to be only the beginning
point of his inquiry into divine things.[51] Irrationality can also occur in the
divine frenzy or inspiration, but so too is it a type of irrationality that
leads the seeker to search out deeper truths and hidden meanings in the
sacred myths. The ordinary human mind alone is insufficient to access
and comprehend the divine mind. The assistance of the gods is imperative.[52] That assistance in seeking is inspiration for the one who is
endowed with superior wisdom.

As another example of the writers in antiquity who describe the
human search for the divine mind, Julian utilizes familiar vocabulary.
Forms and cognates of γινώσκω and τέλος designate the end of the

---

[49]Cf. also Epictetus's discourses. *e.g.*, this is an important term in *Discourse* 3.22 to
describe the ideal Cynic and his work. Cf. also Plutarch *Apud* 385D; Plato *Apol.*
21C-22E.

[50]In this regard, Christian writers like Origen find a parallel. Origen, in his theory on
the three levels of interpretation, regularly emphasizes the command in John 5:39 to
search the scriptures. That command then becomes important in the effort to "ascend to
the Spirit" (*Phil.* 1.30.24). Cf. also *Phil.* 1.21.6; 4.1.3; 5.5.8; *Cont. Cels.* 3.33.16; 5.16.11;
6.7.28; and 6.37.24.

[51]Cf. 216D; 217CD.

[52]Cf. 217CD.

process but also the process itself. Θεός is the object of the search and the bestower of knowledge, and the νοῦς is deployed in seeking knowledge of the gods as it provides the human locus of the search (ἐρευνάω). All of these terms are familiar to the Pauline literature in varying degrees, but Julian also utilizes language not found in Paul. The adjective ἔνθεος, denoting the irrational and frenzied, the seeking verbs ζητέω and σκοπέω, and the sacred stories (μῦθοι) all distinguish Julian from Paul in important ways. Most significantly, Julian understands inspiration in a rather synthetic way. Inspiration occurs both in the mind's scrutinizing and searching as well as in the infusion of divine frenzy. The νοῦς that is most proficient in this arena is likely to belong to a lover of all things Hellenic. Julian's ideas about divine inquiry and inspiration clearly vary from those of Paul's.

Conclusions

These few examples, then, provide a glimpse into a constellation of terms and ideas that cluster around the general rubric of inquiry into the divine mind. In addition, inspiration is understood by these writers in a variety of ways. Plato provides for a searching philosopher as well as an ascending scale of inspiration with the philosopher at the pinnacle. Plutarch describes the displaced mind of the priestess and the seeking of both the priestess and her client. Julian is intrigued by the incongruous riddles of the ancestral myths and exhorts the seeking lover of Hellenism to rely on the power of his νοῦς.

The vocabulary that has frequented these discussions so far includes: parallels and cognates of ἐρευνάω, denoting the search; parallels and cognates of σοφία, usually denoting the desired cognitive result of the search; and parallels and cognates of θεός, obviously denoting the divine role in and the object of the search. In addition, other related ideas frequently enter the discussion. For example, the notions of error (ἁμαρτάνω) and of humanity's innate incapacity to discern the ultimate truth without divine aid appear regularly.

In sum, these various Greek writers provide for the inspiration of different types of persons as well as for inspiration in varying forms. In Plutarch, the frenzied priestess's νοῦς is displaced, but in Plato, the philosopher's νοῦς is optimized or heightened. It is also important to note that thus far the focus seems to be more cognitive than articulative.

In other words, the prophet/seeker desires to obtain knowledge; little has been said about the subsequent communication of that knowledge to others. It is now instructive to turn to the texts of several Jewish writers in order to broaden further this investigation of inspiration and the search for the divine mind.

Chapter 2

Ancient Inquiry into the Divine Mind
The Jewish Tradition

In this chapter, I examine descriptions of inspiration in two Jewish writers of the first century CE, namely Philo and Josephus, and also survey apocalyptic literature and the LXX. Again, attention is focused not only on inspiration but on particular instances when these writers describe the human search for the divine mind. We are continuing to seek an understanding of who is inspired and how such inspiration occurs in an effort to broaden the cultural background against which to read 1 Cor 2:6-16.

Philo

Philo represents the most useful Jewish subject for this investigation since he frequently discusses the human mind and its contemplation of the Deity. In other words, Philo likes to ponder inspiration and the human search for the divine mind. Especially important in these discussions are forms and cognates of ἐρευνάω, which are commonplace in Philo, a fact that separates him from most other writers of his time.[1] In nearly all cases, Philo uses forms of ἐρευνάω in discussions of the quest for truth, and he frequently utilizes it to describe what he himself is doing in

---

[1]Philo uses some form or cognate of this verb more than 125 times, a number unrivalled by any other writer included in the Thesaurus Linguae Graecae list for this same era. *E.g.*, Plato uses it twenty-nine times and in a variety of ways; Plutarch uses some form of this verb about twenty times, Epictetus only once (*Discourse* 2.11.13), and Dio Chrysostom but three times (*Or.* 6.38–6.39; 35.5). At *Or.* 35.5, Dio uses this language to describe a person's "search for" (ζητέω) and "questions of" (ἀνερευνάω) a philosopher or speaker whom the seeker hopes has something to "reveal" (ἀποκαλύπτω) for the seeker's benefit. In the two instances in *Oration* 6, the verb ἐρευνάω is used to describe a physical search for enemies and food.

particular passages where he is "scrutinizing," "examining," or "investigating" some matter.[2] This type of usage does not apply to many other writers. For example, Plutarch normally uses this verb to refer to a military search or a more general scrutiny rather than that inquiry involved in the quest for truth.[3]

Moreover, for Philo, the mere use of forms of ἐρευνάω often indicates a discussion of the human search for knowledge of and from the divine. For example, at *Leg. All.* 3.84, Philo writes,

> For when the mind (νοῦς) does not, like a master, frighten the soul with threats, but governs (ἄρχω) it as a father (πατήρ), not granting (χαρίζομαι) it the things that are pleasant to it, but giving it even against its will the things that are good for it; when in all matters turning away from what is base and from all that draws it to things mortal, it soars aloft and spends its time in contemplation of the universe and its different parts; when, mounting yet higher, it explores (ἐρευνάω) the Deity (τὸ θεῖον) and His nature, urged by an ineffable love of knowledge (ἐπιστήμη); it cannot continue to entertain the principles it imbibed originally, but in its desire to improve itself seeks (ζητέω) to change its abode for a better one.

In this section of his allegorical interpretation, Philo considers the evil origin of pleasure and the variety of original endowments given by God to various entities at creation. For example, Er and the Serpent were created evil. Here, Philo discusses the endowment of Abram, who was created with a good endowment and led to a prosperous city. This observation leads Philo to comment on the etymology of "Abram," which means "father high-soaring." Thus, Abram was given to soar like the νοῦς.[4]

In this text, the language of the search appears again. The role of the mind (νοῦς), the search (ζητέω, ἐρευνάω), knowledge (ἐπιστήμη), and the divine nature (θεῖον), as well as the human incapacity

---

[2]*E.g.*, among the many uses, cf. *Abr.* 3.2; *De Som.* 1.41.1; 2.17.3; and *De Fug.* 194.2. Clement of Alexandria also likes this verb, using some form of it about twenty-five times, many of which, as in Philo, also describe what he is doing in his writing. *e.g., Strom.* 1.2.21.1; 1.21.109.1

[3]*E.g., Them.* 10.4; *Luc.* 19.4.

[4]For other interpretations of Abram, cf. *Cher.* 4; *Gig.* 62; and *Mut.* 66.

for complete knowledge, all occur here as they do elsewhere. Moreover, Philo provides some important clues as to how this language functions in his writing and thought. First, as usual, he is interpreting or dealing with an Old Testament text, a fact that distinguishes him from the other writers under consideration. Consequently, Philo's understanding of the Deity reflects the God of Abraham and Judaism, active in the world. Clearly it is this God who is the object and focus of the search for things ultimate.[5] In this case, the Old Testament text is Gen 3:14. The curse of the Serpent leads to Philo's consideration of original endowments, which leads to Abram. Abram's name reminds Philo of the mind's ascent.

Second, the prominent role of the νοῦς is quite typical in Philo's writings. For Philo, the mind and its role in humans is crucial for understanding the construction of reality, human existence, and access to knowledge.[6] Here, it is the mind that is soaring to new heights, seeking

---

[5]This is not to discount the Platonic notion of the transcendent Supreme Being/First Cause as also being present in Philo's conception of God. This pairing of Hebrew and Platonic concepts seems somewhat paradoxical to the modern reader. Cf., *e.g.*, *Conf.* 136-37 where God is both everywhere and nowhere. It is important not to overstate this paradox, however, for Judaism and the Hebrew Scriptures certainly exhibit a notion of the transcendence of God. Another way of looking at this paradox in Philo is given by A. M. J. Festugière, O.P., *La révélation d'Hermès Trismégiste, IV (Le Dieu inconnu et la gnose)* (Paris: Gabalda, 1954) 1-51, who notes that there were two predominant strands of thought about God in pre-Philonic Greco-Roman philosophy: that of the Pythagoreans who stressed the unknowability of God and that of the Stoics who emphasized the pantheistic and pervasive nature of God. Festugière argues that the two strands remained separate until they were fused by Philo and Pseudo-Aristotle. In doing so, it seems that Philo would then be seeking to combine in philosophy what he already saw present in Judaism, namely the diverse and paradoxical nature of God.

[6]Considerable scholarly debate still exists regarding the philosophical influences on Philo's construction of reality. David Winston, *Logos and Mystical Theology in Philo of Alexandria* (Cincinnati: Hebrew Union Press, 1985) argues that Philo is an ardent Platonist seeking to reconcile his ancestral heritage with his philosophical system; Valentin Nikiprowetzky, *Le commentaire de l'écriture chez Philon d'Alexandrie: Son caractère et sa portée* (Leiden: Brill, 1977) argues that Philo is first and foremost a Jew who has complex reasons for seeking to reconcile Hellenism and Judaism. Other opinions are set forth by Burton Mack, "Under the Shadow of Moses: Authorship and Authority in Hellenistic Judaism," in *SBL Seminar Papers 1982*, ed. Kent Richards (Chico CA: Scholars Press, 1982) and John Dillon, *The Middle Platonists: A Study of Platonism 80 BC–AD 220* (London: Duckworth, 1977). Because it takes all three elements of Philo's thought equally seriously, I prefer the model of David Runia where three elements are

(ζητέω), contemplating, and exploring (ἐρευνάω) the Deity.[7] The mind governs the soul for Philo, not vice versa. It is important that the νοῦς here ascends; it is not displaced nor is it overtaken as it is in Plutarch's descriptions since Plutarch emphasizes the ψυχή. The νοῦς probably is not aware of its material surroundings, but it is still active. This action is focused on searching for God and divine knowledge. Thus, Philo seems to have a quasirational view of inspiration here rather than the clearly irrational view of Plutarch. The νοῦς is active and conscious but in an unusual and abnormal way that is highly mystical.

Finally, the mind is ultimately frustrated in its attempts here to know the divine mind, reflecting Philo's conviction that the human mind can travel into the divine realm only so far before being thwarted. At the end of this passage, the mind wishes to change its abode so that it can go further; alas, that is impossible in Philo's view of reality.[8] Nevertheless,

present in Philo but none has absolute priority: his loyalty to Judaism and the Law, his love of paideia and Greek philosophy, and his concern for the welfare of his people that lends an apologetic tone to some of his writings. These three are held in a dialectical tension as the various elements assume different levels of significance at diverse points in Philo's writings. See David Runia, *Philo of Alexandria and the Timaeus of Plato* (Leiden: Brill, 1986) 541-43. For a full discussion of the philosophical elements in Philo's thought, see John Dillon, esp. 139-83. For introductions to the thought of Philo, see Erwin R. Goodenough, *The Politics of Philo Judaeus: Practice and Theory* (New Haven: Yale, 1938); and Harry A. Wolfson, *Philo: Foundations of Religious Philosophy in Judaism, Christianity, and Islam* (Cambridge: Harvard, 1947).

[7]As the Supreme Form, God is the source of all knowledge who bestows that knowledge on creatures according to their abilities to understand. God is the archetype of rational existence, and humankind is a copy or representation of that archetype. Thus, humans are uniquely able to receive the divine gift of knowledge by virtue of their most God-like part, the mind (or rational part of the soul or reason). It is this part of the human that is able to relate to the Logos and therefore to a portion of God. Again, such knowledge is never full nor complete; rather it is always partial and fragmentary. Because the cosmos is created in such a way as to assist the human quest for knowledge, by the elevation of the mind, the human can contemplate God and ultimate truth. See *Cher.* 120-21; *Opif.* 25; 144; *Som.* 1.239; *Conf.* 147-48; *Spec. Leg.* 1.214; 4.14. Also *Det.* 83-90 where the νοῦς formerly was a part of the divine. Of course, much of this comes from the influence of Plato. Cf. *Tim.* 47a-c.

[8]For Philo, the primary essence of God is wholly transcendent but a portion of that essence is manifested on levels accessible to the human νοῦς. Crucial here is the bridging function of the Logos. Cf. *De Som.* 1.239; *Conf.* 147-8; and *Opif.* 25. For a full discussion of Philo's view of reality and the philosophical underpinnings for his thought,

God endows some people like Abram and Isaac, even before their birth with a "most excellent portion" (3.85). For example, at *Mos.* 2.187-191, Philo broadens this understanding somewhat in his portrayal of Moses, who is the supreme human philosopher, prophet, and seeker.[9] In some cases, Moses's mind is actively engaged and heightened by God; at other times, Moses's mind is completely displaced.[10]

In his allegorical explication of Gen 16:6-12, which focuses mainly on the words "fled," "found," and "fountain," Philo reveals more about his use of the language of the human search and divine inspiration. This particular passage concentrates on the idea of seeking, which is the focus of the larger section *De Fug.* 119-75. Here Philo interprets the story of the Burning Bush.

> But the prophet owing to desire of knowledge (ἐπιστήμης) lifts his eyes above the whole universe and becomes a seeker (ζητεῖ) regarding its Creator, asking of what sort this Being is so difficult to see . . . he prays that he may learn from God Himself what God is: for he had no hope of being able to ascertain (γνῶναι) this from another, from one of those that are inferior to Him. Nevertheless he did not succeed in finding (ἐρευνᾶν) anything by search respecting the essence of Him that is. . . . For it amply suffices the wise man (σοφῷ) to come to a

---

see Winston, *Logos and Mystical Theology.* See also his article "Philo and the Contemplative Life," in *Jewish Spirituality*, ed. Arthur Green (New York: Crossroad, 1987) 198-232.

[9]For an examination of the dynamics involved in Philo's juxtaposing his own authority with the authority of Moses, the author of the texts that Philo explicates, cf. Richard Hecht, "Scripture and Commentary in Philo." *SBL Seminar Papers 1981*, ed. K. Richards (Chico CA: Scholars Press, 1981) 129-64.

[10]Cf. David Winston, "Two Types of Mosaic Prophecy according to Philo," in *SBL Papers 1988*, ed. David Lull (Atlanta: Scholars Press, 1988) 442-55. Winston thinks that Philo appears to distinguish between two types of prophecy at *Mos.* 2.191. (1) προφητεία (ecstatic prophecy) mediates the message through divine possession. It resembles Hellenic oracular forms of prophecy more than does the scriptural portrayal of Moses. Cf. Balaam at *Mos.* 1.274-91. (2) ἑρμηνεία (interpretive prophecy) is the interaction between the divine mind and the human mind like that at the giving of the Decalogue and the question and answer method used at *Mos.* 2.188. Cf. also Noah and the Septuagint translators at *Her.* 260-66. Winston's theory is helpful, although I do not think that Philo consistently distinguishes these two types of prophecy throughout all of his writings. In one case, the mind is heightened; in the other, it is displaced.

knowledge (γνῶναι) of all that follows on after God and in His wake, but the man that wishes to set his gaze upon the Supreme Essence, before he sees Him will be blinded by the rays that beam forth all around Him. (*De Fug.* 164-65)

Again, the prominent role of the search is obvious, but here the seeker is Moses, who now becomes a σοφός hoping to know (γινώσκω). This inclusion of the σοφός is not surprising given Philo's predilection for Platonic ideas and Middle Platonist interpretations, particularly in his portrayal of Moses. The prophet Moses is a seeker who wants to find information regarding the essence of God. Again, that search is fruitful up to a point, but the human is ultimately thwarted in his efforts to acquire information. The prophet is blinded before actually seeing God, not an unfamiliar concept to Jewish readers of Philo who would certainly know of Moses' Pentateuchal physical encounters with God at the burning bush and later on at the mountaintop. On both occasions, the physical presence of God is intense and overwhelming. As in the example from *Leg. All.* 3.84, Philo here again does not have the mind displaced but rather refocused. Furthermore, Philo adds other important terms to his description of inspiration with forms of σοφία and γνῶσις, both of which recur in a number of the writers under consideration here, including Paul.

One should note here also that the seeker realizes that he is dependent upon God for acquiring divine knowledge. Such knowledge is not readily attainable simply to the human who desires or seeks it. Rather, the prophet prays that he can "learn from God Himself" for he knows that no other entity is able to reveal knowledge of God's essence. As we have already seen, human dependence on divine initiative, or grace, also recurs in many of the ancient writers who discuss the human search for knowledge.[11] The human prophet is not only innately incapable of full and complete understanding, but he is also totally dependent upon God for any knowledge at all.[12] Moreover, it is doubtful that Philo would

---

[11]This is a particular favorite in later Christian discussions using this cluster of terms. *E.g.*, Clement's *Strom.* 1.4.27.2; 4.17.108.5; 5.14.129.3; 6.18.166.4; and 8.1.1.2–8.1.2.2; and *Dives* 5.2. Cf. also Barnabas 10.10 and Origen *Cont. Cels.* 6.17.29; *Fragments on 1 Corinthians* §8 and §10.

[12]Cf. *Mig.* 34-5 where Philo describes his own ability in writing as sometimes

extend even this much capacity to humans other than Moses, who acquires semidivine characteristics in Philo's writings. In *Leg. All.* 3.84, however, it is unclear how much of the ascending mind can be achieved only by Abram and how much is attainable to other wise, seeking persons.

Two other examples from Philo will solidify our view of the writer who probably represents the most important parallel for our interpretation of 1 Cor 2:6-16. These two final texts have been selected because they provide important examples of ideas that specifically parallel Paul in 1 Corinthians. At *Opif.* 69-71, Philo again employs this set of language and ideas to describe the ascent of the mind (νοῦς). In this work as a whole, Philo interprets the creation account in Genesis. In this particular passage, he considers humanity to be the crowning achievement of creation (*Opif.* 65-66). This is true because to humans God gave the νοῦς par excellence (*Opif.* 66), which is itself the image of God (*Opif.* 69).

> The Mind (νοῦς) . . . is invisible while itself seeing all things, and while comprehending the substances of others, it is as to its own substance unperceived; and while it opens by arts and sciences roads branching in many directions, all of them great highways, it comes through land and sea investigating (διερευνάω) what either element contains. Again, when on soaring wing it has contemplated the atmosphere and all its phases, it is borne yet higher to the ether and the circuit of heaven, and is whirled around with the dances of planets and fixed stars, in accordance with the laws of perfect music (μουσικῆς τελείας νόμοι), following that love of wisdom (σοφία) which guides its steps. . . . [I]t is seized with Corybantic frenzy (κορυβαντικὴ ἐνθουσία), and is inspired, possessed by a longing far other than theirs and a nobler desire. Wafted by this to the topmost arch of the things perceptible to mind (νοητοί), it seems to be on its way to the Great King Himself; but amid its longing to see Him, pure and untempered rays of concentrated light stream forth like a torrent, so that by its gleams the eye of the understanding is dazzled. (*Opif* 69-71)

"incapable"; at other times he is ἔνθεος so that ideas fall in a "shower from above." Also *Cher.* 27.

Again, Philo emphasizes that the νοῦς is humanity's divine image and endowment. The νοῦς enables the human to contemplate his maker. Here the description clearly transcends the patriarchal exemplars, Abram and Moses. Not only does Philo employ a mysticism to describe the human seeker's quest for σοφία, he also demonstrates a conviction that much of this search and inspiration is at least partially irrational. That irrationality, however, is not like the displaced mind of the mere human vessel in Plutarch. Rather, Philo has the mind leaving the material realm behind to gaze upon the divine. It goes to the "topmost arch of things perceptible" to the human mind (νοήτοι). Philo's mysticism here is unmistakable as the mind travels ever higher into the ether and circuitry of heaven so that it dances with the constellations. It seems that the νοῦς is maximized or heightened rather than discarded. Despite its close relationship to God, the mind achieves much, but ultimately it is dazzled again by intense light as it reaches the topmost level attainable for human comprehension. Furthermore, the irrational "Corybantic frenzy" seizes and possesses the mind, taking it to new heights of experience.[13] Thus, Philo seems to blend the rational and the irrational, perhaps because the description here applies by virtue of creation to all humans rather than simply to the models of Abram and Moses.

Thus far, Philo's descriptions have all applied only to individuals. Furthermore, the focus has been almost exclusively on the reception of knowledge with little attention given to any possible articulation or communication of that knowledge to others. In a particularly important text for the interpretation of 1 Cor 2:6-16, however, Philo writes at *Conf.* 53-59, in his own allegorical interpretation of the Babel events in Gen 11:1-9:

> For what our senses perceive, or our speech expresses, or our emotion
> causes us to feel, and how or why each result is attained, are matters
> which we should scrutinize carefully (ἐρευνάω) and expose every
> error that we find. He who contradicts none of these, but assents to all
> as they come before him, is unconsciously deceiving himself and raising

---

[13]Again, cf. *Migr.* 34-35. For later Christian usage, cf. Clem. *Strom.* 5.14.129.3 where Pindar speaks "as if in a Bacchic frenzy." Here, Clement also parallels Philo's notion of the Greeks' plagiarism of the Hebrews. For a good description of Corybantic frenzy, cf. Dodds, *Greeks and Irrational*, 78-80.

up a stronghold of dangerous neighbors to menace the soul. . . . "We," they will continue, "like instruments of music (μουσικῆς ὄργανα) where all the notes are in perfect tune, echo with our voices all the lessons we have received." . . . [T]he prize is given to those who, after diligent and careful scrutiny (διερευνάω), following the more certain testimony of sight, rather than hearing, have the will to accept the faith (πιστεύω) that mortality is full of unfaith and clings only to the seeming. Wonderful then indeed is the symphony (συμφωνία) of voices here described, but most wonderful of all, exceeding every harmony (ἁρμονία), is that united universal symphony in which we find the whole people (ὁ λαὸς ἅπας) declaring with one heart, "All that God hath said, we will do and hear" (Exod 19:8). Here the precentor whom they follow is no longer the Word (λόγος), but God the Sovereign of all. . . . For other men act after they have heard, but these under the divine inspiration (ἔνθεος) say—strange inversion—that they will act first and hear afterwards, . . . so that they may judge (ἐπικρίνω) their actions, whether they chime with the divine words (λόγοι θεῖοι) and the sacred admonitions.

As Philo interprets Genesis 11 allegorically, he concentrates on the idea of "one lip and one voice." He takes this concept to refer to a chorus or unison of voices, present not only in the Babel multitude but also within each individual as well. He contrasts that chorus of evil with the words of Genesis 42:11 when Joseph's brothers visit him in Egypt (*Conf.* 40): "We are all sons of one man; we are peaceful." For Philo, the "one man" becomes the Logos, who brings peace. The purely theoretical, highest possible attainment of the Logos would be Israel's concord when it pledged at Exodus 19:8 to "do and hear" God's will even before hearing the commandments in Exodus 20.

This text is noteworthy for the context turns from a purely indivi-dualistic mystical pursuit of knowledge to a communal pledge of faithful response to God's revelation, an idea paralleled, as far as I can deter-mine, only in 1 Corinthians. Philo is interested in describing the people of Israel, theoretically existing in perfect harmony and speaking with one voice.[14] Here, the contrast is drawn between those who are willing to

---

[14]Furthermore, Philo uses the image of musical instruments to capture the idea of this communal inspiration. Other writers use the imagery of music, but only Philo and Paul do so in a corporate fashion.

accept the belief (πιστεύω) that the spiritual realm is essentially
different from the material one and those who are not. The spiritual is
eternal and divine; the material is worldly and ephemeral. Philo portrays
the people of Israel, if and when they should come as a body to
recognize these truths and God's sovereignty, as a unison of sound
(συμφωνία) that speaks in perfect harmony with one voice of God's
deeds.[15] Moreover, such a pledge comes "under the divine inspiration"
before they even hear God's commandments in the first place! According
to Philo, they have explored, investigated, and examined together to
arrive at some measure of ultimate metaphysical knowledge and truth
about the Deity. Not surprisingly, this knowledge is given as a prize, as
Philo again stresses the divine role in this acquisition of wisdom.[16]

Philo also introduces the importance of judging or discerning
(ἐπικρίνω) actions and words in order to determine their validity for
divine knowledge. This notion implies the presence, real or potential, of
false teaching and/or actions in need of judgment by the Hebrew
community as described by Philo or perhaps by Philo's audience itself.
This idea also parallels 1 Corinthians where, as I will discuss in detail
later on, forms and cognates of κρίνω recur as Paul exhorts the Corinthians to judge both themselves and their own actions and to discern the
merit of Paul's directives.

Two other concepts here are especially significant. First, Philo
describes the articulation of this divine knowledge rather than just its
reception. The people, a unison (συμφωνία) of voices, *speak* with one
voice. Unlike the other texts where Philo has described the inspired mind
as it acquires knowledge, he moves further here as the people *declare*
with one heart the precept of Exodus 19:8.

Second, Philo utilizes a corporate dimension, displaying only here the
belief that the search and inspiration can involve more than just the
individual. Elsewhere, the search is a private affair between the seeker
and the divine. Both of these ideas will be crucial for the interpretation
of 1 Cor 2:6-16, particularly as Paul makes similar moves with the same
kinds of language but goes still further in the development of the

---

[15]Cf. Plato *Crat.* 405d.

[16]For more on Philo's view of the role of the spirit in accessing divine knowledge,
cf. *Gig.* 9; *Mut.* 6; 56; *Spec. Leg.* 1.46. All of these are grounded in the ancient
philosophical commonplace, especially popular with the Stoics, that like is known by like.

communal dimension. For Paul, it seems that the Spirit simultaneously inspires the community as a whole and the individual members within it. For Philo, inspiration usually involves just the individual while here it is just the community. Philo never describes both at the same time.

Finally, Philo exemplifies virtually all of the common pool of language and ideas under consideration here. The language he uses to describe the human search for the divine mind and subsequent inspiration shows both similarities and differences with those utilized by the Greek writers already discussed as well as the examples in Josephus, the LXX, apocalyptic literature, and Paul in 1 Cor 2:6-16. Like Paul, Philo uses forms and cognates of κρίνω, ἐρευνάω, γινώσκω, χαρίζομαι, θεός, σοφία, νοῦς, κόσμος, μέρος, and τέλος. Unlike Paul, but like many of the other writers in this era, Philo also uses terms and ideas characterized by forms and cognates of φύσις, δόγμα, ἐπιστήμη, ἔνθεος, ζητέω, and συμφωνία. Like Paul, Philo emphasizes the role of God as the giver and the object in the process. Also like Paul, Philo links that process to the human mind (νοῦς) and occasionally uses the imagery of musical instruments. Most importantly, Philo provides our only example of the corporate dimension of the search for knowledge and inspiration.

For Philo, however, much of this searching process is not only mystical but also somewhat irrational, which itself is not really a Pauline parallel. Furthermore, Philo spends considerably more time setting forth the role of the individual than he does exploring any social and corporate aspects of the quest. His interest is not so much like the Pauline effort to modify communal behavior; rather, Philo seeks to describe the individual's quest for divine knowledge. At *Conf.* 53-59, that interest spills over onto Philo's view of the people of Israel as God's inspired instrument.

Finally, one should mention the significance of Philo's choice of literary form, the commentary on scripture. This choice distinguishes him from the philosophical treatises used by many of his contemporary Middle Platonists as well as from Plato's original dialogues, Plutarch's reflective essays, Julian's polemical writings, and Paul's personal letters of pastoral care and exhortation. As Paul occasionally does, Philo frequently uses another text, the LXX, as his springboard for discussion. Philo comments on that text in an effort to elicit the truth embedded there by the Logos since Philo views scripture as a written reflection of the divine Logos. Such convictions are not the case in writers such as Julian or Plutarch.

Thus, in a variety of contexts, spanning Philo's interpretation of scripture from the creation account to Babel, Philo can employ similar language in discussions that center on inquiry and inspiration. He can provide for the inspiration of the paradigmatic νοῦς of Abram, the ultimate human Moses, the generic created human νοῦς, or the corporate body of Israel. For Philo, that inspiration can be ecstatic or irrational. This is true of Philo's description of Balaam, of portions of Philo's descriptions of Moses, and of his depiction of the Corybantic frenzy in *Opif.* 69-71. For Philo, that inspiration can also be optimizing and mystical, whereby the νοῦς is still active but heightened. This type is more often the case in Philo's descriptions of Moses, and it also seems to apply to Philo's description of the inspired Israel at *Conf.* 53-59. In all these cases, a human seeks the divine mind and is subsequently inspired.

Josephus

Josephus provides another example of Jewish usage of language about irrational inspiration although he uses it infrequently.[17] Josephus,

---

[17]At *AJ* 4.104-20, Josephus portrays the events involving Balaam and his inspiration. As in the writings of Philo and others, in Josephus's account, God is clearly in control and gives (χαρίζομαι) the knowledge and inspiration. The emphasis here is on predicting the future, not unlike the emphasis in *BJ* 3.340ff, a text that I discuss below. Furthermore, Balaam's inspiration involves clearly irrational elements. Josephus uses the common term μάντις to describe Balaam, who is overcome by God's Spirit (πνεῦμα) and is unconscious when much of this happens. For Philo's portrayal of Balaam, cf. *Mos.* 1.274-91. A second issue to be considered in interpreting Josephus' language is the matter of prophecy in the ancient world. Modern scholarship has often sought to distinguish between prophets, defined as social and moral reformers, and those figures who predicted the future. Yet it is evident that Josephus' definition of prophecy is much broader than that. He presents Jeremiah as a priest denouncing sin and urging repentance, but he also portrays Daniel as an esoteric wise man who interprets the meaning of dreams and omens, and who understands God's sacred plans. It seems reasonable to conclude that Josephus' understanding of prophecy is quite broad, encompassing a predictive aspect, a need for technical expertise (*e.g.*, dream interpretation), and a certain priestly dimension. Thus, he probably did see himself as something of a forlorn Jeremiah-like prophet who also foretold the future to Vespasian. For more on the comparison with Jeremiah, see Rebecca Gray, *Prophetic Figures in Late Second Temple Jewish Palestine: The Evidence from*

however, demonstrates no interest in the human search for the divine mind. The acquisition of divine knowledge and the idea of inspiration are not ones that frequent Josephus's writings because he is more an apologetic historian than a philosopher or metaphysician. Thus, Josephus exhibits no real concern for the philosophical abilities of the νοῦς.

At *BJ* 3.340-390, Josephus, in a heavily apologetic passage, describes his own personal survival and escape at Jotapata during the Jewish War by claiming that he was inspired by God for a new and higher task, to foretell Vespasian's military and political success. He presents himself as an inspired prophetic interpreter of sacred books, dreams, and ambiguous utterances.[18] It is his capture at Jotapata that is crucial to the present

---

Josephus (Oxford: Oxford University Press, 1993) and also David Daube, "Typology in Josephus," *JJS* 31 (1980): 18-36, who parallels the two men. For a view that varies widely from Daube, see Helgo Lindner, *Die Geschichtsauffassung des Flavius Josephus in Bellum Judaicum* (Leiden: Brill, 1972). Gray also provides an examination of other prophetic figures in Palestine during this same period. For example, she discusses Essenes like Judas, Menahem, and Simon; sign prophets; and other figures like Jesus, Son of Ananias. Cf. also Joseph Blenkinsopp, "Prophecy and Priesthood in Josephus," *JJS* 25 (1974): 239-62; and Richard A. Horsley, "Like One of the Prophets of Old: Two Types of Popular Prophets at the Time of Jesus," *CBQ* 47 (1985): 435-63.

[18]Compare the work of Tessa Rajak, Rebecca Gray, Louis Feldman, and Shaye J. D. Cohen for four different interpretations of Josephus' self-understanding as an author and possibly as a prophet. Tessa Rajak, *Josephus: The Historian and His Society* (London: Duckworth, 1983) believes that it is difficult to say that Josephus consistently saw himself as a prophet. Rajak thinks that any self-reference of Josephus to a prophetic mission bears an element of calculation on Josephus' part. In other words, the prophetic self-referential language in *BJ* 3 is no more than a function of the apologetic nature of the discourse. It simply provides Josephus with an alibi for his actions. Shaye J. D. Cohen, *Josephus in Galilee and Rome: His Vita and Development as a Historian* (Leiden: Brill, 1979) sees in Josephus' writings a chronological development from the early role of a Roman historian to a later role as a religious nationalist. Cohen is particularly interested in noting the developments in Josephus' thought over the thirty years of his literary career, so he thinks that Josephus began to write as a Jewish propagandist and interpreter for the Romans. Therefore, in *BJ*, Josephus really saw himself as a Jeremiah-like prophet rather than as a traitor. Cohen claims that Josephus believed himself to have been one of the few Jews to recognize the inevitability of the divinely sanctioned Roman rule. As such, he was commissioned by God to convey that message, along with a message of acquiescence, to his fellow Jews. Rebecca Gray also deals in detail with this issue. She seeks to sketch the formal distinction between the age in which Josephus lived and those prior ages in which prophets were truly great. This distinction, according to Gray, prevents Jospehus from explicitly referring to himself as a "prophet," although he

discussion for it is in describing that capture that he is most forthcoming about himself and his motives. In this self-presentation, we get a glimpse of Josephus' view of inspiration as he describes something like a prophetic call narrative.[19]

Josephus provides a lengthy account of his survival, his capture, and his subsequent prediction of the ascension of Vespasian to the Roman throne. The self-referential language becomes quite prominent as Josephus portrays himself in a thoroughly prophetic manner. This prophetic self-presentation is important for elsewhere he does not appear to make claims of inspiration for his overall written account of the Jewish revolt in *BJ*. Nor does he use such language for himself in his later works, even when mentioning Jotapata, Vespasian, and the other events and persons so crucial in *BJ*. He never explicitly refers to himself as a προφήτης, but the language is highly suggestive of such a prophetic claim. As he hides from the Romans in a cave with his colleagues, Josephus is "aided by some divine providence" (3.341: δαιμονίῳ τινὶ συνεργίᾳ χρησάμενος). Then he is a priest as well as an interpreter of dreams,

---

employs a number of words and images that reveal that he did at times view himself as such. Louis Feldman, "Prophets and Prophecy in Josephus," *JJS* 41 (1990): 386-422, argues that Josephus was not claiming prophetic powers in a classical sense but rather was simply claiming to be able to interpret dreams and foretell the future. Feldman claims that prophets only began to foretell the future in second-century Christianity, so Josephus' language was meant to appeal to a Greco-Roman audience that would associate predictive abilities with divine endorsement. Feldman sees no grounds for thinking that Josephus thought of himself as a prophet. For a good overall discussion of this phenomenon in both Judaism and Christianity, see also John Barton, *Oracles of God: Perceptions of Ancient Prophecy in Israel after the Exile* (London: Dartman, Longman, and Todd, 1986), who believes that the key issue relative to authority in Josephus' mind was the idea of antiquity. Judaism would therefore succeed or fail by virtue of its response to its own traditions and customs. Thus, Josephus was pointing backward with his prophetic language to those very traditions grounded in the great prophets of old. Cf. also two works of David E. Aune: *Prophecy in Early Christianity and the Ancient Mediterranean World* (Grand Rapids: Eerdmans, 1983) and "The Use of προφήτης in Josephus," *JBL* 101 (1982): 419-21. For a thorough bibliography of research on Josephus, see Louis Feldman, *Josephus and Modern Scholarship (1937-1980)* (Berlin: DeGruyter, 1984).

[19]The notion of the call is a subject that itself deserves more attention although such an examination is beyond the scope of this investigation. For scholarship on this topic, cf. Kurt Deissner, "Das Sendungsbewußtsein der Urchristenheit," *ZSTh* 7 (1930): 772-90; and John Moles, "The Career and Conversion of Dio Chrysostom," *Journal of Hellenic Studies* 98 (1978): 79-100.

skilled in ascertaining the meaning of ambiguous utterances of the Deity. Finally, he is inspired (ἔνθους γενόμενος: *BJ* 3.351-3).

As we have seen, such language has strong precedents in Greek literature, particularly in describing an overtaking of the human by the divine. It is possible that Josephus employs it here because much of his audience was a learned group of Hellenized Romans. After all, this is the account of a war, written by a participant in that war who surrendered to the Romans and then wrote under their patronage. It is generally agreed that Josephus writes with an apologetic slant as he seeks to present Judaism and himself in a positive light. In other words, the language of inspiration may be more a reflection of Josephus' views of his audience than of his own views as a Jew. Josephus may use this phrase to defend his actions, which may have been viewed as cowardly or traitorous, by using language that would connote to his Roman audience the impression of a decision made under ecstatic possession rather than made simply as a human.

Josephus also employs ἔνθους γενόμενος, a phrase common in contemporary secular literature to denote ecstatic utterance and possession, to describe the actions of prophets like Elijah and Saul in the *Jewish Antiquities* (*AJ*). Furthermore, he does not hesitate to call such prophets of old by the designation προφήτης.[20] Nevertheless, Josephus, for all his interesting data about prophecy, does not ever seek to describe a human search for divine knowledge or deep spiritual matters using the same kind of language evidenced by Philo, Plutarch, and Plato. For example, ἐρευνάω is used more than forty times by Josephus but never in a prophetic context.[21] Likewise, βάθος (cf. 1 Cor 2:10) occurs throughout Josephus' writings but not in connection with spiritual matters or the deep things of God.[22] Despite the dearth of common vocabulary, Josephus does place the impetus for inspiration clearly with God, an

---

[20]*E.g.*, cf. *AJ* 6:1ff; 7:300ff; 8:200ff; 9:1ff; and 10:1ff. Such passages reflect concentrations of the use of this designation.

[21]The two most potentially illuminating uses are at *AJ* 8.332 where Josephus describes the prophet Elijah, but the verb ἐρευνάω is used about a search to kill rather than for divine knowledge. At *BJ* 1.599.3, Josephus describes ghosts in the royal court detecting secret mysteries.

[22]This term is used by Josephus almost exclusively to describe buildings, structures, and pits.

emphasis which is by now a common refrain from Plato to Philo. Finally, Josephus does allow for the irrational displacement of the mind (*e.g.*, his portrayal of Balaam) in a way that closely parallels the views of Plutarch, his contemporary. Such a view also colors Josephus's self-presentation in *BJ* 3.34-390 as he depicts himself as an irrationally and divinely inspired prophet. Josephus's description of inspiration centers on the Divine supplanting the human.

The LXX and Apocalyptic Traditions

The Jewish apocalyptic tradition as evidenced in 4 Ezra also draws on the common pool of language concerning inquiry and inspiration.[23] Michael Stone has produced a thorough discussion of the theme of inspiration in apocalyptic literature.[24] Particularly pervasive in apocalyptic literature's discussions of inspiration are emphases on the important roles of angels, daimons, and intermediaries in apocalyptic inspiration, and on the apocalyptic concepts of dreams and visions.

In particular, Stone focuses on the example of inspiration provided in 4 Ezra 14:37-41 as a means of evaluating and interpreting such language elsewhere. This passage describes the inspiration given to Ezra as he is just about to receive the entire Bible and esoteric literature from God and to dictate it to scribes. The stages of inspiration described here include: (1) the onset of inspiration, (2) a feeling of enlightenment following that onset, (3) the retention of the content of revelation in Ezra's spirit, and (4) the inspired ability to articulate and dictate this content.

Stage 1 has parallels throughout apocalyptic literature and often evokes images of divine initiative, often using an angelophany or a vision. This first stage frequently centers on a seer's distressed or

---

[23]Apocalyptic literature particularly describes the phenomena of angels and inspiration. Cf. Ezekiel 40; 1 Enoch 10:3; 72:1; 2 Enoch 1:4; Daniel 8:16; and 2 Baruch 55:3. For another example of inspired speech, cf. the *Testament of Job* 48-52. Martin, "Tongues of Angels," 559, labels this as esoteric speech since Job's daughters speak and sing in heavenly languages.

[24]Michael Stone, *4 Ezra,* Hermeneia (Minneapolis: Augsburg Fortress, 1990) 119-24. Much of my discussion relies on Stone's excursus on inspiration there.

troubled spirit.[25] Stage 2 frequently employs language about the heart and captures the actual act of revelation from the Divine. Stage 3 uses language about the spirit and focuses on the retention of the revealed content. For example, throughout 4 Ezra 14, Ezra prays to God to send His Spirit into him and then is given the cup of inspiration to drink.[26] In contrast, the first four visions of 4 Ezra come as a result of Ezra's troubled spirit rather than from drinking the cup of inspiration. Visions 5 and 6 are dreams. Finally, stage 4 utilizes language about the mouth. For example, 4 Ezra 14:41 states, "My mouth was opened and no longer closed," which serves to introduce the inspired articulation of revealed material.

The vision in 4 Ezra 4 presents an example of the search for comprehension and locates that search at the center of the seer/prophet's dispute with God and His angel. This description typifies 4 Ezra, in which understanding the way of the Most High God is often described as "discovering His judgment." As such, Ezra understands the search for understanding the Divine as the centerpiece of human existence. In fact, Ezra is later granted an interpretation because "you . . . have searched out my law for you have devoted your life to wisdom and called understanding your mother" (13:54-55). Here the search focuses on the Law rather than on God.

Furthermore, 4 Ezra moves beyond the inquiry and reception of divine knowledge to discuss its articulation to others as Ezra communicates his visions. God's revelation of the Bible and esoteric literature to Ezra in 4 Ezra 14 is explicitly said to be partly for public distribution and partly secret. In other words, only a portion of the revealed matter can be articulated. The rest is esoteric and private.[27] Stone also notes that Ezra describes intellectual capacities with references to the heart and breast and describes inspiration with references to the spirit and articulation with references to the tongue. Finally, the theme of humanity's

---

[25]Cf. 2 Enoch 1:3-5.

[26]For inspiration as drinking from the divine, cf. Philo *Ebr.* 146-48 and *Fug.* 162-68; and Ezekiel 2-3. Cf. also Plutarch *Pyth.* 406B; *Defectu* 432E. For the "lamp of understanding" lit within Ezra's "heart," cf. Plutarch *Pyth.* 397C; *Defectu* 433D.

[27]As we will see in my chapter 5 below, this notion has significant parallels and affects the reading of 1 Cor 3:1-4.

inability to comprehend the unsearchable ways and mind of God recurs throughout 4 Ezra.[28]

Other apocalyptic views of inspiration complement that of 4 Ezra. In the *Ascension of Isaiah*, the seer is in a trance but is also able to retain the vision's content and recount it later.[29] Further, Hans Lewy has noted the common tradition that the Sibyl lacked memory while the scribes were unable to keep up with the Sibyl's rapid speech.[30] Ezra reverses this Sibylline tradition by remembering all that he receives and presenting his own experience of revelation in a manner paralleling that given to Moses. Ezra's spirit clearly retains its memory.

Other important Jewish evidence for the idea of the search for the divine mind would also include LXX passages[31] such as Judith 8:14, a text that shows remarkable parallels with 1 Cor 2:10-11, 16a, when it says:

> For you cannot find (εὑρίσκω) the depth (βάθος) of the heart (καρδίας) of man, neither can you perceive the things that he thinks: then how can you search out (ἐρευνάω) God who has made all these things and know (ἐπιγινώσκω) his mind (νοῦς) or comprehend (κατανοέω) his purpose?

Here Judith rebukes the Bethulians for their testing of God for they have given God an ultimatum for action. As a result of their giving of that ultimatum, Judith reminds them of God's inscrutability and the fact

---

[28]Cf. 2 Baruch 20:4.

[29]Cf. *Asc. Isa.* 6:10-16.

[30]Cf. Hans Lewy, *Sobria Ebrietas: Untersuchungen zur Geschichte der Antiken Mystik*, BZNW 9 (Giessen: Töpelmann, 1929): 95 n2.

[31]Of course, a thorough and detailed examination of the broad issue of inspiration in the LXX is far beyond the scope of this investigation. Such an examination would include an analysis of the various ways in which the prophets present themselves as the inspired recipients of God's Word, a phenomenon that is paralleled to some degree at 4 Ezra 14:41. The LXX obviously contains many other disparate descriptions of inspiration. For three introductory discussions of this issue, cf. Aune, *Prophecy*, chap. 4; Gerhard von Rad, *Old Testament Theology*, 2 vols., trans. D. M. G. Stalker (London: Oliver and Boyd, 1962) 1:93-103 and 2:50-98; and Robert R. Wilson, *Prophecy and Society in Ancient Israel* (Philadelphia: Fortress, 1980) chap. 6.

that their action of presuming to know God's mind borders on self-idolatry. In other words, humans *cannot* search the mind of God, and Judith emphasizes the absolute sovereignty of God, whose ways cannot be comprehended by humans. In this respect, Judith 8:14 parallels 1 Cor 2:9 where Paul cites an unknown text in order to describe God's otherness and the hiddenness of God's ways. Likewise, at 1 Cor 2:11, Paul clarifies with his statement that only the Spirit can comprehend the things of God.

In another example of this language in the LXX, the writer of Proverbs makes the human spirit into an agent of the divine, which searches and scrutinizes the innermost parts. "The spirit (πνοή) of a human is a light (φῶς) of the Lord (κύριος), who searches (ἐρευνάω) the inmost parts of the belly"(Prov 20:27). This text is rather ambiguous, however, for it is unclear what the ontological relation between the human spirit and the Lord is. Moreover, it is uncertain whether it is the human spirit or the Lord who searches the innermost depths of a human. Nevertheless, Proverbs does describe the close scrutiny of spiritual, esoteric matters.

In addition, the psalmist prays in Psalm 119 for God's intercession during a time of trouble. The psalmist, however, opens this prayer with modest ethical instruction. "Blessed are they that search out (οἱ ἐξερευνῶντες) His testimonies: they will diligently seek Him (ἐκζητέω) with the whole heart" (Ps 119:2).[32] This is how the LXX usually renders בקשׁ. This passage perhaps best parallels those texts already considered in this book because here the human is encouraged to seek out the divine witness. Doing so leads to blessedness. The context of moral instruction also parallels Paul's hortatory, paraenetic efforts in 1 Corinthians, but the Psalmist's depiction of the human search for the divine mind resembles more those of Julian and Philo since the human is the agent of the search, whereas Paul emphasizes that God is the agent in 1 Cor 2:6-16.

Excursus: Post-Pauline Christian Literature

As evidenced in the notes up to this point, Christian authors after Paul used terms and ideas about inquiry into the divine mind similar to those

---

[32]Cf. Clem. *Strom.* 5.14.129.3 for the use of this same psalm (119) in later literature.

found in 1 Cor 2:6-16.[33] At 1 Clem 21:2, the author quotes the aforementioned Prov 20:27, and 1 Clem 21:9 calls God a "searcher of thoughts"
(ἐρευνητὴς ἐννοιῶν). The context here in 1 Clement is not so much
a philosophical discussion of divine inquiry but a rhetorical and hortatory
effort to modify the Corinthians' behavior. To paraphrase, because God
alone knows all thoughts and observes all human actions, the Corinthians
should therefore act properly. At 1 Clem 40:1, the author also attempts
to modify behavior by telling the Corinthians to do what has been
commanded by God "since we have looked into the depths (βάθη) of
divine knowledge (γνῶσις)." Thus, while 1 Clement 21 says something
of God's searching of humans, 1 Clement 40 reverses that in order to
illustrate that believers have already had access to the depths of God. In
one case, God does the searching, whereas in the other, it is the Christian
who has already searched the deep things of God.

The Epistle of Barnabas likewise uses similar language in its efforts
to warn against any Christian appropriation of an overly legalistic conception of the Old Testament. At 4:1, Christians should "inquire"
(ἐραυνάω) into the things that "are" and "seek out" (ἐκζητέω) only
those things that are able to save. At 10:10, βάθος is used in a similar
counsel to the readers.[34] Believers seek out the salvific deep things of the
divine mind while foolish outsiders do not.

This same language developed still further in the later Christian
writings of Clement and Origen. As noted throughout this investigation,
their use of this cluster of terms and ideas is extensive. In Clement's
Stromata, this language is used repeatedly to describe the efforts of the
true philosopher, the lover of truth. In this regard, Clement more closely
resembles Plato than Paul. Of course, Clement, like Philo, writes in the
Platonistically-charged environment of Alexandria. At *Strom.* 7.15.91,
Clement seeks to show how that same lover of truth distinguishes the true
from the seeming, truth from heresy. At 8.1.1-8.1.2, Clement writes
eloquently that the proper objective of theological and philosophical
inquiry is the discovery of truth. The seeker also asks questions of the
scriptures and is given the gift of knowledge by God.

---

[33]In addition, cf. Justin *Dialog* 56.16; Hermas 10.1.6. In later literature, cf. Chrys.
Hom. 21.1 in Romans.

[34]The notions of "depths" and the "abyss" were particular favorites of Origen as well.
Cf. also 1 Clem 59:3.

For it is impossible to find (εὑρίσκω) without having sought; or to have sought (ζητέω) without having examined (ἐρευνάω); or to have examined (διερευνάω) without having unfolded and opened up the question. (8.1.2)

Seeking here applies to the searching of the scriptures, an idea attributed to scribes and Pharisees in John 5:39 and 7:52. Thus, Clement does not describe God as searching humans as in 1 Clement 21, nor humans searching for the divine mind as in 1 Clement 40; rather, Clement depicts believers who search the scriptures in the hope of finding divine truth. Then the seeker receives the prize of knowledge.

Moreover, at *Strom.* 4.17.107, Clement quotes Proverbs 20:27 regarding his own interpretation of 1 Clement, and at 4.17.108, he quotes 1 Clement 21:9 on the same matter.[35] Thus, the texts dealing with this familiar topic begin to merge as later interpreters utilize earlier texts.

Most importantly, in appropriating 1 Cor 2:6-16, Clement moves to claims that those who possess the Spirit can search the deep things of God (cf. *Strom.* 2.2.7.3). The searching that the Spirit does in 1 Corinthians is explicitly transferred to the Christian who possesses the Spirit. Moreover, the Christian alone can "grasp the secret that is in the prophecies."

Origen, also writing in Alexandria, picks up this same theme at *Cont. Cels.* 6.17.29 when he says that the depths (βάθη) of God are attainable only to those who possess the Spirit that searches all things. Interestingly, Origen's allusion to 1 Cor 2:10 here comes in a discussion chiefly about Moses's superiority as one of the few men to have been enlightened by the Logos.[36] In a sense, then, Origen, also writing in Alexandria, blends Plato, Philo, and Paul.

Finally, as stated before, this familiar language is important throughout Origen's writings about the interpretation and inspiration of scripture. Only the one who "searches the scriptures" can fathom the

---

[35]He also refers to Prov 20:27 at *Strom.* 7.7.37 and to Ps 119:2 at *Strom.* 7.1.1.

[36]For two discussions of Origen's view of inspiration set against the larger cultural context, see Grant, *The Letter and the Spirit,* and Robert J. Hauck, *The More Divine Proof: Prophecy and Inspiration in Celsus and Origen,* AAR Series 69, (Atlanta: Scholars Press, 1989). Grant provides a review of evidence from Homer to Origen for views of inspiration.

depths and hope to attain perfection (see *Phil.* 1.14.9). Again, a post-Pauline Christian writer invokes the Johannine command to search the scriptures.

Hence, post-Pauline Christian literature often spends little time on theories of individual inspiration and devotes more attention to the inspiration of scripture. Clement and Origen stress that scripture is to be searched. Barnabas and 1 Clement, however, provide for humans to search the deep things of God. Nevertheless, there is no talk of irrational or ecstatic inspiration, an absence that probably reflects Paul's influence on later Christian notions of inspiration.[37]

Conclusions

Thus far, this investigation has demonstrated that a variety of writers in antiquity used a common cluster of terms and ideas to describe a common theme, the human effort to discover the mind of God. Writers using some portion of this constellation of ideas wrote in places as varied as Rome, Chaironeia, Constantinople, and Alexandria. Despite geographical, social, and religious variety, these writers utilize in some way the idea of the search along with the related emphases on σοφία, γνῶσις, and the divine initiative. The notion of the search obviously is at the center of this cluster, but so too is the common object of that search (God or gods) and the realization that divine aid is required for humans to acquire any such knowledge.

---

[37]Reiling, *Hermas*, provides an important discussion of how pagan understandings of prophecy and divination could create problems in Christian churches. For example, Reiling cites evidence from Hermas, the Didache, and Chrysostom's homily on 1 Cor 14:20ff to demonstrate early problems with the notion of the Christian μάντις, where a divinatory element is central. See Reiling, chap. 4. Furthermore, Reiling proposes that Hermas' eleventh mandate seeks to address a crisis in Christian prophecy occurring because of the growing presence of Hellenistic divinatory practices in Christianity. Hermas then seeks to differentiate between true Christian prophecy and pagan divination. It is interesting for my purposes here because the inspiration of the prophet is presented not as an act of the Spirit but as the work of an angel of the prophetic spirit. Hellenistic elements are present throughout Hermas' picture of inspiration, but Reiling argues that these elements were not borrowed; rather they were common property used by Hermas to elucidate his understanding of prophecy. See Reiling, chap. 5. Cf. David Hill, "On the Evidence for the Creative Role of Christian Prophets," *NTS* 20 (1974): 262-74.

Some of the writers stress irrationality more than others. For example, Plutarch depicts inspiration as the displacement of the priestess's mind. In Plato's description of the ideal philosopher, the inspiration is like an optimizing or maximizing of the human mind. In other cases, such as that of Philo's ascending νοῦς, inspiration carries a mystical quality that is neither wholly rational nor wholly irrational. For all the writers, the search is an individual endeavor rather than a social one. Furthermore, the writers have little to say about the articulation or communication of any discovered knowledge to others in a meaningful way. The search first and foremost serves the person involved and his interests alone. Only Philo indicates any sense of a corporate dimension in this process, yet he does this on only one occasion. At *Conf.* 53-59, he seeks to describe the inspiration of the people of Israel but in an ideal state. They ultimately fail to attain such a state, however, because of their disobedience. Moreover, unlike Paul, Philo does not provide for the unique notion of the divine inspiration of both the group as a whole as well as each individual within that group.

The language of inquiry and inspiration unites all these texts and writers surveyed. Their understandings of the nature of the divine entity clearly vary, but their interest in the human search for the divine will and in a description of that search does not. With this understanding, I can now turn to Paul and 1 Corinthians in general. In particular, at 1 Cor 2:6-16, Paul employs this same language already evidenced. However, nuances and emphases differentiate his usage in significant ways. The writers already considered can sharpen the focus for a new reading and improved understanding of previously more opaque passages.

Chapter 3
A First Look at 1 Corinthians 2:6-16

In this chapter I identify in 1 Cor 2:6-16 the language often used in antiquity to depict the human search for the divine mind and also points out the parallels between Paul's use of such language and the usage of the other writers surveyed in chapters 1 and 2. In addition, similar language appears in several other New Testament texts that will receive attention here as we seek to draw out the particularities of 1 Cor 2:6-16. A fuller exegesis of 1 Cor 2:6-16 will be the object of chapter 4, so it is the goal of this chapter simply to identify the issues and to raise the questions that will be at the center of chapter 4. In other words, this chapter bridges the broad surveys of chapters 1 and 2 with the analysis of 1 Corinthians in the chapters to follow.

One can easily identify in 1 Cor 2:6-16 a cluster of terms that are infrequent in Paul's writings. This cluster usually appears in other ancient descriptions of divine inquiry and the human quest for inspiration. I have underlined for emphasis those terms that are particularly important for this investigation of inspiration and inquiry language in Paul. "We speak *wisdom* among the *perfect*" (σοφίαν δὲ λαλοῦμεν ἐν τοῖς <u>τελεί-</u> <u>οις</u> : 2:6).[1] "*God* has *revealed* to us through the *Spirit*" (ἡμῖν δὲ

---

[1]Τέλειος here may also be translated as "mature" (RSV, NIV) or "complete." NEB renders this as "those who are ripe for it;" JB as "those who have reached maturity;" and TEV as "those who are spiritually mature." I have chosen to render it as "perfect" (KJV) because of the rhetorical contrast Paul is drawing between those with the Spirit (Christians) and those without it (the pagan world, etc.). "Perfect" heightens the contrast that Paul attempts to convey in this passage's modification of a misunderstanding held by some of the Corinthians regarding status and wisdom. Irenaeus also seems to read this as "perfect." Cf. his *Adv. Haer.* 5.6.1. Cf. also Laurence L. Welborn, "On the Discord in Corinth: 1 Corinthians 1-4 and Ancient Politics," *JBL* 106 (1987): 85-111. Welborn has shown that in Plato's *Laws*, the term describes the "perfect citizen" (*Leg.* 643d; 730d). The term can also denote the politically powerful or influential in writers such as Sophocles (*Aj.* 1352; *Ph.* 385), Herodotus (3.18; 9.106), and Josephus (BJ 1.12.5; AJ 14.12.2). Pearson, *Pneumatikos-Psychikos*, 29-30, provides evidence from Philo that the term τέλειος can also denote religious achievement and that the idea of "perfection" or

ἀπεκάλυψεν ὁ θεὸς δία τοῦ πνεύματος: 2:10a). "For the *Spirit searches* everything, even the *depths* of God" (τὸ γὰρ πνεῦμα πάντα ἐραυνᾷ, καὶ τὰ βάθη τοῦ θεου: 2:10b). "No one *knows* the thoughts of God except the *Spirit* of God" (τὰ τοῦ θεου οὐδεὶς ἔγνωκεν εἰ μὴ τὸ πνεῦμα: 2:11b). "We have the *mind* of Christ" (ἡμεῖς δὲ νοῦν Χριστοῦ ἔχομεν: 2:16b).

One must establish here the parallels and similarities, as well as some of the differences, that the language of 1 Cor 2:6-16 exhibits in comparison with the other texts already examined in this investigation. The language Paul uses here is obviously rare for him, but it is clearly not uncommon in other ancient writers seeking to describe the human quest for knowledge of and from the divine. In such texts, inspiration is understood as seeking and acquiring access to, or information from, the divine mind.

Elsewhere, at Romans 8:27, Paul introduces the idea of God's "searching" (again, ἐραυνάω) of hearts as well as the idea of the "mind of the Spirit" (φρόνημα τοῦ πνεύματος). Later, in Romans 11:25-36, which deals with the salvation of Israel, Paul provides a fuller parallel to the language and ideas of 1 Cor 2:6-16. In Romans 11:25a, Paul sets the stage for the discussion to follow as he begins, "I want you to understand this mystery (μυστήριον)." The ensuing section from Romans 11:25b-32 then deals with the details of this "mystery," the salvific priority of Israel and the Gentiles. Then in 11:33ff, Paul moves into a praising of God, which Nestle-Aland 26 has placed in strophic form.[2] In this hymnic praise, the reader finds much that mirrors 1 Cor 2:6-16 as βάθος, σοφία, γνῶσις, ἀνεραυνάω, and νοῦς all appear, and the quotation from Isaiah 40:13 in verse 34 is nearly identical to Paul's citation of that same passage at 1 Cor 2:16. Paul's praise in Romans 11 lauds the unknowability of God. God's riches, wisdom, and

---

"maturity" there is tied to the achievement of σοφία. Cf. *Mig.* 28ff; 46; *Leg.All.* 1.90-94; 3.196; and *Agr.* 8-9. Pearson posits that τέλειος was not the usual term for those persons initiated into the mysteries; rather that term was usually τετελεσμένος or τελεσθείς or τελούμενος. Therefore, Pearson thinks that such usage was originally Stoic and expanded by Hellenistic Jewish writers like Philo to express religious attainment.

[2] As he occasionally does (*e.g.*, 1 Cor 2:9), Paul appears to quote another ancient source, or more likely a combination of them.

knowledge are deep; God's ways are inscrutable. God is before and above all things, and His mind cannot be known by humans. This language regarding God's sovereignty and unknowability seems to fit well in Romans 11:33ff where the preceding discussion of the mystery of salvific priority is very complex and perhaps only divinely comprehended. In that context, an acknowledgment of God's inscrutability makes sense.

Similar language can also be found in the New Testament at 1 Peter 1:10-12, where the subject matter is clearly prophecy. According to the writer of 1 Peter, the Jewish prophets prepared the way of grace for Christians. Again, the relatively uncommon verb ἐραυνάω plays a crucial role. The author of 1 Peter develops the idea of a prophetic search for knowledge in his description of how the Hebrew prophets sought knowledge in advance of Christ. The prophets searched and inquired (ἐκζητέω and ἐξεραυνάω) about salvation and inquired (ἐραυνάω) about the times of God. Only after such a search did God then reveal divine knowledge to them (1:12). The writer uses this language to describe the Christians' source of hope immediately before he launches into the moral exhortation of 1:13ff.

At Revelation 2:23-4, the Spirit speaks to John regarding false prophecy in an apocalyptic revealing that itself may be prophetic. This specific text is located within the larger letter to the congregation at Thyatira. Here John denounces the false prophetess, called Jezebel (2:20), who by implication knows and speaks of βαθέα. However, these depths are probably βαθέα τοῦ σατανᾶ rather than βαθέα τοῦ θεοῦ. John rebukes this false prophet and her followers, yet it seems likely that βαθέα was a common subject matter for Christian prophets. Moreover, John invokes the language of God's searching powers to warn the audience of the divine judgment of all actions, teachings, and allegiances. Minds and hearts are searched (ἐραυνάω) by God (2:23), and deep spiritual matters (βάθος) are to be learned (2:24). Here, however, God is the one who searches and the prophets who deal in βαθέα. Furthermore, the context is clearly polemical for John uses this language of God's searching to admonish his readers.

Thus, other texts in the New Testament exhibit vocabulary like that in 1 Cor 2:6-16, but the contexts clearly vary and distinguish the usage of such language. As we will see, Paul's usage differs from that in 1 Peter and Revelation despite the obvious lexical similarities. Nevertheless, John does describe early Christian disputes over the possession and communication of spiritual βαθέα, and 1 Peter does provide for a human search (ἐραυνάω) into spiritual matters.

In 1 Cor 2:6-16, σοφία (2:5, 6, 7, 13), ἐραυνάω (2: 10), βάθος (2:10), and θεός (2: 7, 9, 10, 11, 12, 14) are all crucial terms. Σοφία describes a secret knowledge of God that is possessed by Christians (2:6-7). Of course, wisdom is an important issue in the interpretation of 1 Corinthians, but it is also often found at the center of ancient discussions of inquiry into the divine mind. For example, as we have seen, the topos of the true wise man, the σοφός, is central to Plato's *Apology* and to the thought of Philo (e.g., *De Fug.* 64-5). Both Plato and Philo understand the σοφός to be the one who seeks to know ultimate truth. It is no surprise then that σοφία is at the center of the issue of spiritual knowledge in 1 Corinthians 2.

Paul uses ἐραυνάω to depict the Spirit's searching of the divine mind (1 Cor 2:10b). Again, this verb frequents ancient discussions of the search for the divine mind. Along with the related verb ζητέω, ἐραυνάω often captures the active part of such a quest. Yet here in 1 Cor 2:6-16, Paul makes the Spirit the one who searches. In Revelation 2:23-24, it is God who searches; in 1 Peter, it is the Old Testament prophets; in Judith 8:14, it is the prideful Bethulians; and in 4 Ezra, it is Ezra himself who searches. Philo uses ἐρευνάω to describe the efforts of the individual in the search for divine wisdom (*Leg.All.* 384) or to characterize his own work in investigating ultimate matters and truth (*Abr.* 3.2). In other words, the subject of a search can vary broadly.

Significantly, at the same time, Paul reserves the term ἐραυνάω for the activity of the Spirit. "For the Spirit searches (ἐραυνᾷ) everything, even the depths of God" (2:10b). Only Paul places the activity distinctly with the Spirit rather than with God or the human. Paul thereby introduces another agent in the human quest to know the divine mind: the Spirit. It is the *Spirit* who "searches," and "*we*" have received "the Spirit which is from God" (2:12: emphasis mine). Thus, the human is not the one who searches but rather the Spirit; the Spirit then makes the divine mind accessible to the human. In a sense, then, the Spirit bridges the gap between God (and His depths) and humanity. This pneumatology fits well with other Pauline passages that emphasize the agency of the Holy Spirit and its critical role in the Christian life of faith.[3] According to Paul, it is plainly the Spirit of God that enables and empowers the Christian life.

Moreover, only Paul emphasizes the corporate nature of access to the divine mind and inspiration. Unlike Julian or Philo, Paul is not describing here some isolated, individual quest for inspiration. Rather, the quest occurs first of all within the context of the church community in some kind of interactive process. All Christians receive the Holy Spirit at baptism. "We" receive the "Spirit which is from God that we might understand the gifts bestowed on us by God" (2:12). The dispensing of the Spirit is not purely an individual affair. Nor is it purely theoretical and ideal construct like that of Philo at *Conf.* 53-59, where Philo describes the ideal, but unreal, Israel. Rather, it is central to the Pauline definition and founding of the Christian community, for the Spirit bestows the spiritual gifts on Christians (1 Cor 12:7-11); the Spirit pervades the life of the community.[4] The activity of the Spirit is not solely individualistic. Again, it is important to remember that Paul is writing a letter to a specific community of believers when he makes use of the language here.

As would be expected in a discussion of the search for divine knowledge, Θεός is at the center of 1 Cor 2:6-16, both as the object of the search and as the generative source of σοφία. Furthermore, the quotation in 2:9 clearly emphasizes humanity's inability to comprehend the divine without assistance from God, another idea common to such discussions. It is obvious by now how frequently these terms and ideas occur in a variety of ancient writers.

In addition, Paul here speaks of a μυστήριον (2:7), a term that has caused a considerable expenditure of scholarly ink. Like the σοφία it describes, this term seems linked to the cross of Christ, which the "rulers of this age" did not understand (2:8). This theme of two ages, ephemeral versus eternal, has clear apocalyptic parallels. Furthermore, Paul links the

---

[3]At 1 Cor 12:13, by one Spirit are all Christians "baptized into one body" and "made to drink of the one Spirit." At 12:7, 11, the one Spirit bestows the variety of gifts from God. At 3:16, God's Spirit dwells in His temple, the Corinthian congregation. Elsewhere, cf. Rom 5:5; Gal 3:2; 4:6; 5:16ff; Phil 2:1; 1 Thess 4:8; and 5:19, where Paul warns the Thessalonians not to "squelch the Spirit."

[4]Later in the study, I will demonstrate just how critical indeed is this communal dimension. The community, its health, and its upbuilding provide the benchmark against which the search for wisdom and inspiration are to be measured

communication of this divine mystery by God to humanity with the νοῦς (2:16b). Although the νοῦς probably does not play as prominent a role in Paul as it does in Philo (*Leg.All.* 3.84; *Opif.* 69-71), or even Plutarch (*Pyth.* 397C), it is significant that the νοῦς need not be overpowered or idle in order for the human to receive communication of the divine mystery. Perhaps Paul envisions that the human mind is heightened rather than displaced in this activity as it receives the endowment of σοφία from the Spirit in order to have "the mind of Christ" (2:16b). This possibility is made more likely by the Pauline contrast between the active νοῦς in prophecy and the disengaged νοῦς in tongue-speaking. For example, at 1 Cor 14:14-19, the role of the νοῦς seems central to the distinction between these two spiritual gifts. Nevertheless, the νοῦς does not appear as the central agent here as it does in Philo's writings where the νοῦς governs the soul and ascends on high in a mystical experience (*e.g., Leg.All.* 3.84ff; *Det.* 83-90).

Furthermore, Paul moves beyond the mere acquisition of knowledge to its articulation here. The verb λαλέω is prevalent. Of course, Paul develops this emphasis on speech still further in chapters 12–14, where spiritual gifts often involve speech; yet Paul never speaks of the inspiration of the mind (νοῦς) in isolation. Like Plutarch's description of oracles (*e.g., Apud* 384F-385C; *Pyth.* 404B-E), Paul's description of inspiration is linked to some communication with others. In 1 Corinthians, however, no ambiguity exists regarding the clear superiority of intelligible, edifying speech (*e.g.,* 1 Cor 14:4-5). For Paul, the judging of divinely received knowledge and its responsible communication within the community take a priority unparalleled elsewhere in antiquity.

As do most other ancient writers, Paul places the initiative for bestowing, and a status as the source of, divine knowledge clearly with God. It is *God*'s wisdom (2:7), which *God* reveals (2:10), and Paul makes himself an example of *God*'s power (2:4-5). This locus of power in the Deity coincides with Paul's paraenetic aims here. Humans cannot learn the divine mind without divine assistance. "So also no one comprehends the thoughts of God except the Spirit of God" (2:11b).

Paul does not, however, state explicitly the limits of the human acquisition of divine knowledge, an idea that many other writers emphasize. For example, Philo at *Leg.All.* 3.84 allows the mind to ascend only to a certain point before being thwarted in its quest for divine knowledge. Clearly Paul claims that God's σοφία and gifts are given only to some humans (2:14), namely Christians, and he maintains a clear gap between God and humanity. Just how far Paul would allow the human capacity for knowledge of and from the divine to progress, however, is unclear.

Linked to this absence of any explicit demarcation of limits is Paul's omission of any irrational element in his description of this quest for divine knowledge and inspiration. Julian stresses the irrationality of the ancestral myths (*e.g.*, 170AB), Philo describes a variety of frenzied and ecstatic mystical experiences (*e.g.*, *Opif.* 69-71), and Plutarch emphasizes the irrationality of the inspired priestess at Delphi (*e.g.*, *Defectu* 432). Paul, on the other hand, reserves any mention of irrationality for the discussion regarding the phenomenon of speaking in tongues. Unlike Josephus or Julian, Paul never uses many of the words commonly associated with ecstatic inspiration or possession, even for tongue speaking.[5] For example, words such as ἔνθους and μάντις are completely missing in Paul's writings.[6] Rather, Paul emphasizes the rationality of prophecy and most other forms of inspired Christian speech, and therefore, of the search for knowledge and inspiration.

These few observations make it clear that the terms and ideas present in 1 Cor 2:6-16 all point to a reading of this pericope that recognizes the milieu of the ancient search for the divine mind. We must, however, note the obvious: Paul is writing a personal letter to a community that he founded. This genre and agenda alone distinguish his use of such language because his objective is not an allegorical exposition of an Old Testament text, with a frequent digression into philosophical speculation, as in Philo. Nor is Paul seeking to produce a persuasive and reflective, yet measured, essay like those of Plutarch. Rather, Paul seeks to communicate with, inform, reprove, and shape the life of the Christian community at Corinth.[7] The letter was not originally intended for a broad

---

[5]For example, Josephus *AJ* 4.104-20; *BJ* 3.340-90; Julian 222A-23A.

[6]Only at 1 Cor 14:23 does Paul possibly waiver from an absence of these words. There Paul urges the Corinthians not to allow anyone to μαίνεσθαι. Cf. Plut. *Pyth.* 397A.

[7]On the overall purpose and tone of 1 Corinthians, the recent work of Margaret M. Mitchell is very insightful and thorough. See her *Paul and the Rhetoric of Reconciliation: An Exegetical Investigation of the Language and Composition of 1 Corinthians* (Tübingen: Mohr, 1991). For her thesis, Mitchell, 1, persuasively argues that 1 Corinthians should be seen as a unitary letter containing a "deliberative argument persuading the Christian community at Corinth to become reunified." Thus, she sees (against scholars

or general circulation but for a specific community and its particular needs and exigencies. Paul's very appropriation of this common set of terms and ideas within an epistolary setting is unique.

Secondly, by using this language here, Paul provides a clue to the subject matter under discussion: the Christian search for knowledge and inspiration. As this investigation demonstrates, this subject matter runs throughout 1 Corinthians as a whole. Since this language of the human search for the divine mind and for inspiration has clear parallels in other ancient writers, such language would likely not have been alien to at least some of the congregation at Corinth. As we have seen, however, other ancient writers display a variety of understandings of inspiration. Plato alone shows evidence of several discrete understandings and descriptions of inspiration. The focus on the search for the mind of God, employed here by Paul, is but one of those, and the remainder of the book will focus on the specifics of Paul's employment of that theme.

Having now made these observations regarding ancient parallels to Paul's vocabulary, topic, and argument in 1 Cor 2:6-16, I will now move to examine 1 Cor 2:6-16 with greater precision and detail.

---

such as Munck and Fee) 1 Cor 1:10 as the πρόθεσις of the letter as a whole. Paul is concerned first and foremost with the problem of factionalism in Corinth. With only a few exceptions, I agree with her overarching assessment of the letter. I will modify her conclusions somewhat in my chapter 4 when I look at the paraenetic context of 1 Cor 2:6-16. Her model seems a bit rigid in not allowing Paul to deviate at all from deliberative rhetoric or a singular purpose, so I will elaborate on this as I seek to show (with scholars such as Kuck and Fiore) that 1 Cor 1:10-4:21 can be viewed as broadly paraenetic in character without doing damage to Mitchell's view of the primary focus on factionalism. For opposing views, see Johannes Munck, *Paul and the Salvation of Mankind*, trans. F. Clarke (Atlanta: John Knox, 1959) and Gordon Fee, *The First Epistle to the Corinthians*, NIC (Grand Rapids: Eerdmans, 1987).

Chapter 4
I Corinthians 2:6-16
and Inspired Community

In this chapter I focus on the specifics of Paul's appropriation in 1 Cor 2:6-16 of the kinds of language surveyed and examined in chapters 1–3 above. Particularly significant is Paul's locating of this language in his paraenetic address to a specific community. This context of paraenesis is important because Paul modifies common language regarding inspiration and divine inquiry and makes it applicable to all Christians rather than just to a single individual or some select few. He thereby provides for the corporate inspiration of the Christians at Corinth and seeks, in keeping with the overarching purpose of this letter, to modify the Corinthians' propensity for factionalism by locating all Christians on the same spiritual plane.

I Corinthians 2:6-16 within Its Epistolary Setting

Margaret M. Mitchell has persuasively argued that Paul is primarily concerned in 1 Corinthians with addressing and modifying the Corinthian church's factionalism and internal dissension. As such, the letter as a whole finds its foundation and purpose in 1 Cor 1:10: "I appeal (παρακαλῶ) to you, brethren, by the name of our Lord Jesus Christ, that all of you agree (τὸ αὐτὸ λέγω) and that there be no dissensions (σχίσματα) among you, but that you be united in the same mind and the same judgment (καταρτίζω ἐν τῷ αὐτῷ νοῒ καὶ ἐν τῇ αὐτῇ γνώμη)." Mitchell contends that this statement is the πρό-θεσις for the letter and that Paul hereafter uses deliberative rhetoric in order to persuade the Corinthians to resolve their problems with dissension in the future.[1]

---

[1]Again, see her thesis in Margaret M. Mitchell, *Paul and the Rhetoric of Reconciliation: An Exegetical Investigation of the Language and Composition of 1*

Mitchell carefully garners other ancient examples of deliberative rhetoric, including a number of epistolary texts, in support of her reading of 1 Corinthians in this fashion. As a result, she is able to demonstrate effectively that the whole of the letter coheres and need not be viewed through partition theories.[2] She rightly sees the entire letter, including chapters 7–16, as serving the overall function of the address of the problem of factionalism. Hence, 1 Cor 2:6-16 is located within a letter whose overarching goal is to resolve internal dissension in the Christian community at Corinth.

At the same time, 1 Cor. 2:6-16 is set within the context of a broadly paraenetic section, 1:10–4:21,[3] which is characterized by νουθεσία (4:14), or strong admonition and instruction often characterized by shaming.[4] Mitchell sees no reason to view 1:10–4:21 as a

---

Corinthians (Tübingen: J. C. B. Mohr, 1991) 1. For the proof that 1 Corinthians is a unified deliberative letter urging concord, see her chapter 4. Her chapter 2 identifies 1 Corinthians as an example of deliberative rhetoric alongside other ancient epistolary examples. Her chapter 3 then locates the language of factionalism and reconciliation in such a rhetorical context.

[2]Mitchell puts to rest once and for all partition theories for 1 Corinthians. Her most significant contribution may well be this proof of the letter's abiding coherence. Three examples of scholars who partition this letter include: Schmithals, *Gnosticism in Corinth*; Robert Jewett, *Paul's Anthropological Terms: A Study of Their Use in Conflict Settings*, AGJU 10 (Leiden: Brill 1971); and Christophe Senft, *La Première Épitre de Saint-Paul aux Corinthiens*, CNT 2/7 (Neuchâtel/Paris: Delachaux & Niestlé, 1979). A seminal view of the potential partitioning of 1 Corinthians was set forth in Johannes Weiss, *Der Erste Korintherbrief*, MeyerK 5:9 (Göttingen: Vandenhoeck und Ruprecht, 1910, Repr. 1970).

[3]There is nearly universal scholarly agreement that this is the first major section of 1 Corinthians. Even partitionists, like Schmithals and Senft, agree that this is the first such section. For more on the nature and overall character of 1:10–4:21, see Nils A. Dahl, "Paul and the Church at Corinth According to 1 Corinthians 1:10–4:21," *Studies in Paul* (Minneapolis: Augsburg, 1977) 40-61 and John Fitzgerald, *Cracks in an Earthen Vessel: An Examination of the Catalogues of Hardships in the Corinthian Correspondence*, SBLDS 99 (Atlanta: Scholars, 1988). Particularly helpful is Fitzgerald's consideration of Seneca's *Epistle* 94 and Seneca's comments there on the necessity of admonition as well as Seneca's contrast drawn between the perfect wise man and the imperfect, weaker individual. See Fitzgerald, 117-28.

[4]This type of discourse was intended to reprove error, and it often became too harsh if unrestrained. Thus, the admonisher often was despised for being abusive instead of beneficial. Nevertheless, the aim of νουθεσία was to help the audience rather than to lapse into reviling and fault-finding. In the NT, cf. also 1 Thess 5:12-14; Rom 15:14; and

discrete section of paraenesis; rather she views 1:18–4:21 as a rebuke of factionalism and as a proof of the need for Paul's instruction. An inclusio, however, denoted by παρακαλῶ (1:10 and 4:16), brackets the section as a whole and serves to indicate Paul's agenda in this block of moral exhortation, instruction, and reproof (4:14).[5] Furthermore, the subject matter clearly changes at 5:1. It seems likely that this section from 1:10–4:21 is something like παράκλησις.

Such παράκλησις is quite characteristic of paraenesis in antiquity, and this type of address often was associated with that discourse between a father and son.[6] Hence, it is not surprising that Paul uses the imagery of children in this section (cf. 4:14-15; also 3:1-4 and 4:17).[7] Still other examples of paraenetic material in this section include: the use of

---

1 Cor 10:11. Elsewhere, cf. Dio Chrysostom *Or.* 51.7; 72.13; 77/78.38; Plutarch *De Aud. 39A; Quomodo adulator* 50B; 70-72; and Seneca *Ep.* 94.49-52.

[5]Paul also uses παρακαλῶ to introduce admonition at Rom 12:1; 15:30; 16:17; 1 Cor 16:15; 2 Cor 10:1; Phil 4:2; and 1 Thess 4:1, 10; 5:14. My view of paraenesis is derivative from the work and comments of Abraham J. Malherbe. Cf. his "Hellenistic Moralists and the New Testament," in *ANRW*, 26:1, ed. W. Haase (Berlin: DeGruyter, 1992) 267-333. See especially Part 3: Epistolary Paraenesis, 278-92. See also his *Paul and the Popular Philosophers* (Minneapolis: Augsburg, 1989). Characteristic of such paraenesis was the use of traditional, unoriginal material; a pointing out of the obvious; reminding the audience of what it already had been taught; the use of paradigms and antithetical forms; and extolling the value of personal example. By this time, such epistolary paraenesis was an established form of hortatory address. Cf. Seneca *Epistles* 94 and 95. For 1 Corinthians 1-4, cf. also C. J. Bjerkelund, *Parakalô: Form, Funktion, und Sinn der Parakalô-Sätze in den paulinischen Briefen*, Bibliotheca Theologica Norvegica 1 (Oslo: Universitetsforlaget, 1967) 141 ff. See also the work of Benjamin J. Fiore, *The Function of Personal Example in the Socratic and Pastoral Epistles* (Rome: Biblical Institute, 1986) 168-84, and his article " 'Covert Allusion' in 1 Corinthians 1–4," *CBQ* 47 (1985): 85-102. Fiore carefully shows the nuanced rhetorical argumentation used by Paul in 1:10–4:21, and his work supports understanding this block of the letter as paraenetic in a broad sense.

[6]In the NT, cf. Heb 13:22 and 1 Pet 5:12, where παράκλησις is associated with moral exhortation. At 1 Cor 14:3, the prophet speaks to the congregation for their "upbuilding (οἰκοδομή), and encouragement (παράκλησις), and consolation (παραμυθία)." Cf. Dio Chrysostom *Or.* 77/78.38. For more on the various forms and types of moral discourse, see also Abraham J. Malherbe, " 'Pastoral Care' in the Thessalonian Church," *NTS* 36 (1990): 375-91.

[7]The specific language of 3:1-4 represents more than paraenetic discourse, however. The rhetorical character of this passage is discussed in more detail in my chapter 5 below.

antitheses (*e.g.*, 1:26-27; 2:4; 2:6-7; 3:1-2); reminders of what the audience already knows (*e.g.*, 3:16); and the use of personal example (*e.g.*, 2:1-5; 3:5-6; 4:1ff).

Viewing this section (1:10–4:21) as paraenetic in emphasis is not a significant departure from the broader thesis of 1 Corinthians as a deliberative letter addressing factionalism. Mitchell's reading, however, tends to force the whole of 1 Corinthians into the mold of deliberative rhetoric and does not sufficiently recognize the differences between this section and the remainder of the letter.[8] I contend that this section (1:10–4:21) serves to establish the *bona fides* of Paul in preparation for the ethical instructions and directives that follow in the rest of the letter.[9] Such a view does not undermine Mitchell's thesis that the overarching purpose of the letter's is to address factionalism, since the various issues addressed in chapters 5–16 all can be viewed as contributing to such a problem of dissension. Nevertheless, the paraenesis, whose attributes Mitchell clearly recognizes in 1:10–4:21, serves the subsidiary purpose of establishing Paul's good-faith intention before the Corinthians while at the same time helping to address factionalism.

Most significantly, the paraenesis of 1:10–4:21 focuses on the activity and power of God (*e.g.*, 2:4-5; 3:4-6; 4:20) and also emphasizes personal example in Paul's effort to address the problem of disunity and strife (*e.g.*, 2:4-5; 3:9; 4:12, 16).[10] In fact, Fiore proposes that Paul appears to

---

[8]Mitchell, 50-53, argues that all paraenesis is deliberative rhetoric, thereby subsuming the former classification into the latter. Views such as this often lead Mitchell to overlook the particularities and specifics of 1 Corinthians in her effort to prove the unitary character and deliberative rhetoric of the whole. For example, she does not do justice to the individual topics *in se*, addressed in chapters 7–16 of the letter. Idol meat, the Lord's Supper, and other issues become only issues of factionalism and are not examined in their own right. Nevertheless, her careful and thorough look at the whole is an important and useful contribution. One must exercise care, however, when appropriating its thesis while examining particular passages within that whole.

[9]So, too, David Kuck, *Judgment and Community Conflict: Paul's Use of Apocalyptic Judgment Language in 1 Corinthians 3:5–4:5*, (Leiden: Brill, 1992) 152; Fiore, *Function*, 169-84; and Fitzgerald, 117-28.

[10]At 1:10, the beginning point of this section, the paraenesis urges the end of factional strife and discord via a common mind or purpose. At 4:16, the end of this block, Paul himself is the paraenetic example to the Corinthians. Again, cf. Fiore, *Function*, 168-84. A different view of this section can be found in Michael Bünker, *Briefformular und rhetorische Disposition im 1. Korintherbrief*, Göttinger Theologische Arbeiten 28

use three cycles of argument: (1) Paul first puts forth a general Christian principle in the first person plural, (2) he then applies it to the Corinthian congregation in the second person plural, and (3) he finally articulates his own exemplification of that principle, often in the first person singular.[11] Kuck has shown, however, that Fiore's model breaks down at several

---

(Göttingen: Vandenhoeck und Ruprecht, 1983). Bünker compares Paul's letters to the moral epistles of Seneca and views 1:10–4:21 as a complex rhetorical letter. Bünker argues that 1:18–3:23 addresses factionalism and that 4:1-21 is Paul's personal apology. This view of the structure is less helpful than that of Bünker, who places the issue of wisdom as a complement to the broader issues of factionalism and Paul's authority. A more recent effort at a rhetorical-critical investigation of this letter is that of Stephen Pogoloff, *Logos and Sophia: The Rhetorical Situation of 1 Corinthians*, SBLDS 134 (Atlanta: Scholars Press, 1992). Pogoloff posits that the rhetoric of various speakers causes Corinthian factionalism. Pogoloff's analysis remains far too general to be useful, however, and his investigation concentrates primarily on secondary literature rather than on ancient rhetorical texts and speeches.

[11]The three cycles are: 1:18–2:5; 2:6–3:5; and 3:6–4:5. This schema is developed in considerable detail in the two works of Fiore cited above. I do not agree completely with the arguments made by Fiore. For example, not much of a Pauline personal exemplification of the general principle appears in 3:5. I do think, however, that Fiore's observation of the tripartite structure is both more or less correct and helpful. What is more significant for my purpose here than the specific breakdown of the structure, however, is the paraenetic nature of the material in 1:10–4:21. Contrary to traditional opinion, this language is not apologetic in nature but rather serves to underscore Paul's own personal example to the Corinthians. A good example of one of the definitive works supporting the apologetic character of this section can be found in Nils A. Dahl, "Paul and the Church at Corinth According to 1 Corinthians 1:10–4:21." In this article, Dahl sees the section as apologetic in nature. In other words, Paul endeavors to reestablish his authority as the church's founder. The quarrels are due to opposition to Paul. Dahl's case, however, cannot sustain the apologetic character of this section. There simply is no evidence of Paul's defense from personal attack. As a result, Dahl later changed his mind somewhat. Nevertheless, many commentators and scholars since have adopted his original position. For example, Pearson, 27, sees this section as an apology for Paul's apostolic office and authority. However, I see no substantive evidence that Paul is on trial here or defending himself against charges. Rather, Paul is setting the stage and establishing his foundation for the directives that come in the latter portion of the letter. It is paraenetic in character. In another interesting investigation of the language here, Laurence L. Welborn, "On the Discord in Corinth," draws parallels in this section with the language of Greco-Roman stasis. As such, Welborn sees the Corinthian problem as partisanship and party spirit, so Paul's goal in the paraenesis becomes to urge their uniting in the same mind and purpose. Margaret Mitchell builds on Welborn's base and develops it in a useful way for her reading of 1 Corinthians.

points and that Paul's main concern is factionalism. As a result, Paul's discussion of σοφία and "the false valuation of wisdom" is complementary to the discussion.[12] In other words, by relating Paul's discussions of σοφία in 1:10–4:21 to Paul's discussions of factionalism, Kuck rightly sees the root of factionalism in the Corinthian congregation to be a "tendency for individuals to seek status on the basis of their demonstration of spiritual wisdom."[13] This explains the preponderance of uses of σοφία in this section. In fact, the term σοφία occurs in Paul's writings only three times other than in 1 Corinthians 1–2, a fact that underscores the Corinthian problems regarding the understanding of σοφία.[14] Thus, Kuck's reading both corroborates Mitchell's reading and simultaneously expands it with a specific view of the root causes of the factionalism addressed by Paul in the letter. Factionalism is the primary concern, and a false valuation of spiritual wisdom is one of the chief causes of that factionalism.

Paul speaks of this Christian σοφία in temporal and apocalyptic terms. It was foreordained and determined "before the ages" (2:7). It cannot be comprehended by the "rulers of this age," whom God will destroy (2:6, 8; cf. 15:24). Nor is Christian σοφία accessible to "this age" in general (2:6). Paul has already developed this notion in considerable detail in 1:18-31. Jesus Christ is "our wisdom" (1:30). Moreover, Christian σοφία consists not only of Jesus Christ but also of his crucifixion (2:8; cf. 1:18, 23). Throughout 1:18-2:16, Paul repeatedly draws antithetical distinctions between illumined believers ("we") who are being saved and the unbelieving inhabitants of "this world" who reject the gospel and are doomed to perish.[15]

---

[12]Kuck, 154.

[13]Kuck, 155.

[14]Cf. 1 Cor 12:8; 2 Cor 1:12; and also Rom 11:33. Σοφία obviously was important to the Corinthians for Paul uses the term almost exclusively in the Corinthian correspondence. He uses it elsewhere only in a citation from an outside text at Rom 11:33. Nevertheless, I am unable to see how J. A. Davis argues for Paul's offering a corrective from a "Torah-centric wisdom" to a "Christ-wisdom." I see no evidence that Torah was an issue of dispute in this letter. Cf. J. A. Davis, *Wisdom and Spirit: An Investigation of 1 Corinthians 1:18–3:20 Against the Background of Jewish Sapiential Traditions in the Greco-Roman World* (Lanham, NY/London: University Press of America, 1984) 78.

[15]See the antitheses in 1:18, 21, 22-24, 25, 27; 2:4, 5.

In making these antithetical distinctions, Paul uses thoroughly apocalyptic language throughout the section, particularly as he describes the hidden, mysterious wisdom of God (2:7). Such wisdom is possessed only by insiders. Paul reinforces this apocalyptic theme with the concentration of judgment language in 2:14-15. Forms of ἀνακρίνω cluster as Paul emphasizes that the πνευματικός is judged by no one, a statement that Paul uses to his own advantage in 4:3-5 when he asserts that he also is judged by no one but the Lord. Judgment belongs only to God. The effect of such apocalyptic language and rhetoric is to create a dualistic view of the world where believing members of the community are on God's side in a nonbelieving world that opposes God and therefore stands under God's judgment.[16] As such, Christian σοφία is not the possession of only a *few within* the community; rather the possession of Christian σοφία *defines* the community itself. Hence, σοφία should unify believers rather than cause intracommunity factionalism.

The overall purpose of this section from 1:10–4:21, then, is twofold. First, Paul establishes his *bona fides* for the instruction that comes in the latter part of the letter (chaps. 5–15). Paul himself is the Corinthians' paraenetic personal example of God's activity and power (cf. *e.g.*, 1:17; 2:3-4; 3:5-6; and 4:1). Second, he admonishes and appeals for unity and the end of factionalism, ideas that indicate the broad theme of the entire letter.

In Fiore's model, the second cycle of Paul's argument, from 2:6–3:5, sets forth a statement of a general principle in this particular pericope (2:6-16). Here Paul shifts from a negative description of human wisdom (σοφία) to a positive one. After having described in some detail the negative character of this-worldly wisdom and its adverse effects on those who embrace it (*e.g.*, 1:20-25), Paul's argument changes gears here as he describes a general principle of Christian knowledge, beginning with the adversative δέ in 2:6. The antithesis in verses 6-7, in which the second element is "a wisdom of God, hidden in mystery," underscores the emphasis on the wisdom of God as the positive pole. Again, the negative

---

[16]This is a common effect and/or goal of apocalyptic literature and language. Cf. Wayne A. Meeks, "The Social Functions of Apocalyptic Language in Pauline Christianity," in *Apocalypticism in the Mediterranean World and the Near East: Proceedings of the International Colloquium on Apocalypticism, Uppsala, August 12–17, 1979* (Tübingen: J. C. B. Mohr, 1982) 687-705.

pole would be the wisdom of this world and this age. The θεοῦ in 2:7 is emphatic, and it may be both a possessive and a source genitive.[17] In other words, the wisdom clearly belongs to and originates in God.

As he has done in the preceding material (1:18–2:5), Paul here again makes God the focus of the argument and the locus of activity and power. This emphasis on God is crucial to Paul's paraenetic discussion of the Christian life and his own personal example. The roles of God, the Spirit, and Christ in the second parts of the antitheses in verses 7, 11, 12, 13, and 16 accentuate that emphasis. It is *God*'s wisdom, known only by *God*'s Spirit that is given and taught by *God*'s Spirit. In verse 10, it is *God* who has revealed wisdom through the agency of *His* Spirit.[18] In verse 12, it is *God* who has bestowed the gifts. Finally, in verse 16, the citation from Isaiah 40:13 demonstrates and underscores the idea that no human instructs the Lord; instead the flow of knowledge is just the opposite of that: humans are simply the recipients of *God*'s revelation, not vice-versa. The Spirit "searches"; humans merely receive. Clearly Paul emphasizes the role of God.

Such an emphasis is not unlike that seen in the writers discussed earlier. Like Philo, Plutarch, and Julian, all of whom emphasize that humans require divine assistance and initiative in the quest to obtain access to the divine mind, Paul clearly de-emphasizes the role and status of humans in this process. At the same time, only Paul makes a nonhuman the agent of the search for the divine mind. As we have already seen, the verb ἐρευνάω in the non-Christian writers surveyed here applies only to human activity. In 1 Cor 2:10b, however, "the Spirit searches (ἐραυνάω) everything."[19] Elsewhere in the New Testament, this verb can apply to human activity (1 Pet 1:10-12) or to God's work (Rom 8:27; Rev 2:23) but not to the activity of the Spirit.[20] Such an

---

[17]With Fee, 104 n26.

[18]As stated before, this agency is integral to Pauline theology. Such an idea is useful in refuting Widmann's notion that this pericope is a non-Pauline interpolation.

[19]Cf. Wis 7:22–8:1 for the well-known Jewish praise of wisdom as all-encompassing Spirit. However, only Prov 20:27 approaches, and then only doubtfully so, the ascription of such a searching function to the Spirit of God.

[20]At Rev 2:23-24, however, John, who is "in the Spirit," warns the Thyatirans not to listen to the spiritual βαθέα provided by the prophetess, "Jezebel." John wields the notion that only God can search (ἐραυνάω) in order to rebuke Jezebel and caution the Thyatirans. Likewise, here in 1 Cor 2:6-16, Paul asserts that only the Spirit can search

observation serves as the baseline for my discussion in the next section regarding the function of the language of inspiration and divine inquiry in 1 Cor 2:6-16.

The Language of Inspiration and Inquiry in I Corinthians 2:6-16

The parallels in both vocabulary and thought between Paul and other ancient writers have already been demonstrated in the earlier chapters of this investigation. Scholarship's previous inability to recognize the broader conceptual background of such parallel literature has led to a general agreement that the relatively rare vocabulary here in 1 Cor 2:6-16 must therefore be that of the Corinthians themselves.[21] Moreover, scholars who see 1:10–4:21 as chiefly apologetic in nature tend also to view 2:6-16 as reflecting Paul's refutation of his supposed opponents. In doing so, these scholars explain the relatively rare vocabulary utilized here, but not elsewhere by Paul, as Paul's seeking to use the language of his opponents while either reinterpreting or rejecting it. For example, Schmithals and Wilckens argue that the language here reflects that of Paul's gnostic opponents. Birger Pearson sees Paul appropriating the language of his opponents but radically reinterpreting it with his own apocalyptic twist.[22] Judith Kovacs rightly rejects a reading that emphasizes and requires a theory of opponents here. She proposes instead that 2:6-16 is Paul's own apocalyptic interpretation of the cross and death of Christ.[23]

----

the βαθέα τοῦ θεοῦ so that there are no grounds for any human claims to the ability to search the divine mind. "Jezebel" would be just as reproved here by Paul's rhetoric as she is by John's in Rev 2:23-24.

[21]E.g., Jannes Reiling, "Wisdom and the Spirit: An Exegesis of 1 Corinthians 2, 6-16," in Text and Testimony: Essays in Honor of A. F. J. Klijn, ed. T. Baarda, A. Hilhorst, G. P. Luttikhuizer, and A. S. Van der Woude (Kampen: Vitgeuers—Maatschappij J. H. Kok, 1988) 200-11; Pearson, 27, 31; and Lührmann, 114ff.

[22]Again, Pearson, 27, 31. Lührmann, 114ff, argues that Paul emends a piece of his opponents' esoteric preaching.

[23]See Judith Kovacs, "The Archons, the Spirit, and the Death of Christ: Do We Need the Hypothesis of Gnostic Opponents to Explain 1 Corinthians 2:6-16?" in Apocalyptic and the New Testament, ed. Joel Marcus and Marion Soards (Sheffield: JSOT, 1989)

Nevertheless, despite the presence of very clear apocalyptic ideas, including the prominent theme of the disclosure of revelation, this investigation has demonstrated that the terms in 2:6-16, which indeed are rare for Paul, need not be explained as those merely of "opponents," of "gnostics," or as peculiarly "apocalyptic." Rather, this language enjoyed a much larger provenance than any single area of thought. Quite simply, Paul appropriates language, terms, and ideas from the larger environment in order to calm an internal turbulence in Corinth by reasserting the Christians' fundamental equality and unity. His use of dualistic, apocalyptic language here undergirds that purpose. The general thrust of 1:18–2:16 is to remind the Corinthians that *all* Christians are part of God's age and are possessors of God's σοφία, and they are joined together in opposition to a skeptical, self-exalting, artificially wise world.

Hence, no reason exists to ascribe such an idea to the Corinthians alone, for Paul here is expressing a common understanding of inspiration as searching for and finding truth. In doing so, Paul utilizes language and concepts not only with parallels in gnostic texts, apocalyptic literature, and the mysteries but in a number of other ancient texts of varied religious provenance. The language was common cultural property and utilized by a variety of writers and communities.

Thus, while this passage uses language from the culture, Paul modifies it to suit his own purposes. For example, by making the Spirit the agent of the search, Paul subtly devalues *individual* human claims to access to the divine mind and places such an activity in the Spirit available to *all* Christians by virtue of baptism. No human can claim direct access to the mind of God; such access is mediated only by the Spirit, and God gives that Spirit to all Christians at baptism. The use of δέχομαι in 2:14 carries the connotation of a *reaction* to a prior action, whereas the use of λαμβάνω would have connoted a more proactive

---

217-36. Kovacs bases this reading on the apocalyptic language here and the emphasis on the hidden and mysterious character of the message. She turns to Jewish apocalyptic texts rather than to Gnostic material for assistance, and she rightly rejects the need for opponents in order to make sense of this passage. Pearson, 32, also looks to apocalyptic literature for help, and he claims that Paul employs an apocalyptic preaching form common in the early church. The apocalyptic literature is indeed helpful, but a still broader conceptual background can provide more clarity here.

sense.[24] In other words, humans merely react to the self-revelatory and self-disclosing action of God so that the ψυχικός does not react to the initial action of God, but "we" πνευματικοί, who have the Spirit, do (2:12). The initiative resides with God. Therefore, human claims to special σοφία or access to the divine mind are unfounded and out of order. Christian σοφία is the rightful property of the believing community.

The reception of such revelation enables the recipient to comprehend divine wisdom, that is, to have "the mind of Christ." The cognitive element is pervasive.[25] This pericope, particularly in relation to the discussion that has preceded it, paraenetically contrasts the wisdom of this age and its rulers with the wisdom of God, which is communicated through the Spirit to humans. The created, natural endowment in the human mind is insufficient to grasp this divine wisdom, which must be received from the Spirit. Divine wisdom, put forth by God before the ages (v.7), includes recognition of the "Lord of glory" (v.8),[26] the depths (βάθη) of God (v.10), the thoughts of God (v.11), and the understanding of God's gifts (v.12). Such knowledge has not been seen, heard, nor conceived by humans (v.9) until the revelation provided by God (v.10). The endowment from God makes such inspiration possible, for the emphasis is on the receiving here. Ψυχικὸς δὲ ἀνθρώπος οὐ δέχεται τὰ τοῦ πνεύματος τοῦ θεοῦ (2:14). This idea is reminiscent of Philo's discussion at *Leg. All.* 3.84, where he considers the variety of original endowments at creation. Abram was created good, and his νοῦς was able to soar to divine heights. Likewise, Plutarch discusses how some are born with the predisposed capacity for inspiration and prophecy. For Paul, however, the crucial endowment comes later than at creation, for it is the gift of the Spirit, which the ψυχικός (non-Christian) does not possess. Only this baptismal endowment with the Spirit makes comprehension of the divine mystery possible.

---

[24]This is the only use of δέχομαι in 1 Corinthians. For more on the distinction between these two verbs, see Walter Grundmann, "δέχομαι," *TDNT* 2:50-54. Cf. also LSJ, 382.

[25]Note the cognitive terms (often forms of γινώσκω) throughout this pericope: 2:8 (ἔγνωκεν, ἔγνωσαν); 2:11 (ἔγνωκεν, οἶδεν); 2:12 (εἰδῶμεν); 2:14 (γνῶναι); 2:16 (ἔγνω).

[26]Cf. Jas 2:1; also Eph 1:17 and Acts 7:2.

In order to paint this contrast more starkly, Paul uses specific terms to designate and classify humans.[27] Christians are πνευματικοί (2:13-15; 3:1; cf. 14:37; 15:44-46)[28] and τέλειοι (2:6; cf. 13:10; 14:20)[29] for they have received the Spirit and should act accordingly. At 14:20, Paul again exhorts the Corinthians to be τέλειοι rather than νήπιοι or παιδία in another paraenetic appeal that appears in a context regarding their behavior in worship. Those persons who have not received the Spirit are described with the more *neutral* term, ψυχικός (2:14; 15:44-46).[30] Such a term indicates the condition of humanity before the gift and reception of the Spirit. Finally, those who act *contrary to* the

---

[27]Such a classification was picked up and developed later in gnostic literature based on an exegesis of Gen 2:7 from the LXX. See Pearson, 51-81. In 1 Corinthians, however, the classifications are a function of the rhetorical character of the letter and Paul's aims rather than any ontological or metaphysical statement. Paul shows no interest in setting forth a system of widespread applicability for the classification of human existence. Again, he is trying to shame the Corinthians for their divisive behavior.

[28]There is some ambiguity regarding the translation and meaning of this term in a number of instances where it is unclear whether the term is neuter or masculine. For example, in 1 Cor 2:13b (πνευματικοῖς πνευματικὰ συγκρίνοντες), scholarly debate has vacillated on whether this usage indicates two neuters ("interpreting spiritual things with spiritual things"), or one neuter and one masculine ("interpreting spiritual things for/to spiritual people"). I opt for the latter, thereby reading this as depicting communication *between* Christians. I will discuss this phrase in more detail below. Cf. David Hill, "Christian Prophets as Teachers or Instructors in the Church," *Prophetic Vocation in New Testament and Today*, ed. Johannes Panagopoulos, NovTSup 45 (Leiden: Brill, 1977) 108-30. Hill also sees πνευματικοί as a general term for all Christians with spiritual gifts. So too Wendell Willis, "The 'Mind of Christ' in 1 Corinthians 2,16," *Biblica* 70 (1989): 110-22. Also Reiling, *Hermas*, 145-46, sees this term as describing all Christians who have the Spirit as opposed to humans without it (ψυχικοί). Later, at 1 Cor 12:1 and 14:1, this term could again be translated potentially as "spiritual people" rather than the more likely "spiritual gifts." For another example of this term's juxtaposition with σαρκινός, cf. Rom 7:14.

[29]Cf. Rom 12:2 where the will of God is τέλειος. At Phil 3:15, the term is again used in a paraenetic context.

[30]Paul uses ψυχικός only in 1 Corinthians. Some scholars have read this then as an indication that it is a Corinthian term that Paul appropriates. *E.g.*, Reiling, "Wisdom," 208. It is also interesting that Paul drops this term after 2:14 until it reappears in chapter 15. It seems significant that it is not present in 3:1-4 where the admonitory tone increases and the Corinthians are called σαρκικοί.

Spirit, or in opposition to God, are σαρκικοί (or σαρκινοί)[31] or νήπιοι (3:1; cf. 13:11).[32] These final two terms carry clearly negative connotations for Paul and serve to color the rhetorical canvas on which Paul paints the embarrassment and scandal of the Corinthians' behavior. The Corinthians' factionalism and dissension represent a fundamental betrayal of the gospel so that their behavior resembles that of the world more than that of the body of Christ. Hence, Paul is not dividing Christians into two or more categories, divisions, or levels; rather he is contrasting them to the fleshly, material world and appealing for their behavior and thinking to reflect more the "mind of Christ" than the "rulers of this age."[33]

Again, all of this language reflects the antithetical character of Paul's rhetoric throughout 1:18–2:16. Paul is drawing and reinforcing social boundaries for the community over against the world and is thereby seeking to eliminate such boundaries that currently exist *within* the community. Paul is seeking to remind the Corinthians that their existence as the believing church is fundamentally different from that of the world. As a result, their σοφία and their behavior are to be markedly different from the world's. The Corinthians as baptized believers are neither σαρκικοί nor νήπιοι; rather they are τέλειοι and πνευματικοί. Paul reminds them that their behavior ought to reflect such a status.

Again, inspiration in 2:6-16 is understood as searching for and finding truth. Further, it is not merely a human enterprise. The *Spirit* searches, then reveals; humans receive from the Spirit. Moreover, inspiration pertains first of all not to speech but to the very revelation and discovery of knowledge about the divine. The emphasis here is first of all cognitive. Paul reiterates this point later, in 1 Corinthians 14, where

---

[31]There is a textual variant in 3:1-3 between these two terms, although the net rhetorical effect is the same regardless of the actual reading. The point is clearly a contrast between the spiritual, eternal, and divine as opposed to the material, worldly, and perishable. Cf. also Rom 7:14; 2 Cor 1:12; 10:4.

[32]Cf. Gal 4:1-3 where Paul writes, "When we were children (νήπιοι), we were slaves to the elemental spirits of the universe." Cf. also Rom 2:19-20 where Paul refers to the "instructors of children" alongside other functions like being "a guide to the blind, and a light to those who are in darkness, a corrector of the foolish." Again the term seems to denote an inferior state.

[33]See also Sandnes, 90. He agrees that the argument here shows that Paul's intention was to deal with the issue of factionalism.

revelation *comes* and the prophet must *learn first* (14:29-30). Further, Paul also admonishes the prophets to remember that such revelation came *to* them not from them (14:36). Such an admonition in 1 Corinthians 14 fits with the ideas established here at 2:6-16 regarding the discovery of the divine mind and Christian σοφία.

Like Philo, but unlike Plutarch, Paul links this divine communication with the mind (νοῦς) in 2:16.[34] Paul, however, here likely displays a view of the inspiration of the νοῦς that is even more rational than that of Philo. Paul gives no indication that he envisions the νοῦς discarding its mortal nature in an effort to "change its abode for a better one" (*Leg. All.* 3.84).

This crucial role for the νοῦς is found elsewhere in Paul. In fact, Paul cites this same Isaiah passage regarding the mind of God (Isa 40:13) at Romans 11:34[35] where Paul again is elucidating a "mystery" (μυστή-ριον: 11:25; cf. 1 Cor 2:1, 7).[36] Yet at Romans 11:34, Paul describes the "mind of the Lord" rather than the "mind of Christ." Immediately following, in Romans 12:2, Paul then appeals (παρακαλῶ: 12:1) to the Romans to "be transformed by the renewal of your mind (νοῦς) that you may prove what is the will of God."[37] Also, in Philippians 4:7, Paul assures the congregation that the "peace of God . . . will keep your hearts and your minds (νόημα) in Christ Jesus." Thus, Paul himself provides parallel passages where the νοῦς is actively engaged by God. Paul's notions of faith and salvation have a clearly rational cognitive dimension.

---

[34]When Philo does this, however, the role of the νοῦς is much more prominent as is Philo's mysticism. For Philo, the νοῦς is active and conscious but in an abnormal way so that it can mystically ascend to divine heights. Of course, as I have shown, Plutarch describes the νοῦς as necessarily disengaged when inspiration occurs. Later writers such as Marcus Aurelius (12.26.1) also adopt terminology like that of Paul.

[35]The citation in Romans more accurately reflects the text of the LXX than does that in 1 Cor 2:16. At Rom 11:35, Paul also adds a citation from Job 41:3.

[36]At Rom 11:33, it is obvious that the traditional terms for inquiry and inspiration occur as well. Again, Paul draws on the common milieu for his language. Note the presence of βάθος, γνῶσις, σοφία, and ἀνεξεραυνάω (11:33) and νοῦς and γινώσκω (11:34). At 1 Cor 2:1, there is a textual variant regarding μυστήριον. Nestle-Aland selects μυστήριον, as an anticipation of 2:7 against μαρτύριον, which would look back to 1:6.

[37]Here again the contrast is with "this age" (12:2). See also Rom 7:23 where Paul contrasts the law in his "members" (μέλη) with that of his "mind" (νοῦς).

Even more significantly, the initial exhortation at 1 Cor 1:10 urges the Corinthians to be "united in the same mind (νοῦς) and the same purpose." Hence the role of the νοῦς described in 1 Cor 2:16 links this pericope clearly with the paraenetic aims of 1 Cor 1:10–4:21 as a whole. Paul thereby blends his view of God's engagement with the human νοῦς and the wholly rational inspiraton of the νοῦς by God's Spirit with his overarching rhetorical aims in the letter. Because it is the νοῦς that is engaged by God and inspired by the Spirit, the νοῦς should be properly cultivated in God and Christ in order for the gospel to take full root and to bear fruit. Such cultivation includes nonfactional behavior in the community.

This "united" mind of 1:10 is therefore probably the "mind of Christ" (2:16). Wendell Willis has demonstrated that scholarship historically has tended to view the actual content of the "mind of Christ" in terms of theological doctrines and tenets. Willis offers a corrective to such a reading and demonstrates that Paul's concern here is more with the community's behavior and ethical living out of the gospel than with any holding of right ideas.[38] Given the paraenetic aims of this passage and this section of the letter, along with Paul's criticism of their *conduct* at 1:11 and 3:3, it seems likely that Willis is correct to read 2:16 as referring to the goal of action in the mutual interest of the community. Thus, the one having the "mind of Christ" focuses on community life rather than on petty individual claims to special wisdom and exclusive access to the divine mind. To achieve this end, Paul appropriates common cultural language, probably at least somewhat familiar to the Corinthians, in his effort to modify their behavior. At the heart of Paul's effort is an altering of their understanding of inspiration and spiritual status.

Through the work of the Spirit, God engages the νοῦς to provide humans with divine σοφία. The human νοῦς does not *search*; rather

---

[38]Willis demonstrates how Paul's modification of the LXX quote is crucial. At 1 Cor 2:6-16, Paul changes the νοῦς κυρίου of Isa 40:13 to νοῦς Χριστοῦ, when he does not do so at Rom 11:34. Willis then links 1 Cor 2:16 to 1 Cor 1:10, and its appeal for a common mind, and to 1:13, where Christ is not divided but rather is one. Therefore, Willis thinks that 2:16 seeks to undergird Paul's appeal for unity by reinforcing the notion of the common mind as that of the mind of Christ as well. Having the mind of Christ, then, does not mean "to think the thoughts of Christ after him, nor to have special ecstatic experiences, nor to know proper dogma." Willis, 119. See also Jewett, 450.

it *receives* from the Spirit. The νοῦς is not disengaged; rather it is quite active and conscious. Moreover, the νοῦς is not leaving the mortal nature behind but instead is shown a new way of being in this world. This is the νοῦς τοῦ Χριστοῦ (2:16).

The Church as Inspired Community

Although some scholars have argued that in 1 Cor 2:6-16 Paul distinguishes between two classes of Christians and teaching,[39] and others believe that Paul is staking a claim to the divine authority of his own speech alone,[40] I contend that this pericope describes a concept applicable to all Christians. This widespread availability is the key distinctive element in Paul's appropriation of traditional inquiry language in 2:6-16. The other ancient writers discussed earlier in this study do not apply claims regarding access to the divine mind to a group as potentially large and inclusive as Paul's in this situation. For writers like Plato, Plutarch, and Josephus, the quest for the divine mind is an individual affair.

The agency of the Holy Spirit in this pericope is crucial for my understanding of this passage as applicable to all Christians. All Christians receive the Holy Spirit,[41] and the agency of the Holy Spirit is a crucial theme throughout the letter.[42] Indeed, at 3:16, the corporate Corinthian body is a temple in which God's Spirit dwells. This is true because, at 1 Cor 12:13, by one Spirit all Christians are "baptized into one body" and "made to drink of the one Spirit." In fact, at 12:7, 11, the

---

[39]*E.g.*, Conzelmann, 57-59. C. K. Barrett, *The First Epistle to the Corinthians*, HNTC (New York: Harper and Row, 1968) 69, argues for degrees of maturity. He, too, draws a contrast between τέλειος (2:6) and νήπιος (3:1). Wilckens, *Weisheit*, 52-53, bases this division on Paul's gnostic characteristics, which he sees coloring the whole passage.

[40]*E.g.*, Sandnes, 79. Cf. Reiling, "Wisdom," who consistently refers to this passage as describing Paul's "preaching." Gillespie, "Interpreting," 156, also regards this passage as referring to Paul. He reads it as an "editorial we" and views λαλοῦμεν (2:6) as a resumption of κηρύσσομεν (1:23).

[41]Cf. Reiling, "Prophecy, the Spirit, and the Church," *Prophetic Vocation in New Testament and Today*, ed. Johannes Panagopoulos, NovTSup 45 (Leiden: Brill, 1977) 58-76. Reiling makes this same general observation but fails to make the connection with 1 Cor 2:6-16.

[42]Cf. 6:11, 19; 12:7, 11, 13. Also 3:21-23 where "all things are yours . . . you are of Christ, and Christ is of God." Cf. also Rom 8:15; 2 Cor 11:4; and Gal 3:2.

one Spirit bestows the variety of gifts from God. The one Holy Spirit unites all believers for it forges them into a single body just as they partake of the one Spirit. The Spirit mediates access to the mind of God so that no Christian alone has the Spirit; rather, all do. Therefore, there is no special access to the divine mind for any elite person or group within the Corinthian church.

Again, it is the Spirit who searches. God then reveals His wisdom (σοφία) through that Spirit (2:10). The first position in 2:10 of ἡμῖν as those who are the recipients of revelation through the Spirit reinforces the belief that this is hardly an action that Paul would limit to himself or some select group. In fact, later, at 12:13, Paul says, "For by one Spirit *we all* (ἡμεῖς πάντες) were baptized into one body Jews or Greeks, slaves or free—and *all* were made to drink of the *one Spirit*" (emphasis mine). It seems reasonable then that because *we all* have received the Spirit, "*we* speak wisdom among the mature," "*we* speak a wisdom of God, hidden in mystery," and "*we* speak this not in words taught by human wisdom but in words taught by the Spirit" (2:6, 7, 13: all in first plural present).[43]

Moreover, as I have already shown, Paul consistently distinguishes in 1:18–2:16 between the σοφία of "this age" and the σοφία of God. He paints this contrast using antitheses that often reflect apocalyptic influences. As such, Paul differentiates between the believing community and a hostile, unbelieving world. The believers are those illumined by the Spirit (2:10, 12), those being saved (1:18, 21), those called by God (1:24, 26), and those able to judge all things (2:15). Most probably then, Paul is arguing for a common Christian σοφία that consists of the cross (1:18, 23; 2:8). This cross-centered σοφία is the distinctive possession of believers. In fact, it is the constitutive element of the community as Christian in the first place. As such, Paul uses this idea of common σοφία in his effort to unify the Corinthian believers. They all have received the Spirit and its gifts as their rightful inheritance as believers. They have accepted and understood God's σοφία, which is Christ (1:30). In effect, the σοφία of God distinguishes them from this world and defines their very community.

---

[43]The italicized emphases are my own.

Furthermore, P. J. Du Plessis has demonstrated that τέλειοι in 2:6 does not refer to a separate class of Christians, but should be taken as a general Pauline term for all Christians.[44] Du Plessis draws parallels between τέλειοι and terms such as ἅγιοι (1:2; 3:17),[45] πίστοι, and κλήτοι (1:9, 24, 26), and he focuses chiefly on 1 Cor 2:6-16 and Philippians 3:15 in order to emphasize the contrast Paul makes between pagan religiosity and Christian perfection. Unlike pagans, Christians are "perfect because they receive the full donation of the redemptive work of Jesus Christ" (205). In other words, that which is understood and communicated here by the τέλειοι hinges on the salvific aspects of the cross, which is human folly but God's σοφία. By accepting and under-standing the crucified Christ as God's σοφία, the Corinthians became, and still are, τέλειοι.

The idea that this pericope and its depiction of the search for and the reception and subsequent articulation of divine knowledge apply not only to Paul and some express group of preachers, apostles, or prophets, but also to all Christians finds corroboration in other ways as well. The shift from the first person singular to first person plural in 2:6 and back to first singular in 3:1 fits Fiore's argument mentioned above, which describes this pericope as the statement of a general principle for all Christians. The earlier references in 1:18 (τοῖς δὲ σῳζομένοις ἡμῖν) and 1:30 (ἡμῖν) are clearly to *all* Christians. Finally, the aforementioned use of λαλέω, here used three times in the first person plural, reinforces this universality through its connections with chapter 14 where prophecy and tongues are certainly potentially available to *all* Christians (cf. 14:1, 5, 24, 31).[46]

---

[44]Cf. Paul Johannes Du Plessis, *Teleios: The Idea of Perfection in the New Testament* (Kampen: J. H. Kok, 1959) 176-205. Cf. also Phil 3:15.

[45]Cf. also 6:1-2; 14:33.

[46]This idea is developed more fully in my chapters 6 and 7 below. For example, λαλέω appears thirty-four times in 1 Corinthians, only three of which are outside 1 Cor 2:6-16 and chapters 12–14. One of these three uses is in 3:1, a passage clearly related to 2:6-16. Cf. also 9:8 and 15:34. For a table of linguistic parallels between 1 Cor 2:6-16 and chapters 12–14, see Sandnes, 103. For a broader discussion of the relevance of 2:6-16 to chapters 12 and 14, see Gillespie, "Interpreting the Kerygma," 161-66. Cf. also Gerhard Dautzenberg, "Botschaft und Bedeutung der urchristlichen Prophetie nach dem ersten Korintherbrief (2:6-16; 12–14)," *Prophetic Vocation in New Testament and Today*, ed. Johannes Panagopoulos, NovTSup 45 (Leiden: Brill, 1977) 131-61. For still another view,

Furthermore, it seems rhetorically unlikely that Paul would seek to describe multiple levels of Christians in a letter in which his primary aim is to appeal for the cessation of factionalism. By making the Spirit responsible for imparting σοφία, Paul is able to level the playing field for all the Corinthians since all Christians have access to that same Spirit. Special claims to σοφία and status simply cannot be sustained because all Christians possess the σοφία of God by virtue of their reception of the Spirit at baptism.

Here again, Philo provides a useful text for comparison. Unlike his contemporaries for whom the search for the divine mind and any subsequent inspiration are solely individual affairs, Philo does provide a single example for the possibility of a communal or corporate dimension. As I have discussed earlier regarding *Conf.* 53-59, Philo describes the ideal Israel as searching together and speaking with inspiration. In a move that resembles Paul's antithetical distinctions between believers and an unbelieving world, Philo distinguishes at *Conf.* 53-59 between those who recognize the difference in the spiritual and material realms and those who do not. Philo's discussion remains on the purely theoretical level, however, whereas in a personal letter Paul holds corporate inspiration before the Corinthian congregation as the standard or touchstone by which their behavior is to be judged. They all are inspired by the same Spirit; they all possess the same Christian σοφία; and their behavior ought to reflect that. Moreover, as we will discover in the examination of 1 Corinthians 12 and 14, Paul provides not only for the inspiration of the community as a whole but also for the simultaneous inspiration of individuals within that community.

Unlike most of the other ancient texts already discussed, in 1 Cor 2:6-16 this reception of revelation enables the recipient not only to know Christian σοφία but also to articulate it with inspiration. After all, "we *speak*" (2:6, 7, 13) provides the initial issue of the discussion in 1 Cor 2:6-16. As my broad survey has corroborated, Gillespie and Sandnes have argued correctly, but only partially so, that the unlabeled subject of 2:6-16 is early Christian prophecy, a subject that Paul develops more fully later in 1 Corinthians 12–14. I am unwilling, however, to restrict the expression of such Christian inspiration to prophecy alone. This pericope

see Pearson, *Pneumatikos-Psychikos Terminology*, 44-50.

clearly erects a general framework that links God's revelation to humans through the Spirit with the discussion in chapters 12–14 of speaking in tongues, the interpretation of tongues, teaching, prayer, and singing, as well as prophecy.[47] In other words, the forms of inspired Christian speech are much broader than the category of prophecy alone.

It is also important to note here that Paul has already identified the salvific message of the gospel as "the *word* (λόγος) of the cross (1:18)," and has said that "we *preach* Christ crucified" (1:23: ἡμεῖς δὲ κηρύσσομεν Χριστὸν ἐσταυρωμένον).[48] Also, "I determined to know nothing among you except Jesus Christ and him crucified . . . my *speech* (λόγος) and my *message* (κήρυγμα) were not in plausible words of wisdom" (2:2-4). The salvific word of the cross is Paul's lone message to unbelievers, and it is not spoken (λαλέω) but preached (κηρύσσω or καταγγέλλω).[49] It is this message that leads to belief, conversion, and salvation.

By contrast, in 2:6-16, σοφία is spoken (λαλέω) rather than preached and is expressly linked to the activity of the Holy Spirit (2:10-13; cf. also 12:3; 14:3). In 1 Corinthians 14, κηρύσσω and καταγγέλλω are absent because the discussion focuses on the worship *of Christians*. Thus, λαλέω is used in chapter 14 to delineate the varieties of inter-Christian speech. Likewise, the discourse under discussion here in 1 Cor 2:6-16 is communication *between* Christians, or "πνευματικοῖς πνευματικὰ συγκρίνοντες" (2:13).[50] It is not

---

[47]Again, Reiling's study of Hermas is noteworthy here for Hermas believes that the Spirit is received at baptism by all Christians and forges them all into one body. However, that is the daily Spirit active in the Church. This same daily Spirit makes some Christians accessible to the prophetic Spirit when they are chosen to speak to their fellow Christians. Thus, Reiling contends that Hermas distinguishes between all believers' permanent endowment, which pervades daily Christian life, and a momentary inspiration specific to prophecy. The Christian prophet therefore depends on the church for his/her inspiration by the prophetic Spirit, which occurs only in ecclesial gatherings. See Reiling's chapter 6. Iren. *A. H.* 1.13.4 distinguishes between prophecy and teaching by viewing prophecy as occurring only when God sends the ability to prophesy whereas teaching is not under the same restrictions.

[48]Again, the italicized emphases are my own.

[49]Cf. 1:23; 2:1; 9:14, 27; 11:26; and 15:11,12.

[50]The gender of the dative here has been the subject of much scholarly debate; this phrase, of course, has been translated and understood variously by interpreters. *E.g.*,

preaching in order to convert that Paul describes here, but rather it is more like teaching (cf. 2:13: ἃ καὶ λαλοῦμεν οὐκ ἐν διδακτοῖς ἀνθρωπίνης σοφίας λόγοις ἀλλ' ἐν διδακτοῖς πνεύματος).[51] Such communication is also like the prophecy that edifies and builds up.[52] Since it is internal, intracommunity, inter-Christian communication that Paul describes here, he clearly is not staking an exclusive claim in 2:6-16 for the divine inspiration of his own speech in preaching. Rather, he instructs the Corinthians that all Christians, in varying ways, are inspired, and that such inspiration can generate not only prophecy, but also teaching, tongue-speaking, and other forms of expression or communication.

On the surface, however, the argument of 3:1-4 might seem to preclude the Corinthians' being included in those who have the "mind of Christ." The verbs that deflate the Corinthians' puffed-up status, however, are in past tenses (ἠδυνήθην, ἐπότισα, ἐδύνασθε). As I demonstrate in the next chapter, these references to past events indicate Paul's initial address to the Corinthians at the founding of the church rather than any address after their conversion. The lone exception occurs in 2b (ἔτι νῦν δύνασθε). This present-tense phrase in 2b and 3a, however, seems to be a rhetorical device to reinforce Paul's criticism of the ζῆλος and ἔρις present among them in the immediately following clause of 2:3b (cf. 1:10-11). It likely is an example of rhetoric like that found at 4:8-13 and 6:1-11. I develop this reading in more detail in the following chapter.[53]

Barrett, 76; Conzelmann, 67; and Fee, 115, translate it as neuter. Gillespie, "Interpreting," 160, and Weiss, 65, take it to be masculine. I opt for the latter and translate 2:13b as "interpreting spiritual things for spiritual people."

[51]Fitzgerald, 121 n13, sees it as a "post-conversion period of teaching."

[52]Cf. 12:7; 14:3-5, 12, 26, 31.

[53]The irony in 2:6-16 and 3:1-4 is the emphasis of Robert Funk, "Word and Word in 1 Corinthians 2:6-16," *Language, Hermeneutic, and the Word of God: The Problem of Language in the New Testament and Contemporary Theology* (New York: Harper and Row, 1966) 275-305. See esp. 300-303. See also Reiling, *Hermas*, 145.

Conclusions

Thus, I read this pericope as indeed a statement of a Pauline general
principle in which Paul draws on common language from his milieu in
order to describe the search for knowledge of and from God. As such,
Paul argues that Christian σοφία is grounded in the revelatory action of
the Spirit. This σοφία is not that of the world but of God, and it is
focused on the cross of Christ. Such divine action inspires the human
mind not only to receive and understand divine wisdom but also to
articulate that wisdom with inspiration. Paul then uses this premise in his
effort to modify the Corinthian congregation's behavior by enlarging their
understanding of inspiration to include the entire community. God
inspires not a select few but the church as a whole through the endowment of God's own searching Spirit. Therefore, their self-exalting
behavior and false valuation of spiritual status, which ultimately results
in factionalism, betrays God's action in Christ and the Holy Spirit. Paul
exhorts the Corinthians to cease their fleshly behavior and to embrace the
unity and equality of Christ. In other words, they are to have "the mind
of Christ." This argument ultimately rests on Paul's notion that the Spirit
available to himself, the apostle and founder of the Corinthian church, is
also available to all believers.[54]

---

[54]For a thorough discussion of how this passage has functioned in theological debates
throughout history, see Peter Stuhlmacher, "The Hermeneutical Significance." There,
Stuhlmacher also uses the text to support his own "faith theory of knowledge . . . where
faith is not a hindrance but liberation to realistic thought" (341).

Chapter 5
I Corinthians 3:1–4 and Communal Division

This chapter takes up Paul's continuation of the argument from 2:6-16 in the ensuing passage, 3:1-4, and seeks to demonstrate how Paul carefully uses the ideas from 2:6-16 in order to modify the behavior of the Corinthians. This modification again centers on the continuing presence of strife and factionalism in the Corinthian congregation, the overarching theme of the entire letter as stated in 1:10 and established as such in the work of Mitchell.[1] Moreover, the rhetorical nuances of 3:1-4 illustrate and corroborate the reading of 2:6-16 advocated above.

Paul's Use of Irony

In 3:1-4, Paul remembers his time with the Corinthians and their initial reception of the gospel from Paul's own preaching before and at the founding of the church.[2] The past tenses in 3:1-2 (ἠδυνήθην, ἐπότισα, and ἐδύνασθε) confirm the recollective nature of Paul's message here. Since, at the time of Paul's initial preaching, the Corinthians could not already have been Christians, Paul clearly could not have spoken to them then (cf. λαλέω in 3:1) as he does now after their conversion (cf.

---

[1]Regarding this passage in particular, see Mitchell, 85, where 3:1-4 is read as establishing the slogans of 1:12 as those of "children." Thus, for Mitchell, factional activity is viewed in itself as childishness.

[2]Scholarly opinion is divided as to how this passage functions in its literary setting. For example, Kuck, 159, argues that it provides a transition between the first major section of teaching in the letter, 1:18–2:16, and the second, 3:5–4:5. So too Conzelmann, 71, and Bünker, 39. I think that 3:1-4 is intimately attached to 2:6-16 as the direct application of that pericope's general principle. Of course it is linked to what follows as well, but that does not remove its clear connection with what has preceded it. Cf. Richard Horsley, "Wisdom of Word and Words of Wisdom in Corinth," *CBQ* 39 (1977): 224-39; esp. 224. See also Martin Winter, *Pneumatiker und Psychiker in Korinth: Zum religionsgeschichtlichen Hintergrund von 1 Kor 2:6–3:4*, Marburger Theologische Studien 12 (Marburg: N. G. Elwert, 1975) 208.

the same verb in 2:6). In fact, in 2:1-5, Paul says he came to them and
spoke, but he never describes that speech using λαλέω. Moreover,
before they were Christians, they could not have been πνευματικοί
(3:1) since such a term signifies existence in the Spirit. I established
above that 2:13b refers to communication between Christians (πνευματικοί) as does the verb λαλέω throughout 2:6-16 and the remainder
of 1 Corinthians.[3] It makes sense here in 3:1, then, that Paul's initial
address to the Corinthians before their conversion was not in the form of
speech designated as λαλέω but rather must by definition have been
speech that Paul elsewhere designates by κηρύσσω, εὐαγγελίζω, or
καταγγέλλω.[4] Again, intra-Christian community discourse (*e.g.*, prophecy, instruction, etc.) is described in the Corinthian correspondence by
Paul as λαλέω.[5] Pre-Christian discourse requires other forms of speech.
Preaching and instruction that lead to initial conversion, often depicted
as a coming to repentance and faith, are designated by κηρύσσω or
καταγγέλλω.

Now, however, the Corinthians are (or "should be" according to
Paul's rhetoric here) Christians; yet their behavior reveals that somehow
such a status is either endangered or unwarranted. Paul clearly is using
praise and blame, or νουθεσία, to shame the Corinthians' conduct in a
nuanced rhetorical manner. Their very actions betray the call to faith to

---

[3]Paul heightens the contrast here with his use of λαλέω in 3:1, a verb that occurs
fifty-two times in the seven generally accepted letters of Paul. Of those fifty-two
occurrences, forty-four are in the Corinthian correspondence. It is possible that such
evidence indicates that this verb was a part of the problem group's vocabulary in Corinth.
This may or may not be so; however, as we have seen, closer examination of its usage
in 1 Corinthians indicates that it designates for Paul intra-Christian speech. In this way,
it seems that Paul is contrasting in 2:6-16 and 3:1-4 the inspired speech of himself and
others (potentially all Christians as seen from 2:6-16) with the spoken claims of
allegiance, made manifest in factions and jealousy among the Corinthians.

[4]For such uses of κηρύσσω, cf. Rom 10: 14-15; 1 Cor 15:11; 2 Cor 1:19; 11:4; Gal
2:2; and 1 Thess 2:9. For καταγγέλλω, cf. Rom 1:8; 1 Cor 2:1 and 9:14. For
εὐαγγελίζω, cf. 1 Cor 9:8; 15:1; also Rom 10:14-15; 15:20; 2 Cor 10:16; 11:7; Gal
1:16; 4:13.

[5]Cf. also 1 Cor 9:8; 14:2, 3, 6, 9, 19, 28, 29, 34, 35; 2 Cor 2:17b; 4:13; 12:19; 13:3.
It should be noted, however, that usage in 1 Thessalonians offers contradicting evidence,
for there Paul appears to use λαλέω in reference to his initial proclamation at the
Thessalonians' initial conversion. Cf. 1 Thess 1:8; 2:2, 4, 16.

which they, and he, lay claim (*e.g.*, 1:2). ἔτι γὰρ σαρκικοί ἐστε. This statement in 3:3 is not without some paradox. Paul knows they are Christians and uses a variety of ways to describe them as such throughout the letter.[6] Now, however, their present behavior endangers their status as Christians (πνευματικοί) and leads Paul to use irony to urge their reform. Of course they are Christians, but they act as if they were not.[7] In a real sense, the ζῆλος and ἔρις present in the community resemble their (and others') activity as this-worldly humans before accepting the gospel. The location of this ironic rebuke and instruction fits naturally within the broadly paraenetic section from 1:10–4:21 as Paul exhorts the Corinthians to unity and reminds them of what they should already know.

This use of irony measures the fractious Corinthian behavior against the standard set in 2:6-16 where Paul locates all Christians on the same spiritual plane with equal inspiration and status before God. All Christians can claim similar access to the divine mind through the Spirit. Paul's rhetoric seeks to demonstrate the irony that factionalism has reduced the Corinthians from their status as τέλειοι and πνευματικοί to the level of νήπιοι and σαρκικοί.[8] Despite the claims of some within the community to a superior status, perhaps as self-described πνευματικοί or τέλειοι, such claims only reveal their childishness and worldliness. This state of affairs is still more ironic since the Corinthians, or at least some of them, seem to be claiming a unique access to the divine mind when that very claim reveals a lack of understanding and inspiration rather than a superior access.

This technique of seeking to admonish the Corinthians for behavior that does not reflect who they are as Christians is consistent with Aristotle's view of shame in *The Art of Rhetoric*. For example, at 2.6.12, he suggests

---

[6]*E.g.*, 1:4, 30; 3:16-17, 23, 27; 15:1.

[7]Cf. also 15:2.

[8]Technically, there is a distinction between σάρκινος, which refers to fleshly, material substance, and σαρκικός. However, Paul seems to use the two terms interchangeably. Thus, there is some disparity in the textual manuscript tradition regarding the actual terms used in 3:1, 3. Because of Paul's blurring of the distinctions, the variants are not material for my reading of this passage. Cf. Kuck, 160 n40 and James Francis," 'As Babes in Christ'—Some Proposals Regarding 1 Corinthians 3:1-3" *JSNT* 7 (1980): 41-60. Against such a position, Fee, 124, wants to differentiate clearly between these two terms' connotations within this pericope.

It is shameful not to have a share in the honorable things which all men, or all who resemble us, . . . have a share in. By those who resemble us I mean those of the same race, of the same city, of the same family, and generally speaking, those who are on an equality. . . . All those things are the more disgraceful if the fault appears to be our own.[9]

It seems reasonable to see Paul applying a similar line of argument here as he contrasts πνευματικοί and τέλειοι with the this-worldly behavior of σαρκικοί and νήπιοι. In fact, Paul employs a similar tactic in the discussion of lawsuits in 1 Corinthians 6.[10] In 6:1-11, Paul admonishes the Corinthians for their inability to settle disputes internally (6:2) as well as for simply having such cases at all (6:7). In doing so, they are failing to act like ἅγιοι, like those who have been washed, sanctified, and justified "in the name of the Lord Jesus Christ and in the Spirit of our God" (6:11).[11] Rather, their behavior is like that of the ἄδικοι and ἄπιστοι (6:1, 6), who will not inherit the kingdom of God (6:9). Before their conversion, the Corinthians were such persons; but the point is: now they are not. They are indeed those who have been washed, sanctified, and justified in the name of Christ. Moreover, Paul says this to their "shame" (ἐντροπή).[12]

Hence, Paul ironically reproves the Corinthians' divisive behavior as antithetical to their Christian status and existence several times in this letter. Such a strategy reflects an idea regarding shame present even in Aristotle, that is that people are ashamed when they do not have a share in the honorable things that are shared by their kindred. In this case the Corinthians' behavior is shameful for it jeopardizes their share in the

---

[9]Cf. also 2.23.6 where an argument based on the consideration of time accentuates the contrast between how things were and how they now are. This form of enthymeme also parallels that which Paul is doing here in contrasting the Corinthians before they believed and after.

[10]For this parallel I am indebted to Wayne A. Meeks who first suggested it.

[11]The use of τολμάω as the very first word in this discussion (6:1) underscores the brazennness that Paul sees in the Corinthians' behavior here. Cf. 2 Cor 10:12; 11:21.

[12]Cf. also 15:34. Mitchell, 231, notes how Paul uses irony in 6:5 in order to shame the Corinthians' behavior and thereby dissuade them from it. Fee, 229, labels the sarcasm of 6:5 as the "most biting" in the letter.

kingdom of God just as their internal lawsuits in chapter 6 do the very same thing.

Paul's Modification of Communal Behavior

The designation of the Corinthians as σαρκικοί is directly connected in 3:3 to their behavior as it manifests itself in ζῆλος and ἔρις.[13] The use of σαρκικοί here denotes activity in direct opposition to the Spirit, behavior that prevents or inhibits the baptismal endowment of the Spirit and its ramifications as set forth in 2:6-16.[14] Such a term moves beyond the more neutral term ψυχικός of 2:14 to a harsher, negative indictment of the Corinthians' fleshly worldliness. All Christians are πνευματικοί by virtue of their reception of the Spirit. Activity that is antithetical to the Spirit and to God is that which divides or creates factional allegiance (cf. 1:13; 12:13, 25). Thus, Paul builds here on the language of 2:6-16 in an explicit effort to modify the Corinthians' discordant behavior.

After establishing in 2:6-16 that all Christians are πνευματικοί and at least potentially have the capacity for inspired speech (λαλέω), Paul uses those two key terms from 2:6-16 (πνευματικοί and λαλέω) in 3:1 in his effort to exhort the Corinthians to unity. He surely uses πνευματικοί in an ironic sense here since his point is that although all Christians are πνευματικοί, the Corinthians' behavior precludes his addressing them as such.[15] This direct exhortation to the Corinthians is reinforced by the explicit use of the second person plural throughout 3:1-4. Paul is now addressing them directly rather than setting forth a

---

[13]Cf. Gal 5:19-20 where these two terms are characterized as "works of the flesh (ἔργα τῆς σαρκός)."

[14]Cf. also Mitchell, 81-82, where ζῆλος and ἔρις are seen as "subscribing to earthly and secular values of political glory and strength." Mitchell rightly notes the *topos* in Greco-Roman literature where factionalism is described as a "human" failure and concord is exemplified by the divine entities. Cf. Thucydides 3.82.2 and 84.2; Xen. *Hier.* 7.3; Dion. Hal. *Ant. Rom.* 6.66.1; 8.52.1; Dio Chrys. *Or.* 38.11; 48.14; and, in the NT, Jas 3:13-18. More importantly for my purposes, Laurence L. Welborn has demonstrated that the description of factional contenders as disputing children is another commonplace in Greco-Roman literature. Cf. Dio Chrys. *Or.* 38.37 and Aristid. *Or.* 23.62. See L. L. Welborn, "A Conciliatory Principle in 1 Cor 4:6," *NovT* 29 (1987): 320-46.

[15]With Fee, 123-24. Against Barrett, 79-82, who insists on distinguishing between various levels of Christians.

general principle such as that in 2:6-16. In 2:6-16, all Christians are given the same access to the divine mind. In 3:1-4 that equality is wielded by Paul in a harsh, antithetical way against the Corinthian propensity for factionalism.

Paul does occasionally use irony in 1 Corinthians and nearly always does so using direct first person address to an explicitly second person, plural audience. For example, in the sarcastic irony of 4:8-13, Paul turns the argument directly on the Corinthians themselves, much as he does in 3:1-4 with the initial vocative of 3:1, in order to point out the irony of the Corinthians' puffed-up behavior. At 4:8, Paul says, "Already you are filled! Already you have become rich! Without us you have become kings! And would that you did rule so that we might share the rule with you!" Then at 4:10, "We are fools, . . . but you are wise in Christ." The irony, of course, is that Paul, the fool, is their founding father (4:14-15). Likewise, at 6:5, Paul relates the same irony that among a group that thinks of itself as wise (4:10), there are none wise enough to adjudicate disputes. In these cases, Paul appeals with irony directly to the Corinthians rather than in a third person mode.

Irony is notoriously difficult to identify, particularly by modern readers of ancient texts.[16] As a comparison for 1 Cor 3:1-4, however, Cicero's *Pro Legario* provides some useful formal indicators for the presence of irony. In this speech before Caesar (ca. 46 BCE), Cicero defends Ligarius against the accusations of Tubero. Ligarius affronted Tubero by refusing him landing in the province of Africa in which Ligarius was serving as legate even though Tubero had been appointed the governor of the province. Tubero seeks to gain retribution several

---

[16]Cf. the work of Paul Duke, *Irony in the Fourth Gospel*, (Atlanta: John Knox Press, 1985) 8-18. Duke, 10, notes that "the use of irony in antiquity far outstripped any conscious concept of it." However, Duke demonstrates that irony usually came to signify saying one thing and meaning another. Aristotle provides some early examples, but irony is developed in a fuller way in Cicero. Cf. also W. Buechner, "Über den Begriff der εἰρωνεία," *Hermes* 76 (1941): 339-58. Buechner contends that self-depreciation is central to ancient irony. This element is certainly present in 4:8-13 but is present in the irony of 3:1-4 only to the extent that 3:5-9 can be viewed as Pauline self-depreciation. Cf. also Christopher Forbes, "Comparison, Self-Praise, and Irony: Paul's Boasting and the Conventions of Hellenistic Rhetoric," *NTS* 32 (1986): 1-30. Forbes also surveys ancient literature for discussions of εἰρωνεία and εἴρων, and he seeks to elucidate 2 Corinthians 10-12 in particular.

years later by having Ligarius charged with having supported the African King Juba in a war against Rome.

Scholars have long noted Cicero's skill in handling Tubero with irony in this speech.[17] In particular, Cicero rhetorically seeks to reduce all of Tubero's charges against Ligarius to a single charge of simply having been in Africa in the first place (*Pro Lig.* 1; 9).

For my purposes, however, this speech provides formal parallels with the argument of Paul in 1 Cor 3:1-4, parallels that help demonstrate that 3:1-4 is indeed irony. First, in the particularly ironic section of *Pro Lig.* 9-10, Cicero speaks from his own perspective rather than from that of the defendant, Ligarius, as he does in much of the oration. In doing so, Cicero turns to address the accuser, Tubero, rather than the judge, Caesar, and Cicero employs numerous vocatives in doing so. "When your sword, Tubero, . . ." "But what was our aim, Tubero, . . ." "And in the present suit, Tubero, . . ."

Cicero also employs rhetorical questions here, most of which have obvious answers that implicate or impugn Tubero rather than Ligarius. For example, Cicero begins this section: "My question, however, is this: who thinks it is an indictable offense in Ligarius 'to have been in Africa'?" The answer is clearly Tubero.

Moreover, Cicero gradually increases the tension and gravity of his argument by using dramatic build-up. Cicero does this as he points out the irony of Tubero's failure to recognize his own culpability in various traitorous activities against Caesar, the very same activities that Tubero seeks to use against Ligarius. For example, Cicero gradually builds the drama as he says, "While I do in some degree miss . . . far more sadly (*sed multo magis*) do I miss." Cicero immediately proceeds from this statement to a climax that highlights just how preposterous are Tubero's actions in charging Ligarius at all.

Finally, Cicero introduces the richly ironic section of *Pro Lig.* 9-10 with the conjunction *sed*. This contrastive and adversative conjunction sets the irony of 9-10 off from its context and also serves to set off

---

[17]Cf. *e.g.*, George Kennedy, *The Art of Rhetoric in the Roman World: 300 BC–AD 300* (Princeton NJ: Princeton University Press, 1972) 262-78. Also H. V. Canter, "Irony in the Orations of Cicero," *AJPh* 57 (1936): 457-64; and Auguste Haury, *L'ironie et l'humour chez Cicéron* (Leiden: Brill 1955) 113-14.

Cicero's initial rhetorical question as he launches into his ironic impli-
cating of Tubero in order to defend Ligarius. "*Sed hoc quaero.*"

Each one of these formal traits of Cicero's irony has a parallel in 1
Cor 3:1-4. First, as noted already, Paul moves back into a first person
singular address as he begins 3:1-4 with κἀγώ in 3:1. Second, Paul
employs the vocative, ἀδελφοί, to open the passage, just as Cicero
employs the vocative to address Tubero in his irony at *Pro Lig.* 9-10.
Third, as does Cicero, Paul poses rhetorical questions that obviously
implicate and convict the Corinthians themselves in 3:1-4. Furthermore,
Paul gradually builds the drama and gravity of his argument as he uses
ἔτι νῦν in 3:2 and ἔτι in 3:3. Finally, Paul introduces 3:1-4 with the
contrastive, adversative κἀγώ.[18]

Of course, none of these parallels with Cicero's ironic form alone
automatically signifies the use of irony by Paul. Given the confluence of
these several formal clues, however, along with the content of Paul's
argument, which I have already demonstrated to bear the marks of irony,
the evidence seems to lead to an ironic reading of 3:1-4.

The ironic paradox of the Corinthians' behavior as measured against
the proper, perhaps even ideal, Christian activity like that set forth in
2:6-16 is highlighted in other ways as well. For example, it is paradoxical, and somewhat ironic, that Paul shames the Corinthians in 3:1-4
yet continues to acknowledge their status as Christians by using terms
and phrases that elsewhere apply to Christian existence. In other words,
Paul simultaneously depicts them as Christian and non-Christian, thereby
indicating the tension in which their behavior necessarily locates them.
For example, he uses the phrase ἐν Χριστῷ to qualify their childishness in 3:1. Such a phrase recurs throughout all of Paul's letters to
describe the Christian state.[19] So too does the verb περιπατέω (3:3),
which is often used to depict the daily life of faith.[20] Furthermore,

---

[18]For other NT examples of the adversative κἀγώ cf. Acts 10:28 and Jas 2:18. Cf.
also Phil 2:28 and 1 Thess 3:5. As I will contend in more detail later in the investigation,
Paul can use κἀγώ in an ironic context in other parts of this same letter. Cf. 7:40;
15:8; and perhaps 16:10. Cf. also 2 Cor 11:16-22. See my discussion of 1 Cor 7:40 at the
end of my chapter 7.

[19]*E.g.*, 1 Cor 1:2, 30; 4:15, 17; 2 Cor 1:21; Rom 16:3, 7, 10; Gal 3:26; Phil 1:1; 4:21;
and 1 Thess 4:16.

[20]*E.g.*, Rom 6:4; 2 Cor 5:7; Gal 5:16; Phil 3:17; and 1 Thess 4:1.

ποτίζω (3:2) depicts Paul's and Apollos' work in creating the Corinthian community at 1 Cor 3:6-8 and the common Christian partaking of
the Spirit in 1 Cor 12:13.[21] Hence, Paul carefully and subtly oscillates
back and forth between their true status as Spirit-endowed Christians and
the fact of their ill-begotten behavior in order to capture their redeemed
yet tenuous status. Often the contrast is side-by-side. In some measure,
Paul's continued use of such terms also seems to soften the harshness of
his rhetoric somewhat and perhaps it eases the discomfort or shock
received from the shame of being called νήπιοι and σαρκικοί. By
intermingling typically Christian vocabulary within his reproval, Paul
subtly reassures the Corinthians that they can still count themselves
among the redeemed. However, he simultaneously issues the call to have
that assurance reflect itself in their attitudes and behavior.

This need for modified behavior is evidenced in one other subtle yet
significant way when Paul employs the verb λέγω in 3:4 to denote the
expression of attitudes or allegiances that are antithetical to the Spirit.
When a person claims an allegiance to Paul, to Apollos, or to others, the
verb designating such a claim is not λαλέω, which again symbolizes
intra-Christian community discourse.[22] Rather Paul uses in 3:4 the verb
λέγω, a more generic verb for speech as well as one that generally
applies in and to the world of those who are "merely humans" (3:4:
ἄνθρωποί). He thereby highlights the difference between inspired
speech, like that described by λαλέω in 2:6-16, and the Corinthians'
fleshly, divisive speech (cf. 12:3).[23]

Related to Paul's rhetoric urging unity and common purpose is his
use here of rhetorical questions, a phenomenon examined by Wilhelm
Wuellner.[24] Wuellner's thesis, that rhetorical questions are deployed by

---

[21]Cf. E. R. Rogers, " Ἐποτίσθημεν Again," *NTS* (1983): 139-41.

[22]These claims of allegiance go back to 1:10-12, but there is insufficient evidence to
posit strictly divided loyalists. These phrases could simply be slogans for persons who see
themselves as aligned with a particular preacher on a single issue or as generally seeking
to follow the way preached by an evangelist. In fact, Paul goes on in 3:5-9 to correct their
flawed views of preachers and leaders, namely Apollos and Paul. Cf. Fee, 55-59; 127-35.

[23]Cf. 1:12. Of course, Paul does not always use λέγω in a negative way since it is
a quite general verb. However, here it is a subtle clue as to the point of his argument.

[24]Wilhelm Wuellner, "Paul as Pastor: The Function of Rhetorical Questions in 1
Corinthians," in *L' Apôtre Paul: Personnalité, Style et Conception du Ministère*, BETL
73, ed. Albert Vanhoye (Leuven: Leuven University Press, 1986) 46-77.

Paul in his pastoral care of young churches, fits well with what is clearly occurring in Corinth. The use of such questions in 3:3-4 could be read as softening the blow of Paul's rebuke of their behavior, thereby making his criticism and shaming easier to receive. By phrasing his criticism in the form of a rhetorical question, Paul is able to allow the Corinthians to express some assent to his assertions rather than having them receive shame in a more direct, imperative form that might worsen an already difficult situation. Likewise, the rhetorical questions fit with the paraenetic tone of 1:10–4:21 as Paul sometimes subtly, and often quite overtly, tells the Corinthians that they simply ought to know better. The use of rhetorical questions also underscores the assumed familiarity of the audience with this material and instruction. They should already know such things, either from their previous instruction from Paul, from other Christian training, or from the more general presence of such material in common philosophical literature and teachings. Moreover, the use of rhetorical questions underscores Paul's irony here.

The better educated and more rhetorically sophisticated among the Corinthians would likely have recognized the rhetorical character and nuances of what Paul is doing here. They would have seen Paul's gradually leading the Corinthians through the general principles of Christian existence, inspiration, and access to the divine mind in 2:6-16 and then ensnaring them in something of a trap in 3:1-4 where his criticism and shaming becomes more explicit and directed toward their own behavior. Some, or perhaps many, of the Corinthians fancied themselves superior or elitely accessible to inspiration via the divine mind; therefore Paul relocates all Christians on the same plane of access and inspiration in 2:6-16. The same group(s) of believers probably also constituted something of a party or faction(s) within the church in Corinth, so Paul uniquely rebukes such a faction with his shaming rhetoric here in 3:1-4.

The Topoi of Two Levels of Teaching and Secret Doctrines

The shaming in 3:1-4 is advanced by the use of common ideas and terminology for education and training in antiquity. Paul introduces in 3:1-2 the metaphors of babes (νήπιοι), milk (γάλα), and solid food (βρῶμα). Such metaphors are a commonplace in the literature of the first century as writers such as Epictetus and Philo utilize this kind of imagery to describe their notions of education and philosophical training.[25] Consequently, scholars have often turned to philosophical material, particularly Stoic writings, to elucidate this passage. The results have varied widely, however.

For example, John Fitzgerald sees the child-like metaphor here as evidence of typically Pauline parental imagery in which Paul "fathers" Christian communities and disciples.[26] In nearly all such parental cases, however, Paul employs τέκνον rather than other terms such as νήπιος.[27] From a different vantage point, Birger Pearson appeals to the typically Stoic background of such language to claim both that the terminology is that of Paul's "opponents" and that Paul is concentrating on the contrast between τέλειοι and νήπιοι.[28]

Looking for assistance in material with Stoic influences proves useful, for the Stoics invariably use the term νήπιος in a pejorative context and sense. In such Stoic instances, the term usually highlights the state to be abandoned in favor of seeking true virtue. Epictetus at *Diss.* 3.19.1 depicts the νήπιος as uneducated in life. At 2.16.25, he belittles the child's being persuasively influenced by his attachment to a biscuit, and does so in order to teach that the true philosopher and intelligent human should be influenced by true judgments.[29] Philo also uses νήπιοα in similar ways. For example, at *Agr.* 9, he writes:

> But seeing that for babes (νήπιοι) milk (γάλα) is food, but for grown men (τέλειοι) wheaten bread, there must also be soul-nourishment, such as is milk-like suited to the time of childhood, in the shape of the preliminary stages of school-learning, and such as is adapted to grown men (τέλειοι) in the shape of instructions leading the way through wisdom and temperance and all virtue.

---

[25]For a detailed list of ancient sources in which this metaphor appears, see W. L. Knox, *St. Paul and the Church of the Gentiles* (Cambridge: Cambridge University Press, 1939) 111.

[26]Fitzgerald, 118.

[27]Cf. 1 Cor 4:14ff; 2 Cor 6:13; Gal 4:19; 1 Thess 2:7, 11; Phil 2:22; and Phlm 10. Cf. Fee, 124-25, and Francis, 44-45.

[28]Pearson, 27-30.

[29]Cf. also 2.16.39. For a fuller look at the Stoic and Cynic influences and characteristics in Epictetus' writings, cf. Margarethe Billerbeck, *Epiktet: Vom Kynismus* (Leiden: Brill, 1978).

Pearson contends that Philo here displays Stoic characteristics, and earlier I have noted that Philo blends a variety of philosophical traditions. More important than the specifically Stoic character of Philo's argument is the fact that, like Epictetus, Philo here distinguishes between immature babes and full-grown adults in describing education, training, and the acquisition of virtue.[30] Unlike Epictetus, however, Philo is concerned expressly with religious attainment rather than purely philosophical education. The status of the νήπιος is one to be avoided by seeking out advanced instruction. What is crucial is that the criterion for such a differentiation is education in pursuit of the possession of virtue. This education, with its related gradations in difficulty, is a process that slowly leads to the attainment of virtue. For Paul, however, the difference between the νήπιος and the τέλειος is simply belief/faith in Christ and one's status as a πνευματικός.[31] Although Paul certainly provides for the notion of increase in faith (as well as other Christian attributes),[32] there simply is no indication that Paul envisions an elaborate educational process that parallels the Stoic pursuit of virtue. Furthermore, Philo and Epictetus are concerned solely with individuals whereas Paul exhibits a clear social and corporate concern for the behavior and attitudes of a community.

Whereas the language of a child-like state and rudimentary curricular principles functions in writers such as Epictetus and Philo to illustrate differences in gradation of instruction, such language in Paul here in 1 Cor 3:1-2 is focused less on the content of instruction and more on the portrayal of the advanced state of moral and spiritual development of the Christian. In other words, the language captures the pre-Christian state that should have been left behind by the Corinthians upon their conversion and founding as a congregation. Just as Paul preached (κηρύσσω or καταγγέλλω) to convert them rather than instructed or spoke (λαλέω), so too they were then νήπιοι but now should be πνευματικοί or τέλειοι by virtue of their converted status as

---

[30]In Philo, cf. also *De Cong.* 19 and *Quod Omn. Prob.* 160. Cf. also Richard Horsley, " 'How Can Some of You Say That There Is No Resurrection of the Dead?' Spiritual Elitism in Corinth," *NovT* 20 (1978): 203-31.

[31]Cf. 1 Cor 2:5; 15:14; 2 Cor 4:13; 5:7; 13:5; Gal 3:2, 9, 23-26; Phil 3:9.

[32]Cf. 1 Corinthians 13 and 2 Cor 10:15.

Christians. Again, such a reading hinges on the general principle outlined in 2:6-16 where all Christians are πνευματικοί and τέλειοι.[33]

Another distinction between two types of teaching, as open/revealed versus secret/hidden, also has long been considered a philosophical commonplace, particularly among Pythagoreans, Stoics, and Epicureans. Clement of Alexandria comments on these very groups' propensity for secret doctrines in his effort to justify the Christian use of allegory.[34] Similarly, Sallustius and Julian explicitly comment on the pervasiveness of secret doctrines in ancient philosophy.[35] George Boas, however, has demonstrated the improbability that such secret doctrines existed in these groups themselves but more likely were the constructs of later writers such as Clement, Julian, Sallustius, and others.[36] For example, Diogenes Laertius especially promulgates this idea that earlier philosophers held back or concealed some of their doctrines and tenets.[37]

Instead, Boas proposes that the primary distinction made by the philosophers themselves was that between difficult and easy instruction, or that for the "many" and that for the "few." For example, Aulus Gellius tells us that Aristotle presented two types of teaching in the Lyceum: (1) ἐξοτερικά, which included his afternoon lectures to all comers without selection, and (2) ἀκροατικά, which Aristotle gave in the morning for those whose ability and rudimentary knowledge he had examined. These latter lectures were more abstract and subtle and were intelligible "only

---

[33]Cf. also Kuck, 160, who agrees that the contrast here emphasizes not different groups of teachings but rather is "a picturesque way of describing the goal of deeper intellectual insight and moral maturity." Likewise, J. Francis, 56, who sees the dietary distinction not so much as a difference in teaching content but "a difference in experience between ignorance of the gospel's existence and the hearing of it and belief in it."

[34]Cf. Strom. 5.9.58.

[35]Cf. Julian's comments on the Pythagoreans at 7.239A. Also Sallustius De Diis 3 and 4.

[36]George Boas, "Ancient Testimony to Secret Doctrines," Philosophical Review 62 (1953): 79-92.

[37]Cf. Diog. Laer. 3.63 (Plato); 8.15, 42 (Pythagoras); and 10.5 (Epicurus).

to those who have heard us."[38] The distinction is clearly a function of the audience's prerequisites and readiness.

Paul employs no original idea here in his rebuke of the Corinthians. He uses these common notions of distinguishing between listeners and their abilities in order to contrast the state the Corinthians left behind when they accepted his gospel and that state that all Christians assume with the baptismal endowment of the Holy Spirit. This distinction is advanced by the description of Paul's preaching (κηρύσσω) to them, which is something like Aristotle's ἐξοτερικά available and accessible to the nonbeliever. After conversion, Paul then can λαλέω.

That a group of the Corinthians is claiming a privileged, advanced status relative to their fellow believers thereby ironically illustrates that they have little understanding of the true fundamental status of all Christians. The statement of a general principle of wide applicability in 1 Cor 2:6-16, and the explicit rebuke of the Corinthians' divisive behavior in 3:1-4, both address such a position directly.

Still later, in 1 Cor 13:11, as Paul wraps up his poetic or hymnic lauding of ἀγάπη in chapter 13, he contrasts himself as a νήπιος as

---

[38]Two works quote a letter from Alexander the Great to Aristotle. Aulus Gellius *Noct. Att.* 20.5; cf. also Plutarch *Vit. Alex.* 7.3. Aulus Gellius provides Aristotle's reply. For the tradition surrounding a Pythagorean classification of instructees into two categories (μαθηματικοί, advanced ones who have fuller knowledge, versus ἀκουσματικοί, who are outsiders that receive only cursory instruction), cf. Iamblichus *De pythagorica vita* 81-82 and Porphyry *De vita pythagorae* 37. For an example of the idealized biography of a silent philosopher during the time of Hadrian, to whom legend attributes a Pythagorean lifestyle, see *Secundus the Silent Philosopher: The Greek Life of Secundus,* ed. Ben Edwin Perry, Philosophical Monographs 22 (Ithaca NY: Cornell University Press, 1964). In contrast, Lucian *Demonax* 11 says that the Cynic speaks to all. In another Cynic example of this universal accessibility, the first-century writer of Socratic *Epistle 1* says he gives his "philosophical instruction in public" and does not "practice philosophy shut up inside, as Pythagoras is said to have done." For a commentary on this epistle, cf. Johannes Sykutris, *Die Briefe des Sokrates und die Sokratiker*, Studien zur Geschichte und Kultur des Altertums 18 (Paderborn: Schöningh, 1933) 13-25. For an introduction to the Cynics, see Abraham J. Malherbe, "Cynics," *IDBS* (Nashville: Abingdon, 1976) 201-203. Cf. also Harold W. Attridge, *First Century Cynicism in the Epistles of Heraclitus*, Harvard Theological Studies 29 (Missoula MT: Scholars Press, 1976). For other ancient views on this matter, cf. Dio Chrys. *Or.* 33.8; Epictetus *Diss.* 1.29.30-32; and Philo *Post. Cain* 141.

opposed to his present status as an ἀνήρ.[39] Thus, he implicitly exhorts the Corinthians themselves to grow up and put on the ways of God as embodied in ἀγάπη. Paul calls them to put aside the childish ways of factionalism and claims to spiritual superiority in order to move toward the ideal, which is action in the mutual interest of ἀγάπη. This dualism is evidenced already in 2:6-16 where Paul antithetically contrasts the wisdom and thinking of this age with that of God and Christ. The wisdom of God is not made manifest in worldly behavior and fleshly dissension. Rather it defines and unifies τέλειοι and πνευματικοί.

Conclusions

Thus, in 1 Cor 3:1-4, Paul contrasts his own inspired communication to the congregation during his initial preaching and formation of the church, his own subsequent inspired instruction to them, as well as the inspired speech of Corinthians within their own worship services, with the Corinthians' fleshly and worldly behavior, attitudes, and communication. He also contrasts the Corinthians' pre-Christian state with their Christian status as τέλειοι, or πνευματικοί, a status that is being jeopardized by their divisive behavior. While they cling to jealousy and strife, the Corinthians are still merely humans (3:3-4). Paul calls them to return to the deeper life in the Spirit as those who have the "mind of Christ" (2:16).

---

[39]For another NT example of a contrast between the child-like state (νήπιος) and maturity (τέλειος) linked to the concept and possession of ἀγάπη, cf. Eph 4:13-14. For another NT example of such states and dietary distinctions, cf. Heb 5:12–6:3.

Chapter 6
The Inspired Body of Christ
in 1 Corinthians 12

In this chapter I seek to demonstrate that clear lexical and thematic similarities link the discussions in 1 Corinthians 12 and 1 Cor 2:6-16. In fact, in 1 Corinthians 12, Paul develops the foundation laid in 1 Cor 2:6-16 in significant ways in his presentation of the body of Christ and his discussion on spiritual gifts or persons. Of particular importance is Paul's employment of the concept of communal inspiration from 1 Cor 2:6-16. In doing so, Paul's concern again is the modification of communal behavior, including control of the exercise of spiritual gifts and the resolution of the issue of factionalism and discord within the Corinthian congregation.

The Issue of Inspired Speech (1 Cor 12:1-3)

The introductory verses in chapter 12 immediately pick up the theme of inspired speech and intra-Christian communication.[1] In 12:3a, Paul employs the verb λαλέω to refer to Christian speech "in," or "by," the Holy Spirit (ἐν πνεύματι θεοῦ λαλέω). Specifically, he contrasts speech under the direction of the Holy Spirit with speech that can "say"

---

[1]12:2 is notoriously difficult both to translate and to understand. For an examination of this verse and its possible interpretations and connotations, see Terence Paige, "1 Corinthians 12.2: A Pagan *Pompe?*" *JSNT* 44 (1991): 57-65. Paige contends that Paul here alludes to ancient civic religious processions rather than simply to pagan religious practice. As such, Paul thereby depicts the Corinthians' pre-Christian existence as a subjection to evil powers that led them about in a fashion that they did not completely comprehend just as the public is led by officiants in a pagan *pompe*. Paige then moves to claim that 12:1-3 therefore introduces 12–14 as a discussion of what it "really" means to be "led by God" and to be under the direction of the Holy Spirit. For a discussion of the equally intriguing curse in 12:3, and its nuances, see Jouette M. Bassler, "1 Cor 12:3: Curse and Confession in Context," *JBL* 101 (1982): 415-18.

(λέγω) a curse against Jesus (λέγω Ἀνάθεμα Ἰησοῦς). As Paul did in 3:4, he again here supplies a subtle clue regarding his distinction within 1 Corinthians between inspired Christian speech (usually designated as λαλέω) and ordinary, non-Christian, or even anti-Christian, speech (often designated by λέγω). Again, such an understanding of the use of λαλέω is grounded in the foundational work of 2:6-16 where "we speak a wisdom among the perfect."[2]

Obviously, other clear lexical links connect 12:1-3 with 2:6-16. In 12:1-3, Paul uses cognitive language like that set forth in 2:6-16. Of course, such language is not surprising in an epistolary setting of instruction.[3] In a phrase befitting an often paraenetic and equally pastoral letter, in 12:1, Paul does not want the Corinthians to be ignorant (ἀγνοέω) regarding spiritual gifts or persons (πνευματικοί).[4] In 12:3, he wants them to know (γνωρίζω) the difference between two kinds of speech. The rulers of this age do not know (γινώσκω: 2:8), while the Spirit understands the thoughts of God (2:11: ἔγνωκεν). Furthermore, Paul exhorts the Corinthians in 2:16 to assume the "mind of Christ" (νοῦς τοῦ Χριστοῦ), a thoroughly cognitive expression as demonstrated by my discussion above in chapter 4. Cognitive language plays an important role in both of these instances as well as in other locations throughout the letter.[5]

Thus, 12:1-3 sets the stage for the remainder of chapter 12, but it does so in a way that is reminiscent of, and probably based upon, the crucial discussion in 2:6-16. Spiritual persons, πνευματικοί, have spiritual gifts, πνευματικά. Paul has already established in 2:6-16 that

---

[2]Cf. also the distinction between these two verbs at 3:1, 4 as noted in my discussion above.

[3]Περὶ δέ here introduces the entire section of 12–14. See John C. Hurd, *The Origin of First Corinthians*, 2d ed. (Macon GA: Mercer University Press, 1983), esp. 186-95.

[4]This term, πνευματικῶν, can be translated either of two ways. Schmithals, *Gnosticism in Corinth*, 161, translates it as masculine, and as therefore referring to "spiritual people." Most other scholars take it as neuter, "spiritual gifts." I think it is ambiguous, perhaps even intentionally. The term in itself is another lexical link between the two passages, and the ambiguity is heightened that way. So too Mitchell, 266 n448. "Both are equally possible since in this section Paul's whole point is that gifts are incarnated in individuals and cannot be evaluated apart from their value for the social whole."

[5]*E.g.*, 1:21; 8:2; 13:9; and 14:14-19.

all Christians are πνευματικοί, and he reinforces it here in 12:1-3, particularly in verse 3, since all Christians by definition would confess Jesus' status as Lord. Furthermore, he clearly is again concerned with the topics of spiritual speech, inspiration, and communal behavior since the issue is the discernment of what constitutes speech under the direction of the Holy Spirit. Most importantly, however, the simple confession that Jesus is Lord in 12:3 reestablishes what 2:6-16 has already set forth: that all Christians are inspired. It seems likely that all Christians would have said this statement or something closely resembling it at baptism.

Paul's idea that a statement that Jesus is Lord occurs only "in" or "by" the Holy Spirit (ἐν πνεύματι ἁγίῳ) underscores and corroborates several aspects of my reading of 2:6-16. First, all Christians are inspired by virtue of their reception of the Holy Spirit at baptism since it is the Holy Spirit at work here in 12:3. Second, because of this Spirit-endowment, all Christians, at least potentially, have the capacity for inspired speech, even if it comes only in the form of a simple confession. The discussion of inspired speech in chapter 12 begins here with this simple confession and gradually embraces other forms of speech such as the "utterance of wisdom" (12:8), the "utterance of knowledge" (12:8), and tongue-speaking (12:10). God's searching Spirit makes that possible in both 2:6-16 and 12:3.[6]

The Specifics of Communal Inspiration (I Cor 12:4-13)

In 12:4-13, Paul sets forth for the first time the specifics of his broad notion of communal inspiration. There are varieties of gifts, varieties of service, and varieties of working (12:4-6). To each Christian is given one or more gifts, and this endowment occurs via the work of the Spirit (12:7, 11). Such a notion is not surprising given that all Christians have the Spirit by virtue of their baptism (12:13). Thus, the Spirit imbues the community with a variety of gifts and investments. In other words, all Christians are inspired, and therefore, the community is inspired. In fact, all the gifts are to be used for the common good (12:7). Such a claim here is not at all surprising given all that has preceded it in places such as 2:6-16, 3:1-4, and 12:1-3.

---

[6]Cf. also Pearson, 47-50, and Mitchell, 267-70.

The unity of the Spirit is crucial here. In 12:4, the same Spirit gives the variety of gifts. In 12:11, the same one Spirit inspires (ἐνεργεῖν) all the gifts and apportions (διαιρεῖν) to each Christian as the Spirit wants. In 12:13, the one Spirit is the agent in baptism and is also the baptismal drink of all Christians, both of which functions thereby ensure that there is one body. There is one Spirit, one baptism, and one body, but there are many Christians and a variety of gifts.

This unity of the Spirit undergirds the more opaque language used earlier regarding inspired speech in 2:6-16 where the one Spirit searches and understands the thoughts of God. This information, coupled with the more obvious language about the work of the Spirit here in chapter 12, demonstrates more clearly that Paul uses the activity of the one Spirit as a unifying theme. Baptism, the initial rite in Christianity, provides the basis for all the spiritual gifts, including inspired speech because the Holy Spirit is the only avenue to the divine mind. Hence, any claims to a superior spiritual status or a special access to the divine mind are unsustainable since all Christians have received the same Spirit. Thus, the ideas of 12:4-13 and 2:6-16 are intimately wed and elucidate each other in a way that has not heretofore been brought to light.

Of course, this theme of the unity of the Spirit also fits with the overarching issue of the letter, the address of factionalism and dissension. This theme finds expression throughout chapter 12, particularly in the metaphor of the body of Christ in 12:14ff, a metaphor that develops directly out of the rhetorical question of 1:13 and occurs elsewhere in the letter in less developed forms (*e.g.*, 6:12-20; 11:29).[7] Christ is not divided nor should his body, the Church, be. Another important factor affecting this theme of unity is Paul's explanation that the variety of spiritual gifts

---

[7]For a thorough discussion of ancient parallels with the metaphor of the body, cf. Mitchell, 157-64. Mitchell shows conclusively that Paul extends a common political metaphor and Christianizes it for the Corinthian situation. As such, Paul clearly addresses the issues of factionalism and unity. Cf. also Wayne A. Meeks, *The First Urban Christians: The Social World of the Apostle Paul* (New Haven: Yale University Press, 1983) 166. For other ancient examples of similar language, cf. Livy 2.32.12-33.1 for the fable of Menenius Agrippa. Also Dion. Hal. *Ant.Rom.* 6.86; Plutarch *Cor.* 6.2-4; Dio Chrys. *Or.* 1.32; 3.104-107; 33.16; Seneca *Ep.* 95.52; Philo *Spec. Leg.* 3.131; Josephus *BJ* 1.507; 2.264; 4.406; 5.277-79.

are all utilized for the common good (σύμφορος: 12:7).[8] This term provides another familiar landmark to the audience in Paul's appeal for unity. For example, at 1 Cor 10:23, Paul pairs that which is "helpful" (συμφέρω) with that which "builds up" (οἰκοδομέω), a coupling that is indicative throughout the letter for Paul's benchmark against which all behavior is measured: does it build up the community?

The fact that some of the explicit inspiration language used by Paul here in 12:4-13, as well as throughout the entire chapter, does not appear in 2:6-16 is almost ironic. In particular, in an ancient discussion of inspiration, one would expect the commonly utilized term ἐνεργέω, but that term does not appear in 1 Corinthians until chapter 12. In 12:6, God is the one who inspires (ἐνεργέω) all the varieties. In 12:11, the Spirit performs the same function.

This term, ἐνεργέω, and its related word family were commonly used in ancient descriptions of divine or supernatural activity. Aristotle carefully distinguishes between ἐνέργεια, as active supernatural power, and δύναμις, as potentive supernatural power.[9] Not surprisingly, writers in the *PGM* use this same family of words as a technical term for supernatural activity.[10] This same terminology became prominent in early Christian authors as well, including Paul.[11] For example, at Galatians 2:8, Paul describes God as ὁ ἐνεργήσας in relation to God's working through Peter to reach the Jews and through Paul to reach the Gentiles. Later, at Galatians 3:5, Paul then describes God as "the one who supplies the Spirit to you and works miracles (ἐνεργέω δυνάμεις) among you." Finally, at Philippians 3:21, Christ transforms the bodies of believers into the likeness of his glorious body through his ἐνέργεια.

Yet Paul does not use this term in 1 Cor 2:6-16. Why does Paul wait until chapter 12 to utilize such common and explicit language? Why does

---

[8]This is another philosophical and political commonplace. Cf. Epictetus *Diss.* 2.10.4-5.

[9]*Metaphysics* 9.8.13-14.

[10]E.g., *PGM* 4.156-60, 290. I am indebted to James Ware for his assistance in recognizing this parallel.

[11]In the NT, cf. Matt 14:2; Eph 3:7; 4:16; Col 1:29. In other early Christian literature, cf. Clem. *Strom.* 6.7 (on the inspiration of prophets); 7.14; 8.4; Hermas *Mandate* 6.2.2 (on angels). The term can also apply to evil powers as well. Cf. Clem. *Strom.* 2.20; 6.12; Orig. *Cont. Cels.* 1.22, 60.

he not employ this term in 2:6-16, instead of using the set of terms centering on the search for the divine mind? A number of possible answers occur. Perhaps because some of the Corinthians were so enamored of such matters, he used more subtle ways to persuade them before becoming more explicit. By not using what might have been especially loaded words, such as ἐνεργεῖν, early on, perhaps Paul felt that he might be able to persuade them without their knowing all the ramifications. Or, perhaps one of these instances in either 2:6-16 or 12:1ff. represents the use of the Corinthians' vocabulary, while the other is Paul's own corrective or personal preference. Neither set of terms is a particularly frequent one in Paul, but the language of chapter 12 has a number of Pauline parallels, as demonstrated above, whereas the language of 2:6-16 finds Pauline parallels only in Romans 8 and 11.[12]

Nevertheless, as in 2:6-16, 12:4-13 again locates the focus of the action and the locus of power clearly in God and nothing or no one else. ὁ δὲ αὐτὸς θεὸς ὁ ἐνεργῶν τὰ πάντα ἐν πᾶσιν (12:6b). This focus on the action of God is furthered by the use of the divine passive, δίδοται, in verses 7 and 8. Such an emphasis on the primacy of God recurs throughout the chapter as God "composes" the body in 12:24 and "appoints" offices in the church in 12:28. In the paraenetic address of 2:6-16, this focus on the divine is important because it establishes the direction of the flow of inspired knowledge and access to the divine mind. God is clearly in charge (cf. again 2:7, 10, 12). Now in chapter 12, God directs not only the revelation of His mind but also the very composition of the body of Christ, the Church, as well as the inspiration of every single gift within that Church. In other words, Paul uses the idea of God's fundamental and ultimate control over spiritual matters, an idea firmly established in 2:6-16, and develops it specifically with regard to the origin, proper exercise, and understanding of spiritual gifts within the church community. That idea applies in 2:6-16 firstly to the acquisition and reception of divine knowledge and secondly to its articulation. In chapter 12, the idea expands to include all spiritual gifts including every form of inspired speech.

---

[12]In addition, cf. Phil 2:13, where Paul describes the activity of God among the Christians as ἐνεργέω. He uses the same term to describe the activity of the word of God at 1 Thess 2:13. Cf. also 2 Cor 4:12.

Finally, other lexical links connect 12:4-13 with 2:6-16. Among the spiritual gifts listed in 12:8-10 are the speech of wisdom (12:8: λόγος σοφίας) and the speech of knowledge (12:8: λόγος γνώσεως). As we have seen, wisdom and knowledge are important topics in 2:6-16. The proper view of the nature of σοφία is integral to the Christian faith. Moreover, as we have seen, Sandnes and Gillespie have established that part of the frame of reference for 2:6-16 is early Christian prophecy, so it comes as no surprise when another spiritual gift in chapter 12 is that of prophecy (12:10: προφητεία). These words, combined with the pervasive role of the Spirit (πνεῦμα) and the prominence of θεός, establish clear lexical and thematic links with the foundational discussion in 2:6-16.

The Equality of Inspiration (1 Cor 12:22-26)

I include this portion of the broader development of the body of Christ image (12:12-26) only to collate my reading of the undergirding notion of inspiration[13] with Mitchell's primary thesis of this letter's overarching purpose as an appeal for unity. As Paul moves from the specifics of communal inspiration in 12:4-13 into the metaphor of the body of Christ in 12:12-26, he again locates the center of activity in God, who composes the body so that the inferior part receives "the greater honor" (12:24). In doing so, Paul employs these verses 22-26 to level the playing field again and to counter special claims among some of the Corinthians who deem themselves as superiorly endowed. Instead, Paul says, all Christians are endowed. In fact, those who appear to be inferior are actually more honorable (12:23).[14] Thus, worldly values are inverted by God in the Church.

Of course, this rhetorical maneuver allows Paul to address factionalism still again as he does expressly in 12:25 where he admonishes against dissension (σχίσμα). Instead, Paul urges an ethic of mutuality

---

[13]Initially set forth in 2:6-16 and developed here in chapter 12.

[14]Cf. Albert Vanhoye, S.J., "Nécessité de la diversité dans l'unité selon 1 Co 12 et Rom 12," in *Unité et diversité dans l'église*, ed. Henri Cazelles (Vatican City: Libreria Editrice Vaticana, 1989) 143-56. Vanhoye maintains that Paul contends that diversity is absolutely necessary and essential for and within the unity of the body of Christ, the Church.

and regard for all (12:25-6).[15] In doing so, however, Paul also expands
and makes explicit the underlying implications of his message in 2:6-16.
There, Paul initially stakes a claim to the idea that all Christians have the
same access to the divine mind through the agency of the searching
Spirit. Intra-Christian community discourses involve a variety of speech
forms, including not only prophecy, but also preaching, teaching, prayer,
and tongues. Each Christian potentially is capable of any or all of those
speech forms by virtue of the baptismally-endowed Spirit. It is God who
controls the access to the divine mind; now it is God who composes the
body, distributes the spiritual gifts, and dictates their proper status and
order. In other words, God may use you, but God doesn't need you. Paul
continues to locate all Christians on the same spiritual plane and to make
God the lone source of Christian existence and status. In doing so, Paul
again links 2:6-16 with chapter 12.

The Proper Allegiance of Christians (1 Cor 12:27-31)

Finally, in the concluding verses of chapter 12, Paul applies this heretofore quite general discussion of the inspiration, valuation, and exercise of
spiritual gifts directly to the Corinthians and their situation. Again, the
modification of their behavior and related attitudes is his aim. There can
be no mistake as to the audience in this passage. Paul begins with the
second person, plural (ὑμεῖς ἐστε) and an emphatic δέ at the very
outset of 12:27 and concludes chapter 12 with still more second person,
plural address (12:31). He also explicitly states that the matter of his
concern here is the understanding of roles "in the church" (12:28: ἐν
τῇ ἐκκλησίᾳ). The issue here is clearly internal, intracommunity,
and between Christians.

Since Paul has already warned against the phenomenon of discord in
general in 12:25 and called for an ethic of mutual reciprocity in 12:26,
it seems obvious that the issue here in 12:27-31 is the improper valuation
of roles and gifts within the community and a resultant discord and
factionalism. In order to counter such a tendency in the church, Paul lists
these roles, or gifts, in a hierarchical fashion in 12:28. The use of

---

[15]For more on the *topoi* of cosuffering and corejoicing in antiquity, see Mitchell,
162-63. She demonstrates that this is yet another way of appealing for unity. Cf. Dio
Chrys. *Or.* 38.33, 43; 41.13; 48.6; Aristides *Or.* 23.35.

πρῶτον and δεύτερον tips off the reader that these are not listed arbitrarily nor at random. Moreover, *God* has appointed them in this order (12:28). This statement introducing 12:28 provides yet another example of Paul's locating the initial action and ultimate control with God, just as he has done in 2:6-16 and earlier in chapter 12. As God controls human access to the divine mind, composes the body of Christ, and inspires the spiritual gifts, likewise God has already done the hierarchical appointing in the church. As we will see later, it is no coincidence that prophecy is listed second (after only apostleship!) and that tongues are listed last in the divinely appointed organizational chart.[16] Paul implicitly admonishes those who would falsely value a role, particularly that of speaking in tongues, just as he explicitly warns the Romans not to overvalue themselves in the divine schema (Rom 12:3).[17] Such an admonition becomes still more explicit later in 1 Corinthians, when Paul advocates the superiority of prophecy over against tongues in chapter 14.

The parallels with Romans 12:3-8 become still more helpful when Paul moves from the description of the diversity within the body of Christ immediately to an appeal for ἀγάπη in Romans 12:9-10. This move closely resembles that made in 1 Cor 12:31b–13:1ff where Paul moves from a discussion of spiritual gifts and roles within the church (12:1-31a) into his hymnic praise of ἀγάπη in 1 Corinthians 13.[18] He

---

[16]Of course, I am not the first to note the significance of this order.

[17]It is interesting to note how the gifts or roles listed in Rom 12:6-8 vary widely from those listed here in 1 Cor 12:28 and elsewhere. For example, tongue-speaking is absent in the Romans list. Those gifts listed in Romans seem of a different ilk, perhaps influenced by the notion of Paul's subtle appeal for financial support of his campaign and the collection. Note especially the inclusion of ὁ μεταδιδοὺς ἐν ἁπλότητι, ο προιστάμενος ἐν σπουδῇ ὁ ἐλεῶν ἐν ἱλαρότητι in Rom 12:8b. The breadth of these two lists also underscores how Paul's understanding of spiritual gifts spans both the ordinary and the extraordinary, the usual and the unusual.

[18]For the unity of 1 Corinthians 12–14, see Nils Johansson, "1 Cor 13 and 1 Cor 14," *NTS* 10 (1964): 383-92. For more on the development of this theme and connections between 12, 13, and 14, see Carl R. Holladay, "1 Corinthians 13: Paul as Apostolic Paradigm," in *Greeks, Romans, and Christians: Essays in Honor of Abraham J. Malherbe*, ed. David L. Balch, Everett Ferguson, and Wayne Meeks (Minneapolis: Fortress, 1990) 80-98. Holladay contends that 1 Corinthians 13 presents ἀγάπη as the motivation for Paul's own apostolic ministry. Paul then seeks to ground the Corinthians' concrete life of faith in just such a principle. Far from being an ethereal, flighty poem,

then returns to corporate worship, communal behavior, and the proper exercise of spiritual gifts, especially inspired speech, in 1 Corinthians 14. As such, Paul firmly undergirds his specific instruction in chapters 12 and 14, regarding what is important within the community, with an ethic of action in the communal interest, or in the ἀγάπη of chapter 13.[19]

As he does in 3:3-4 (and elsewhere), Paul employs rhetorical questions here to serve his purpose of shaming the Corinthians and modifying their behavior.[20] In 12:29-30, he unloads a barrage of seven such questions, all of which clearly call for a negative reply. The cumulative effect is to allow the Corinthians' chorus of "No, . . . no, . . . no, . . ." to build so that it is almost humorously obvious that the community is diversely inspired. Not everyone is an apostle nor is everyone a tongue-speaker. Again, this method provides Paul with a means of softening the intensity of his rhetoric when it is turned expressly and inescapably on the Corinthians themselves.

In 12:31, then, Paul provides a final clue as to his purpose and intent. He hearkens back to 3:3 when he appeals to the Corinthians to "earnestly desire (ζηλοῦτε) the higher gifts" (RSV).[21] I think, however, that this

---

1 Corinthians 13 is firmly planted in reality and is crucial for a reading of chapters 12 and 14. See also the literature cited by Holladay, especially Fiore, *Function of Personal Example*, 26-44, and Malherbe, "Hellenistic Moralists."

[19]Cf. also Eph 4:11-12 for another Pauline list of gifts followed by a qualifier that such are to be used for "building up the body of Christ." Again, the list of gifts, and their ordering, differs from that found in 1 Cor 12:28. Cf. also 1 Peter 4:10-11 where the only two spiritual gifts mentioned are speech (λαλέω) and service (διακονέω) although God's varied grace is noted in 4:10.

[20]Again, see Wuellner.

[21]This term, ζηλοῦτε, can be interpreted and translated as either imperative or indicative. Most scholars take it as an imperative that calls the Corinthians to a different way. For another view, see Charles H. Talbert, "Paul's Understanding of the Holy Spirit: The Evidence of 1 Corinthians 12–14," *Perspectives in Religious Studies*," 11 (1984): 95-108. Talbert maintains that one must distinguish in Paul between the "gifts of the Spirit" and the "fruits of the Spirit" (*e.g.*, Gal 5:22-23). Consequently, here Paul would not call ἀγάπη a spiritual "gift" when it is a "fruit" of the Spirit. As such, Paul is criticizing the Corinthians by summing up their position in the phrase, "But you pursue the higher gifts," and then contrasts that mindset with that of ἀγάπη. Talbert thereby solves two minor problems by reading 12:31a as a summary of the Corinthian way. First, he removes the seeming contradiction in 1 Corinthians whereby Paul chastises them for valuing some persons, gifts, and offices more than others but then seems here himself to differentiate among gifts. Second, he removes the unclarity centering on whether Paul

sentence can also be rendered as a question: "Are you contending for the 'higher gifts'? I will demonstrate for you a way that is beyond that."[22] This translation captures more effectively the progression of Paul's argument as he rebukes the Corinthians' contentiousness and moves to modify it with the better way of ἀγάπη in chapter 13. In fact, at 13:4, Paul contrasts ἀγάπη and ζῆλος as he uses the verbal form of ζῆλος in a clearly pejorative sense to say what ἀγάπη is not.

Hence, Paul gradually develops this argument against ζῆλος, for at 3:3 Paul admonishes the Corinthians for the presence of ζῆλος in their midst. Christ is not divided (1:13). As we have seen, factionalism and conflicting allegiances are criticized throughout the letter. Then in 12:31 and 13:4, Paul advances his critique of ζῆλος by comparing it unfavorably with ἀγάπη. In 14:1, however, Paul provides for the possibility of a proper object and motivation of ζῆλος. This corrective is made even clearer in 14:12 when Paul summarizes his points and says, "Since you are zealous (ζηλόω) for manifestations of the Spirit, strive (ζητέω) to excel in building up the church (οἰκοδομή)." Thus, ζῆλος itself is not the root of the problem. Rather, the problem lies in behavior that reflects a misunderstanding of God's action in and through the Holy Spirit. Ζῆλος that upbuilds is acceptable. Ζῆλος that results in ἔρις is not. This exhortation can best be read with the understanding of Christian inspiration via the Spirit that I have established above.

Conclusions

All Christians have the Spirit and therefore can manifest it. Such manifestations are proper and valid only when exercised in and for the

---

would consider ἀγάπη a spiritual gift. Rather, Talbert proposes, Paul wants to undergird spiritual gifts with the fruit of the Spirit. I am intrigued and fascinated by Talbert's reading but still find it preferable to let the apparent inconsistency in 1 Corinthians stand. First, Paul does not make mention of fruits of the Spirit in either of the extant Corinthian letters. Second, and more importantly, Talbert seems to ignore that in 12:28 Paul has just stated that God Himself appointed a specific hierarchy of roles or offices. It seems reasonable, then, to read Paul as moving from the hierarchy of 12:28 to a similarly vertical scale where ἀγάπη is of a "higher" order. Finally, Talbert fails to make the connection with 14:1, which seems to serve as an inclusio with 12:31 and brackets the entire discussion.

[22]For this insight, I am indebted to Wayne A. Meeks.

Christian community. Moreover, these manifestations may take a variety of forms, all of which are inspired by the Holy Spirit and appointed by God. Building up the Church, then, is the correct object of one's zeal and allegiance. Because of the readings of 2:6-16 and 3:1-4 presented above, such a Pauline directive permeates this letter more than ever before realized. The Corinthians' inappropriate behavior reflects a misconception regarding the inspiring activity of God. God gives all Christians the same access to the divine mind through His searching Spirit. That access then comes to fruition in οἰκοδομή not ἔρις.

Chapter 7
1 Corinthians 14 and Corporate Worship

In this chapter I trace the presence in 1 Corinthians 14 of those elements first set forth in 1 Cor 2:6-16 and then developed in 1 Cor 3:1-4 and 1 Corinthians 12. Ideas such as the proper object of one's ζῆλος (cf. 3:3; 12:31), the depiction of inspired speech as λαλέω (cf. 2:6-16; 3:1-4; 12:1ff), communal inspiration (cf. 2:6-16), the proper role of prophecy, and basing the benchmark for the community's spiritual discernment on an action's merit for the community (οἰκοδομή) are all central to 1 Corinthians 14. In an effort to demonstrate how Paul's understanding of communal inspiration—particularly as it is articulated in 2:6-16—again operates in a crucial way for a reading of 1 Corinthians, I will here examine how such ideas and issues function in 1 Corinthians 14.

14:1-12: Inspired Speech and ζῆλος Redone

In 14:1, Paul makes a transition from his aretalogy of love in chapter 13 to a discussion of corporate worship and behavior. At the center of this topic, again, is the idea of ζῆλος, and now Paul describes its proper object.[1] As mentioned earlier, this term is used negatively in 3:3 to depict the Corinthians' divisive, factionalized situation, an idea that stems from the very outset of the letter in 1:10-11.[2] Paul then demonstrates the dangers of ζῆλος in 12:31 at the end of his discussion of spiritual gifts. Finally, at 13:4, Paul measures ζῆλος against ἀγάπη.

---

[1]Note how 14:1a concludes the discussion of ἀγάπη while 14:1b returns to the idea of spiritual gifts (πνευματικά), which Paul urges the Corinthians' ζῆλος to embrace. In 12:31 and more explicitly in 13:4, Paul has demonstrated the shortcomings of the Corinthians' ζῆλος when it is measured against the benchmark of Christian ἀγάπη. Now in 14:1, 12, Paul moves to a positive assessment of ζῆλος.

[2]Again, cf. Mitchell's thesis that this is the πρόθεσις for the letter, a thesis that I discuss above.

Ζῆλος assumes center stage here in chapter 14 where it provides an inclusio for reading the entire chapter. In 14:1, the community's ζῆλος is properly to be focused on ἀγάπη, spiritual gifts (πνευματικά), and prophecy (προφητεία). At 14:39, at the end of this chapter's discussion of corporate worship and inspired speech, Paul reiterates that their ζῆλος is to be concentrated on prophecy rather than speaking in tongues. Hence, Paul's concern for ζῆλος unifies chapters 12–14 as he seeks to modify the Corinthians' behavior and attitudes.[3] In doing so, Paul moves from his earlier negative assessments of ζῆλος to a more positive view of ζῆλος that accounts for the common good.

The key point of the discussion in this chapter's attending to ζῆλος and unity in worship hinges on the proper understanding and employment of inspired speech. In chapter 14, Paul explicitly mentions a wide array of inspired speech forms: speaking in tongues (14:2, 4, 5, 6, 9, 13, 14, 18, 19, 22, 23, 26, 27, 39); prophecy (14:1, 3, 4, 5, 6, 22, 24, 29, 31, 32, 37, 39); prayer (14:13, 14, 15); singing (14:15); thanksgiving (14:16, 17, 18); teaching (14:6, 19, 26); revelation (14:6, 26, 30); and the interpretation of tongues (14:5, 13, 26, 27). Nearly always λαλέω is used to describe the activity in performing such inspired speech. In fact, at 14:6, Paul uses only this verb to describe his own inspired speech in a hypothetical "coming to"[4] the Corinthians in order to benefit them with "revelation or knowledge or prophecy or teaching" as well as with a tongue. In other words, all these forms of speech can be viewed as inspired speaking (λαλέω).

In chapter 14, Paul maintains the same distinction that he has asserted throughout this letter between λαλέω as inspired, Christian, intra-community speech, and other verbs, such as λέγω, as noninspired, more general speech.[5] Again, the generality of types of speech that λέγω can

---

[3]See again note 232 above on the unity of chapters 12–14, and see my above discussion in chapter 6, section D, on the how Paul deals with ζῆλος.

[4]Cf. 2:1-5 for Paul's account of his original "coming to" (ἔρχομαι) the Corinthians.

[5]It is interesting to note that of the 296 occurrences of λαλέω in the NT, 52 are in Paul. Of Paul's 52 total uses, 24 are in 1 Corinthians 14 alone, 34 are in 1 Corinthians as a whole, and 10 additional uses are in 2 Corinthians. Paul uses this verb only 8 times outside the Corinthian correspondence. In contrast, the verb λέγω occurs 2,262 times in the NT, about 7 times more often than λαλέω. Paul uses λέγω 95 times, 30 of which are in 1 Corinthians and 13 of which are in 2 Corinthians. He uses λέγω 3 times

describe is emphasized here. Of course, Christians can λέγω; so too can outsiders, non-Christians, or even anti-Christians. Λέγω, and other verbs of speech utilized by Paul, encompass a broad span of usage, much broader than that assigned to λαλέω by Paul in 1 Corinthians. At the same time, the categories within λαλέω expand as well in 1 Corinthians 14 since Paul embraces here a number of forms of inspired speech not mentioned elsewhere in the letter.

Moreover, 14:1-12 introduces the benchmark against which the assessment and valuation of inspired speech is to be measured: the edification or upbuilding (οἰκοδομή: 14: 3, 4, 5, 12) of the community.[6] Earlier, the Corinthian church itself is described as God's οἰκοδομή (3:9). The context of communal gathering is made even more clear as Paul also expressly mentions the ἐκκλησία in 14:4, 5, and 12 in reference to οἰκοδομή. The community of believers is both the proper audience for such inspired speech and the object of it.[7] Inspired speech is rightly exercised with the benefit of the community clearly in mind.[8] Again Paul intermingles the ideas of community and inspiration. The community is both the locus and the focus of inspiraton.

---

in 1 Corinthians 14 (14: 16, 21, 34). In 14:16 it refers to the speech of an outsider, in 14:21 to the Lord's saying in the LXX, and in 14:34 to a saying in the Law. Never does it describe the speech of believers within the Christian community or its worship.

[6]Later in the same chapter, cf. 14:17, 26. In 14:3, Paul also adds two terms to elaborate on οἰκοδομή: παραμυθία and παράκλησις. In 1 Corinthians, παράκλησις functions in two ways. First, as here in 14:31, it describes the communal focus of prophecy. Elsewhere in the letter, Paul uses forms of this verb to describe his own goals in writing the Corinthians. Cf. 1:10; 4:13; 16:12, 15. See my treatment of this in chapter 4, section A above. Related forms of παραμυθία occur elsewhere in Paul to describe proper Christian behavior. Cf. Phil 2:1; 1 Thess 2:12; 5:14. Cf. also 2 Cor 12:19 for the pairing of inspired speech (λαλέω) and οἰκοδομή.

[7]Earlier, this same terminology of upbuilding has been advocated as the standard for believers' behavior regarding the Lord's Supper (10:23) and the consumption of idol meat (8:1, 10). Obviously the ideas of communal reciprocity and accountability run throughout this letter.

[8]The term ἐκκλησία is not particularly common in Paul outside of the greetings and conclusions of letters (e.g., Rom 16:1, 4, 5; Gal 1:2, 13, 22; 1 Thess 1:1). However, it appears 20 times in 1 Corinthians, and 8 times here in 1 Corinthians 14 alone. Consequently, Paul makes clear the context in which he understands inspired speech to occur: it is within gatherings of the Christian community.

In stressing the community and its benefit, Paul emphasizes the distinction between speaking in tongues and prophecy, a distinction that clearly runs throughout the chapter. Prophecy is to be preferred because of its ability to build up. The use of comparatives underscores this point several times (14:1, 5a, 5b). In order to develop this distinction still further, Paul employs in 14:7-8 metaphorical language of musical instruments, a phenomenon paralleled in Plutarch's description of the inspiration at Delphi.[9] Paul likens tongues to instruments that do not give distinct notes and are therefore unintelligible and useless to the hearer. In the same way, Paul observes that one cannot understand the speech in an unknown language of a foreigner (14:10-11).[10] Consequently, tongues do not build up the church.[11]

Paul sums up 14:1-12 in 14:12 where he again uses ζῆλος, πνεῦμα, οἰκοδομή, and ἐκκλησία to recapitulate his point. Moreover, Paul employs additional words in this summation to provide clues to his purpose when he says, "strive (ζητέω) to excel (περισσεύω) in building up the church." Paul often employs ζητέω to characterize what should be pursued and desired in a righteous life.[12] As we have seen,

---

[9]Cf. again *Defectu* 418D; 431A; 436F; 437D. For an examination of the meaning of and parallels with ὅμως in 14:7, cf. Joachim Jeremias, " "Ομως (1 Cor 14,7; Gal 3,15)," *ZNW* 52 (1961): 127-28.

[10]It is interesting to note that in 14:8 Paul refers to the sound of a trumpet (σάλπιγξ) in making ready for battle. This idea occurs also at 15:52 and at 1 Thess 4:16 in reference to Christian eschatology, where the trumpet sounds on that day as the dead rise. Thus, it is certainly speculative, yet nevertheless attractive, to propose that we could have here an allusion to early Christian eschatological instruction. In other words, inspired speech serves to edify the community in order to prepare them for spiritual and eschatological battle, and such speech fails if it cannot be ascertained when it is communicated in unintelligible tongues.

[11]For more on tongues and their social status within the Corinthian church, cf. again Dale Martin, "Tongues of Angels." Martin, 569, argues that Paul's goal in 1 Corinthians 12–14 is "to lower the assessment of glossolalia among the Corinthians and to argue that it is less valuable for the assembly than is prophecy." Martin goes further in demonstrating the high status often accorded to tongue speakers in antiquity and shows how Paul takes the side of lower status members in his effort to modify the behavior of higher status members.

[12]For positive examples, cf. 1 Cor 10:24, 33; 13:5. For negative examples, cf. 1 Cor 1:22; 2 Cor 13:3; Phil 2:21. Cf. also Gal 1:10 and 1 Thess 2:6. This term reinforces his attention to the proper focus of ζῆλος. Περισσεύω is a common Pauline term in

searching and seeking are common ideas in ancient discussions of inspiration. Earlier, in 2:6-16, Paul has sought to remind the Corinthians that it is the Spirit who searches (ἐραυνάω) the mind of God. Here, however, Paul reproves the Corinthians and instructs them to direct their own human search toward the community. In other words, "the Spirit alone searches the things of God; you should seek to build up the community." Leave to God the things that are God's. It is obvious that Paul here is appealing to the Corinthians to modify their corporate behavior and their understanding of inspired speech in order to build up the church. The proper valuation of prophecy is paramount to such an appeal.

14:13-19: The Criterion of the νοῦς

Paul in 1 Cor 2:6-16 clearly locates in God the power and activity required for the revelation of knowledge regarding the divine mind (2:7, 10, 11, 12). As we have seen, this conviction was not uncommon in antiquity. Unlike Plutarch, Philo, Josephus, and others in antiquity, however, Paul does not rate the value of some ecstatic or irrational authentication of inspired speech as supremely validating of the reception and articulation of such revelation; in fact, he makes it secondary at best. God certainly provides the inspiration, but the avenue is not necessarily irrational or ecstatic.

The Corinthians likely overvalued the significance of any vindication of the inspired speaker via an ecstatic state, because in chapter 14 Paul carefully distinguishes between intelligible, communally edifying prophecy and ecstatic, individualistic tongue-speaking. This observation can be seen in several places in chapter 14 but nowhere more prominently than in 14:13-19.

Paul does not understand prophecy to involve an ecstatic or trance-like state where the human vessel is unresponsive to his or her surroundings or where voluntary human functions are replaced by automatic ones.[13] Rather, tongues require such a state of ecstasy. Tongues

---

hortatory directives. *E.g.*, 2 Cor 8:7; 9:8; 1 Thess 4:1.

[13]My discussion of ecstasy in antiquity and 1 Corinthians 14 often parallels the view found in Callan, "Prophecy and Ecstasy in Greco-Roman Religion and in 1 Corinthians." For a similar definition of a trance, which I am making a defining factor in ecstatic

are further defined as: not intelligible, or incomprehensible (14:2, 9, 16); directed toward God rather than humans (14:2); and building up the individual speaker rather than the community (14:4, 5, 6, 17). Tongues only benefit the community when they are interpreted for the group's understanding and benefit (14:5, 13). Most importantly for this discussion, however, Paul claims in 14:14-15 that tongues occur when the spirit is engaged but the mind (νοῦς) is "unfruitful" (ἄκαρπος).[14] The mind fails to serve the community or bear fruit for the benefit of others. In contrast, the Corinthians are exhorted to pray (προσεύχομαι) and sing (ψάλω) "with the spirit" (τῷ πνεύματι) and "with the mind" (τῷ νοΐ). This role of the νοῦς proves crucial when seeking to illumine Paul's understanding of the nature of inspired speech.

Clearly, Paul affirms in 14:14-16 the necessity of expression "with the mind" (τῷ νοΐ) alongside that "with the spirit" (τῷ πνεύματι). This assertion is not surprising given Paul's predilection in this section for giving preference to that action that serves and benefits the community. In order for the community to benefit, a believer's communication obviously must be intelligible to others lest the hearers be left cluelessly in the dark. Moreover, as we have already seen, early on in this letter, Paul has located the basis for his appeals and instructions in the νοῦς. At 1:10, he exhorts the Corinthians to "be united in the same mind" (ἐν τῷ αὐτῷ νοΐ). At 2:16, his argument rests on the idea that Chris-

---

speech, cf. Erika Bourguignon, "The Self, the Behavioral Environment, and the Theory of Spirit," in *Context and Meaning in Cultural Anthropology: In Honor of A. Irving Hallowell*, ed. Melford E. Spiro (New York: Free Press, 1965) 39-60, 41. This view appears to contradict the view of "ecstastic" speech found in Wayne A. Meeks, *The Origins of Christian Morality* (New Haven: Yale, 1993). Meeks, 100, includes all of the speech forms found in 14:26 as "ecstatic." Meeks, 49, cites the possibility that a lower social class "prophet" might receive a revelation "in a trance." Meeks' definitions of ecstasy and trance differ from those I employ here.

[14]This is the only occurrence in Paul of this adjective ἄκαρπος. However, it seems clear that it is used here to emphasize the need for the νοῦς to be used to benefit others in the community. Elsewhere in the NT, this adjective usually applies to ineffective Christian behavior. Cf. Eph 5:11; Tit 3:14; and 2 Pet 1:8. At *Phaedr.* 277A, Socrates maintains that its ability to bear fruit forever proves the superiority of the dialectic method. This method plants seeds in other minds rather than generating "fruitless" thoughts or words. In *Nic. Eth.* 1125a, Aristotle contrasts "useless" things and those things that bring in a return. On the fruitfulness of oracles, cf. Aeschylus, *Eum.* 714.

tians have the "mind of Christ" (νοῦς τοῦ Χριστοῦ). Paul does not divorce the cognitive element from the spiritual activity and communication of Christians; rather rational human cognition plays a vital role.

This insistence on the superiority of rational, nonecstatic behavior and communication has another function as well. The discussion in 14:13-19 is marked by a concern for those outside the Christian community. Behavior in public worship is to be conducted with an eye toward the outsider. In 14:16, the ἰδιώτης cannot participate in the "Amen" since he cannot understand what is being said unless one also speaks τῷ νοΐ.[15] Again, the outsider is not built up, or edified (οἰκοδομέω), just as the community is not built up. Thus, Paul's missionary agenda cannot be served by unintelligible speech, so Paul develops this stance still further in 14:20-25.[16] Paul obviously expects, or is at least willing to allow for the possibility of, the presence of outsiders in Christian public worship,[17] and Christian behavior in worship should exhibit concern for such outsiders.

---

[15]This custom reflects a Semitic Jewish tradition of worship that would therefore have been present to some degree in Corinth. Cf. Meeks, *First Urban Christians*, 148.

[16]It is interesting that Paul makes himself something of an example in 14:18, which may have an ironic flavor and/or a sarcastic twist to it. Paul thanks God that his tongue-speaking is superior to that of *all* of the Corinthians. This could have an ironic tone for Paul portrays himself in a variety of ways throughout the letter, often in a manner to emphasize humility and equality. He also thoroughly devalues tongue-speaking in 14:1-17. Nevertheless, at 14:18, he claims to be superior to all the Corinthians, even the group of hyperspiritual overvaluers of tongue-speaking. Moreover, it is also possible that Paul here is also employing sarcasm whereby he subtly mocks their claims to superiority and counters with his own comparative μᾶλλον. In doing so, Paul would be making a claim, which may or may not be true yet which he demonstrates throughout the letter to be unfitting in a Christian community. Spiritual gifts and inspiration are from God and are no grounds for human boasting. It is interesting that Paul begins the phrase with εὐχαριστῶ τῷ θεῷ, a phrase that characteristically begins the thanksgiving form in Paul's letters. For other examples of the thanksgiving form, cf. 1 Cor 1:4; also Rom 1:8; Phil 1:3; 1 Thess 1:2. Cf. also 1 Cor 1:14; 1 Thess 2:13. For the seminal scholarship on this thanksgiving form, cf. Paul Schubert, *Form and Function of the Pauline Thanksgivings*, BZNW 20 (Berlin: Töpelmann, 1939).

[17]So too Charles Talbert. See his "Paul's Understanding of the Holy Spirit," 101.

14:20-25: Community, Childishness, and Ecstasy

This pericope is important for this investigation first of all because Paul juxtaposes in 14:20 terms like those found earlier in 2:6-16 and 3:1-4. At 14:20, Paul urges the Corinthians to be ἀδελφοί and τέλειοι rather than νήπιοι and παιδία.[18] This language recollects those earlier passages where Paul asserts that all Christians are, or should be, τέλειοι.[19] The Corinthians, although their divisive behavior jeopardizes such a status of perfection or maturity, were νήπιοι before their conversion (cf. 3:1-4) and should now reject such a status of childishness.[20] Hence, in 14:20, in an effort to address the Corinthian problems regarding inspired speech and spiritual status, Paul again invokes the same language developed earlier in the letter. This application in 14:20 fits well with Paul's original use of this language regarding inspiration in 2:6-16 and factionalism in 3:1-4. The Corinthians need to be reminded yet again of their rightful status as τέλειοι, a status that their attitudes and behavior

---

[18]He then juxtaposes οἱ πίστοι with οἱ ἄπιστοι in 14:22-25. This move, however, represents a change back to a missionary concern for the outsider like that above in 14:16ff. Paul wants the Corinthians' behavior to facilitate the conversion of outsiders (see 14:25; cf. 7:12-15). The antitheses like those in 14:22 also provide a glimpse of Paul's defining the social boundaries of the Corinthian believing community as he does elsewhere in the letter using such antitheses. Cf. 6:6; 7:12-15; 10:27. Verses 21-22, however, present something of a problem since v.22 appears to contradict Paul's point in verses 23-25. How can prophecy be a sign for believers in 14:22 but designed for unbelievers in 14:24-25? In fact, Talbert, 102, contends that 14:21-22 are a Corinthian assertion to which Paul responds in 14:23-25. On the other hand, Wayne Grudem, *The Gift of Prophecy in 1 Corinthians* (Washington: University Press of America, 1982) 192-202, contends that σημεῖον can also have a negative dimension, showing not only God's favor but God's displeasure. In other words, a "sign" here is intended to bring judgment on the outsider for (s)he does not understand what is occurring and is therefore clearly outside the believing community. On the other hand, prophecy, because it is intelligible, can lead the outsider to faith. Fee, 682, and Barrett, 323, and I agree.

[19]Ἀδελφοί is a frequent Pauline term used to describe the position of, and Paul's own relationship with, all Christians. In 1 Corinthians, for example, cf. 5:11; 6:5-8; 7:12-15; 8:11-13; 15:6; and 16:11-12. For τέλειος cf. 2:6; 13:10.

[20]It is interesting that this is the only occasion in which Paul uses the common noun παιδίον in the seven generally accepted authentic letters. When Paul addresses the Corinthians in a pastoral sense as his "children," he uses τέκνον. See my discussion above in chapter 5, section C. For νήπιος, cf. 13:11 where the term is again juxtaposed with τέλειος. Cf. also Gal 4:1, 3.

in worship betray.[21] Paul is likely impugning childishness on the part of (some of) the Corinthians as displayed in their understanding and conduct regarding access to the divine mind and inspired speech (2:6-16), unity (3:1-4), spiritual gifts (12:1-31), and public worship (chapter 14). Furthermore, just as he has done in 2:16 and 14:13-19, Paul continues to appeal to their rational, cognitive capacity when he says, "In *thinking* be perfect" (emphasis mine).

Paul also exhibits more concern in 14:23-25 for the impressions of any outsiders present in worship much like that concern exhibited in 14:16. In 14:23-25, Paul plainly hopes that the outsider, the ἰδιώτης, or the unbeliever, the ἄπιστος, is swayed by the corporate behavior in worship so that "conviction" (ἔλεγχος and ἀνάκρισις) and "prostrate worship" (προσκυνέω) of God occur.[22] Thus, Paul's concern goes beyond a mere apologetic desire to impress outsiders, or simply to assuage their concerns about Christianity, to a deeper missionary desire for the conversion of outsiders.[23] Paul, although using what is for him uncharacteristic vocabulary for a very characteristic topic, obviously uses the language of the conviction of sin and conversion here.[24]

This impression is reinforced by the two terms chosen by Paul to depict the desired effect on outsiders, ἀνακρίνω and ἐλέγχομαι. The parallels with 2:6-16 help with the interpretation of 14:20-25. At 2:14-15, as we have already seen, only the believing πνευματικός can ἀνακρίνω.[25] The ψυχικός cannot ἀνακρίνω for (s)he does not have "the things of the Spirit of God" (τὰ τοῦ πνεύματος τοῦ θεοῦ: 2:14). Moreover, the πνευματικός is judged (ἀνακρίνομαι) by no one in 2:15, a fact that Paul employs to his advantage at 4:3-4. He too is judged by no one other than God. In other words, ἀνακρίνω

---

[21]Paul is concerned again with the community's public worship. For example, at 14:23, he employs συνέρχομαι to refer to their gathering as a community. He uses this term earlier to refer to their gathering together for the Lord's Supper (11:17-34).

[22]This is the only time in Paul that forms of ἔλεγχος and προσκυνέω occur.

[23]Meeks, *Origins of Christian Morality*, 49, 63, notes that shame would result from outsiders' perception of the worshipers' madness.

[24]In the later Pauline tradition, ἔλεγχος is used in similar ways. Cf. 1 Tim 5:20; 2 Tim 4:2; and Titus 1:13. Elsewhere in the NT, cf. John 3:20; 8:46; and 16:8.

[25]Note also the presence of καρδία and κρυπτά in 14:25, terms like those used to depict the gaining of access to the divine mind in 1 Cor 2:9-10. Cf. also 4:5.

often has salvific and spiritual connotations for Paul. Although Paul does not deploy ἐλέγχομαι elsewhere, the term takes on similar connotations in the deutero-Pauline tradition such as that represented at Ephesians 5:11-13.[26] In sum, it is significant that Paul moves beyond a simple reproval of the Corinthians' misbehavior and misvaluation of inspired speech to imply that such ill-begotten conduct jeopardizes not only their own status as τέλειοι but the very salvation of those outsiders whom the community of faith is expected to be able to convert.

The presence of μαίνομαι in 14:23 also highlights Paul's revaluation throughout this passage of ecstatic, trance-like behavior and speech.[27] This term, which occurs nowhere else in the extant Pauline corpus,[28] enjoyed widespread usage in a variety of ancient writers to describe the irrational, ecstatic activity of prophets and other communicants with the divine. As we have already seen, the role of the ecstatic μάντις pervades Plutarch's discussions of the Delphic oracles as well as many other descriptions of inspiration and prophetic activity in Hellenistic antiquity.[29] For example, the term also frequents Plato's discourses on prophetic activity.[30] Thus, with these examples, it becomes clearer that

---

[26]It is interesting that at Eph 5:11, the writer urges for "unfruitful (ἄκαρπος) works of darkness" to be "exposed" (ἐλέγχομαι) by the believing community. Cf. 1 Cor 14:14, 24.

[27]Sandnes, 92, points out that this was the "usual term for prophetic ecstatic inspiration." Cf. Aune, *Prophecy*, 21, 33-34, 41; Crone, 11-39.

[28]The only other occurrences in the NT appear at John 10:20, where Jesus is criticized by the Jews for being mad; at Acts 12:15, in the portrayal of Rhoda; and at Acts 26:24-25, where Festus accuses Paul of being mad. In all three instances, the term carries a clearly negative and pejorative sense.

[29]In addition to those texts cited in chapters 1 and 2 above, cf. Lucan *De Bello Civili* 5.160-200 for a graphic but poetic account of Apollo's dislodging of the mind of the Delphian priestess. Apollo assumes control so that the priestess has a wild frenzy characterized by foaming lips. For another example of the employment of foaming lips, this time in a satirical setting, cf. Lucian, *Alexander* 12. For other descriptions of the role of irrational ecstasy, cf. Cicero *De Div.* 1.2.4 where Cicero comments on the ancient view that the human mind was inspired in two ways when in an "irrational and unconscious state" (*sine ratione et scientia*). This occurred first, by frenzy, and secondly, by dreams. Also Philo *Quis Her.* 265-266; *Spec. Leg.* 1.65; 4.49; *Mut.* 1.39; and *Mos.* 1.281.

[30]See my discussion above in chapter 1. Again, cf. *Phaedr.* 244A-45A, where Socrates says that the greatest of blessings come to us through madness (διὰ μανίας), which is sent from the gods. He goes on to say that the Delphic priestess bestows few benefits

Paul seeks to distinguish Christian prophecy, in the context of public worship, from other phenomena in the cultural environment.[31] Unlike tongue-speaking, Paul's idea of Christian prophecy emphasizes rational, intelligible communication in which the νοῦς is fully aware and conscious.[32]

Such a view is also consistent with the Septuagintal uses of μαί-νεσθε and μανία, where the terms are always used pejoratively and often to distinguish the sound state of the true prophet from the madness of pseudoprophetic impostors.[33] For example, at Jer 36(29):26, Jeremiah refers to the need to control "any madman" (παντὶ ἀνθρώπῳ μαί-νομαι) who "plays the prophet" (παντὶ ἀνθρώπῳ προφητεύω). In this sense, Paul's view of μανία is faithful to the Old Testament in not including prophecy as a trance-phenomenon.[34]

In summary, Paul's view of prophecy is that it can potentially come to any member within the community. The prophetic endowment appears

---

when "in her right mind." Cf. also *Tim.* 71E-72A; and *Ion.* 534C-D where Socrates again speaks on this matter.

[31]Sandnes, 92, takes this to mean that Paul is countering a Corinthian view that prophecy is ecstatic. This may or may not be so. Paul could also simply be introducing this emphasis on rationality in order to draw out the finer points of exactly why prophecy is to be preferred in communal gatherings to speaking in tongues.

[32]B. C. Johanson, "Tongues, A Sign for Unbelievers?: A Structural and Exegetical Study of 1 Corinthians 14:20-25," *NTS* 25 (1979): 180-203, uses this information to argue that the Corinthians wanted a typically Hellenistic ecstatic validation of tongues. So too Thomas Gillespie, "A Pattern of Prophetic Speech in First Corinthians," *JBL* 7 (1985): 74-95. This certainly is possible, but I think it is more likely that Paul is arguing at a broader level as he elevates traditional nontrance forms of Jewish, and now Christian, prophecy above the position of Hellenistic phenomena such as those more comparable to speaking in tongues. Of course the Corinthians valued tongues; Paul seeks to correct it. His goal is to differentiate between tongues and prophecy.

[33]Cf. Wis 14:28; Hos 9:7-8; both of which also contrast these ideas. For other negative uses in the LXX, cf. Ps 39(40):4; Jer 32(25):16; Wis 5:4; 2 Macc 4:4; and 4 Macc 7:5; 8:5; 10:13.

[34]Cf. Callan, 136. Callan also appropriates the work of Robert Wilson, "Prophecy and Ecstasy: A Reexamination," *JBL* 98 (1979): 321-37. Callan argues that the LXX reverses the typical Greek usage of προφήτης since the OT conception of prophecy rarely includes trances while other Hellenistic writers, including Philo, usually do. However, even Philo portrays Moses primarily as a nontrance prophet. Callan could have strengthened his case by appealing to the LXX usage of μαίνομαι or μανία to corroborate this view.

to have been primarily revelatory, instantaneous, and temporary (14:30-31). Moreover, the prophet's mind (νοῦς) is involved in the process, (s)he is conscious and able to control bodily functions (14:30), and his/her speech is rational and intelligible. Prophecy also can have a missional function (14:25), it can teach (14:31), and it can reveal the secrets of the heart while also pointing toward or revealing God (14:25).[35] Such prophetic speech is also subject to the community's discernment and evaluation, particularly as that discernment is found in the views of those who are known for their prophesying (14:29, 31-32). Therein lies the point: God provides prophecy for an orderly edification of and for the community.[36]

Communal Reciprocity in 14:26-36

Paul continues to focus on communal gatherings for public worship in 14:26-36, again using a form of συνέρχομαι in 14:26 both to introduce the subject at hand and to indicate the context of the actions he is describing.[37] This passage, however, raises several interpretive and theological issues that have fueled considerable debate throughout the centuries and still do so today regarding the controversial subjects of tongues and women's role in worship. I will not attempt to be exhaustive on each of these; rather my focus will continue to be on the principles set forth in 2:6-16 and how their implications affect our reading of 14:26-36.

In 14:26-36, Paul clearly places the discussion of inspired speech in the setting of public worship as he specifically considers those inspired forms of speaking found in tongues and prophecy along with their proper valuation and role in the church (14:26b). He specifically includes in public worship the use of hymns (ψαλμός), teachings (διδαχή),

---

[35]Cf. again 2:6-16, esp. 2:9.

[36]Cf. Antoinette Clark-Wire, *The Corinthian Women Prophets: A Reconstruction through Paul's Rhetoric* (Minneapolis: Fortress, 1990) 157, who contends that Paul's chief goals throughout this section are to promote order, to prevent overlapping voices and extended sessions of any kind of inspired speech, and to forbid any lack of reflection and interpretation.

[37]For a sociological and anthropological examination of how Paul deals with the household, particularly in 14:33b-36, see Stephen C. Barton, "Paul's Sense of Place: An Anthropological Approach to Community Formation in Corinth," *NTS* 32 (1986): 225-46.

revelations (ἀποκάλυψις), as well as tongues, their interpretation, and prophecy. Moreover, Paul continues to wield the critical importance of the measure of any activity's efficacy πρὸς οἰκοδομήν (14:26c). That alone is the goal.

In so doing, Paul issues directives for the management of worship and the deployment therein of spiritual gifts and inspired speech. The desired results are edification and order (14:26c, 31, 33). The exercise of the gift of tongues in public worship requires the subsequent exercise of the gift of interpretation in order to benefit the community (14:27). Without someone to διερμηνεύω, the tongue speaker is to remain silent in public worship, choosing instead a private, individual conversation with God (14:28).[38]

Paul also seeks to control the exercise of prophecy despite his previous advocacy of prophecy's superiority for upbuilding the community. Even prophecy cannot go unchecked and unfettered. Communal discernment is no less important for prophecy than for tongues (14:29).[39]

---

[38]Cf. again 14:2, 4. For a judicious discussion of the efficacy of tongues for worship from both a historical and theological standpoint, I recommend Fee, 652-712, esp. 659-60. He also provides well-reasoned and measured words for the use of tongues in modern churches. For a look at how this passage has been interpreted in church history, cf. Robert A. Kelly, "Luther's Use of 1 Corinthians 14," *Church Word and Spirit: Historical and Theological Essays in Honor of Geoffrey W. Bromiley*, ed. James Bradley and Richard Muller (Grand Rapids: Eerdmans, 1987) 123-34.

[39]Paul here uses the active form of διακρίνω. At 1 Cor 6:5, the Corinthians are to be ashamed for not having anyone wise enough to "adjudicate" (διακρίνω) intracommunity disputes. This reflects the term's frequent judicial connotations in antiquity. At 11:29, the Corinthians are exhorted to "discern" at the Lord's Supper and at 11:31 to "discern" or "judge" themselves properly. He uses this verb in other letters only in Romans but there only in its middle/passive forms (cf. Rom 4:20; 14:23). It is interesting how often forms and cognates of κρίνω occur in 1 Corinthians. Cf. ἀνακρίνω (2:14-15: see my earlier discussion of this verb), which Paul uses only in 1 Corinthians; συγκρίνω, which occurs only at 2:13 and 2 Cor 10:12; and κρίνω, which occurs fourteen times in 1 Corinthians, twice in Corinthians, and elsewhere only in Romans. This frequency suggests obvious problems of discernment in Corinth both of the Corinthians' propensity for the judgment of other persons, including of Paul himself, as well as spiritual discernment problems in a number of areas. Since such terminology is found elsewhere only in Romans, which was probably authored from Corinth, the situation in Corinth is only magnified. It seems likely that the Corinthians' κρίνω problems hinged at least partially on the hyperspiritualists' overvaluation of themselves and their view of their own unique access to the divine mind. Of course, 1 Corinthians

Again, communal edification is the watchword.[40] As an added measure
to secure order and edification, Paul makes any prophet subject to other
prophets (14:32).[41] In other words, any act or message of prophecy is
subject to the discernment of the community, all of whose members
potentially possess the ability to prophesy. Of course, some within the
community may have been more frequent prophets than others. Paul's
directives, however, caution that the prophet's role is not to be
overvalued or unduly recognized.

Paul's treatment of the issue of women, and their speech in public
worship, raises thorny problems for the interpreter as well.[42] Nevertheless,

5–15 treat a number of specific topics, many of which can be understood as problems of
discernment. I would not, however, exclude other potential issues of division. For
example Gerd Theissen makes a strong case for problems deriving from social class
divisions in Corinth. See his *The Social Setting of Pauline Christianity: Essays on
Corinth*, trans. John H. Schütz (Philadelphia: Fortress, 1982). See esp. chaps. 2–4.

[40]Cf. 1 Thess 5:21 and 1 John 4:1, both of which are cases where δοκιμάζω is used
to describe communal discernment.

[41]Others disagree taking this in a more metaphysical sense so that a prophet's own
πνεῦμα is subjected to himself. I do not think this fits the obvious context of 1
Corinthians 14, which stresses reciprocity and communal accountability. Fee, 696, takes
πνεῦμα in 14:32 in a dual sense, referring both to the prophet's spirit as well as to the
Holy Spirit. Such a view probably necessitates seeing the subjection here as I do, as
subject to the community of prophets.

[42]This portion of the passage, from 14:33b-36, has generated a variety of scholarly
theories for interpretation. Five in particular are noteworthy. First, many take this section
as a post-Pauline interpolation and compare its interpolator to the composer and thought
world of the Pastoral Epistles. Cf. Jerome Murphy-O'Connor, "Interpolations in 1
Corinthians," *CBQ* 48 (1986): 81-94; Winsome Munro, "Women, Text, and the Canon:
The Strange Case of 1 Corinthians 14:33-35," *BTB* 18 (1988): 26-31; Dennis R.
MacDonald, *The Legend and the Apostle: The Battle for Paul in Story and Canon*
(Philadelphia: Westminster, 1983) 86-89; cf. also Munro's *Authority in Paul and Peter:
The Identification of a Pastoral Stratum in the Pauline Corpus and 1 Peter*, NTSMS 45
(Cambridge: Cambridge University Press, 1983) 101-103. Second, Elisabeth Schüssler
Fiorenza takes this passage as authentically Pauline and as reflecting within Paul himself
the struggle against the egalitarian nature of early Christianity that he inherited. In
particular, this passage reflects Paul's references only to Corinthian wives and their
interruptions of worship. Cf. her "Rhetorical Situation and Historical Reconstruction in
1 Corinthians," *NTS* 33 (1987): 386-403, and also her *In Memory of Her: A Feminist
Theological Reconstruction of Christian Origins* (New York: Crossroads, 1983) 230-33.
Cf. also Gerhard Dautzenberg, *Urchristliche Prophetie: Ihre Erforschung, ihre
Voraussetzungen im Judentum und ihre Struktur im ersten Korintherbrief*, BWANT 104

even in 33b-36, communal accountability continues to be at the center of the discussion here. Moreover, it is important to note how Paul locates the origin of inspired speech clearly with God (14:36) just as he has already emphasized in 2:6-16.[43]

Curiously, however, Paul specifically uses his Corinthian designation of inspired speech as λαλέω in both 14:34 and 14:35 when he places restrictions on women's speech in worship. He expressly forbids women to λαλεῖν ἐν ἐκκλησίᾳ (14:35). I am most attracted theologically to Clark-Wire's thesis that Paul is more concerned with order than with women prophets in particular, and could perhaps envision, unlike Clark-Wire, a specific group of disruptive women speakers. The λαλέω here could even possibly refer to other inspired speech forms, like tongue-speaking, which is also prominent in the discussion of 1 Corinthians 14. Paul could be seeking to silence a discrete group (whose

---

(Stuttgart: Kohlhammer, 1975) 253-88. A third view can be found in David W. Odell-Scott, "Let the Women Speak in Church: An Egalitarian Interpretation of 1 Cor 14:33b-36" *BTB* 13 (1983): 90-93. Odell-Scott sees the disjunctive particle in verse 36 as signifying a refutation of what precedes it. In other words 33b-35 is a Corinthian assertion or slogan. This view also finds support in Charles Talbert, "Paul's Understanding of the Holy Spirit," 105. A fourth view is represented by Robert W. Allison, "Let Women Be Silent in the Churches (1 Cor 14:33b-36): What did Paul Really Say, and What Did It Mean?" *JSNT* 32 (1988): 27-60. Allison contends that this is indeed an interpolation but from an earlier Pauline letter. The passage has therefore been placed here because of its linguistic similarities and parallels with the literary context in chapter 14. Allison builds on the observation of Wayne Meeks that the repetition of the three main verbs from the preceding context often misleads the reader to overlook the very different principles underlying 33b-35 and its context. Cf. Meeks, "The Image of the Androgyne: Some Uses of a Symbol in Earliest Christianity," *History of Religions* 13 (1973): 165-208, esp. 201-202. A fifth and final view is that of Antoinette Clark-Wire, *Corinthian Women Prophets*, 152-58. She accepts this text as genuine but wants to read Paul as a "less self-possessed persuader" for whose mind the "women prophets of Corinth may be largely on the margin." More simply, Paul's motives here are to promote order and prevent overlapping voices rather than to issue universally binding directives regarding women. Also useful here is Wire's chart, 283 n13, where she outlines the possible ranges of inspired speech for women, ranking the various types of inspired speech from most destructive to most constructive. Clark-Wire's broader thesis is that the women prophets in Corinth probably were not a self-conscious band of a set number but rather women in general, who were accessible as the spirit moved them to prophesy.

[43]See my discussion in chapter 4 above.

composition both he and the original audience clearly know) who is
disrupting worship with any of a variety of inspired speech forms.

Nevertheless, I find this passage to fit exegetically more closely with
Fiorenza's overall proposal that Paul himself struggles with the egalitarian strains within early Christianity.[44] I have already argued that 2:6-16
makes inspired speech potentially available to all believers, as does the
discussion of spiritual gifts in chapter 12. However, this text unmistak-
ably forbids women to λαλέω in public worship. Paul has allowed in
11:5 that a woman can prophesy, although the context of public worship
is less clear in 11:2-16 than it is in either 11:17-22 or 14:26-36. I therefore prefer the option of letting the tension stand as just that, a contradiction. Again, it seems at least possible that a select group of women
speakers were disrupting public worship, and Paul's concern for order
and the mutuality of all participants moves him to silence such a group.

Recapitulation and Sarcasm: 14:37-40

Verses 39-40 clearly summarize and recapitulate what Paul has set forth
in chapter 14. For example, 14:39 uses nearly all of the key words of
chapter 14 in putting to rest what is at the center of the discussion here.
In particular, the use of ζηλόω in 14:39 forms an inclusio with the
introduction to the chapter at 14:1, which itself brackets chapter 13 by its
own inclusio with 12:31. This "zeal" has been crucial to reading not only
chapters 13 and 14 but also that which has gone before. In 14:39, the
Corinthian "brethren" (14:6, 20) should make "prophecy" (14: 1, 3, 4, 5,
24, 31, 32) the object of their ζῆλος (12:31; 14:1) although speaking in
tongues (λαλέω γλώσσαις) is not to be forbidden. This is proper for
God desires order (14:33, 40).

1 Corinthians 14:37-38 represents something more, however, than just
Paul's attempt at sealing his argument. Most scholars take these two
sentences as Paul's staking a claim to a unique spiritual authority,[45] but

---

[44]I agree with Fiorenza that one cannot support the notion of an interpolation in this
passage on textual-critical grounds, so it is exegetically preferable to accept it as
authentic. I am not persuaded, unlike Talbert and Odell-Scott, that the presence of ἤ
alone in 36a is sufficient evidence that this is a Corinthian assertion.

[45]E.g., Clark-Wire, 158, thinks that "Paul puts his spiritual authority on the line."
Aune, *Prophecy*, 257, takes it as Paul's claiming that the foregoing injunctions have the

I think there is more here in addition to the claim to authority. The rhetoric evokes a sarcasm and a harsher rebuke of the faction of individuals claiming spiritual superiority and unique access to the divine mind.

In 14:37a, Paul says, "If any one thinks (δοκέω) that he is a prophet (προφήτης), or spiritual (πνευματικός), he should acknowledge that what I am writing to you is a command (ἐντολή) of the Lord." Other scholars have noted that Paul commonly uses what Clark-Wire calls the "argument dissociating thought from reality."[46] At 1 Cor 3:18, 8:2, and 10:12, Paul contrasts what one may "think" (δοκέω), particularly of one's own status, with how things really are. For example, "Therefore let any one who thinks that he stands take heed lest he fall" (10:12).[47] This usage of δοκέω serves to reverse patterns of thought that not only do not reflect reality but often are puffed-up and self-exalting patterns. This usage occurs regularly enough in 1 Corinthians that it seems quite likely that Paul here subtly but sarcastically reproves the spiritualists in a stinging way.

On one level, all the Corinthians are πνευματικοί and potential prophets, so of course they will recognize Paul's authority and the efficacy of his directives. Moreover, it is probable that Paul is speaking as a prophet here.[48] On still another level, Paul reproves those Corinthians who elevate themselves to a self-defined and exalted position as prophets and πνευματικοί, a position that Paul has already corrected in 2:6-16 and 3:1-4. They have no basis for such inflated self-definition. Moreover,

---

status of prophetic speech. However, I think that Aune's conception of "prophecy" is almost too broad to be of use in this particular instance. For example, he takes 12:3 as a prophetic utterance because it is "inspired by the Holy Spirit." This investigation has shown that, at least in 1 Corinthians, Paul can provide for the inspiration of the Holy Spirit in a wide variety of speech forms.

[46]Clark-Wire, 155.

[47]Cf. also Gal 6:3 where Paul says, "For if any one thinks he is something when he is nothing, he deceives himself." For other examples of the contrast between thought and reality, cf. 1 Cor 11:16; 12:22-23; 2 Cor 11:16; and Phil 3:4.

[48]I am indebted to Wayne A. Meeks for the insight that 14:37ff is a partial parallel to 14:32. Paul envisions himself as engaged in the discernment of efficacious prophecy just like that which he exhorts the Corinthians to do. Thus, this is no claim to a special apostolic authority but rather to the authority of a prophet whose accuracy should certainly be recognized by any in the Corinthian community who think they are prophets. Any prophet should recognize a true spirit of prophecy.

their self-centered claims betray the fact that they are acting as those who are not πνευματικοί. Thus, they may "think" (δοκέω) they are πνευματικοί, but the reality of their actions does not bear out such a status. At the same time, of course, Paul also implicitly, as well as quite explicitly, elevates the status of his own claims and instructions. Although all Christians are πνευματικοί, Paul's directives are, after all, the ones being written by the church's own founder and read in the community as a whole. That authority, however, is tempered by Paul's insistence on subjecting his own prophecy to the discernment of other prophets (14:38) just as he has commanded the Corinthians to do in 14:32.

This reading of sarcasm follows my assertion in the introduction that 1 Cor 7:40b is no Pauline claim to spiritual authority or divine inspiration as Stuhlmacher interprets it. Rather, in 7:40, Paul again sarcastically employs δοκέω to point out with a dual edge that he "*thinks*" that he *too* has the Spirit of God. As a believer, and even more so as the founding father of the Corinthian church, of course he has the Spirit. Paul's sarcasm, however, presents him as humbly seeking the approval of the higher status Corinthians and makes light of their doubt that the church's founder might not have the Holy Spirit (cf. 4:8-13). He subtly mocks those who claim unique access to the divine mind via the Spirit, for all believers have access to the divine mind. This sarcasm rings true since Paul will soon follow that up in 8:2 with, "If any one thinks that he knows something, he does not yet know as he ought." Their puffed-up claims to exclusive possession of the Spirit reflect the fact that they do not understand as they should. In other words, how silly it is for others to claim that somehow they have a unique access to the divine mind that Paul himself, as well as others, could not have. "I *think* that I *too* have the Spirit of God" is at one and the same time a self-depreciating claim and a mighty, felling blow to the puffed-up claims of others.

Conclusions

Thus, in chapter 14, Paul again seeks to correct the misguided notions and behavior of the Corinthians, particularly those Corinthians who are laying claim to a unique access to the divine mind. It seems likely that such a claim coincided with an overvaluation of the spiritual gift of speaking in tongues along with a related propensity to wield that overvaluation for self-exaltation and the denigration of the spiritual status of others who were deemed to be not as spiritual.

Moreover, these tendencies were also leading to the disruption of public worship even to the point of failure in the missionary agenda. Therefore, Paul issues directives to address the proper exercise and control of spiritual gifts, especially inspired speech such as tongues and prophecy, in the Corinthians' worship. Paul also provides for a number of other forms of inspired speech such as teaching, prayer, and singing. In making these directives, Paul again sets out directions regarding the proper object of one's zeal, the notions of communal accountability and reciprocity, and the tension between childishness and maturity/perfection.

As the capstone of chapters 12–14, 1 Corinthians 14 reminds the Corinthians that ἀγάπη is to govern their behavior, especially in corporate worship settings. Moreover, ἀγάπη dictates that no gift is the exclusive possession of a single person or elite group of believers. Rather, all gifts, including all forms of inspired speech, come from God and God's Spirit. That Spirit, which alone searches the mind of God, is the gift of God to believers at baptism.

Conclusions

Paul does indeed provide a discussion of the idea of divine inspiration although he does not make explicit claims for the inspiration of his own writings. When Paul does consider the phenomenon of inspiration in 1 Cor 2:6-16, he describes it using the common ancient idea of the human search for the divine mind. In other words, Paul describes divine inspiration as the search for access to the thoughts of God.

This ancient idea of the search for the mind of God has not been recognized by scholarship as the proper background for reading 1 Cor 2:6-16. Such recognition has important implications for scholarship since most previous readings of this passage have insisted on locating the cultural or religious backdrop of its language in gnosticism, the mystery cults, or in Hellenistic Judaism. This investigation has shown, however, that the terms used and ideas expressed by Paul in 2:6-16 enjoyed a much broader cultural usage. A variety of writers, including Philo, Plutarch, Julian, apocalyptic authors, and even some classical Greek dramatists, all describe the human search for the divine mind. Moreover, they often utilize terms like those used by Paul, such as ἐραυνάω, βάθος, σοφία, and θεός. In doing so, these writers also consistently emphasize the need for divine assistance in order for humans to gain any access to the mind of God. This broad background provides an important lens through which to read 1 Cor 2:6-16.

In order to sharpen the focus for reading 1 Cor 2:6-16, however, it was also crucial to examine how various ancient writers described who was inspired and how so, for in this area, Paul differs significantly from most other writers in antiquity. For example, Plato provides something like an ascending scale of inspiration, at the top of which is the philosopher whose mind is optimized or maximized by a μανία in order to understand deeper matters. Plutarch describes the inspiration of the priestess at Delphi as having her mind completely displaced by the divine. Philo depicts the human νοῦς as it mystically ascends to the divine realm before ultimately being thwarted as the divine prevents any complete human access or comprehension. In all of these examples, as well as in others, the human mind, its will, and its consciousness are either completely disengaged/displaced or only partially active. Moreover, most of these writers provide essentially only for the inspiration of the individual who seeks the divine mind largely for his/her own benefit or for the benefit of a select few. Finally, many of these descriptions are highly theoretical.

In contrast, Paul uses this common ancient idea of inspiration as the search for the divine mind in order to modify the behavior and attitudes of the Corinthian congregation. In fact, Paul uses it to shame the Corinthians for their divisive behavior. In keeping with the overarching themes of 1 Corinthians (to combat factionalism and to encourage unity), Paul deploys the idea of inspiration in 2:6-16 in order to counter some among the Corinthians who were claiming a unique inspiration and an exclusive access to the mind of God. Paul counters such claims in 2:6-16 with his argument that it is a common Christian search not a solely individual one. Moreover, the Spirit of God mediates that search for the Spirit alone searches the mind of God. As the rest of the letter demonstrates, the goal of that inspiration is to build up the community rather than to divide it. In other words, the Spirit is active in the community not just in individuals, the Spirit inspires all believers but in diverse ways, and since inspiration is a gift of the Spirit, no one has grounds for boasting about superior inspiration.

In making this argument in 2:6-16, Paul includes all Christians in the "we" who speak a wisdom (2:6), rather than just himself or some select few. These "we" are those who have received the Spirit that is from God (2:12), those who speak of these things in words taught by the Spirit (2:13), and those who have the mind of Christ (2:16). All Christians are πνευματικοί and τέλειοι by virtue of their reception of the Spirit at baptism. In addition, the claim to have the "mind (νοῦς) of Christ" clearly locates inspiration in the active, conscious human νοῦς and explicitly links inspiration to the concrete reality of the Corinthians' behavior. Here divine inspiration can be, and often is, a wholly rational, nonecstatic process, although Paul can also allow for the ecstatic inspiration that is central to speaking in tongues. Paul's point is that inspiration is designed both to unify and to edify the community. Therefore, the "mind of Christ" designates an ethic of communal ἀγάπη and its corresponding behavior rather than some body of ethereal tenets or heady Christ-like thoughts.

Furthermore, in 1 Cor 2:6-16, Paul elaborates on the idea of σοφία, an idea that he seemingly has denigrated in 1 Cor 1:18-2:5. Christians do possess their own unique σοφία, but it is a wisdom of God not of this world. Christian σοφία is grounded in the revelatory action of the Spirit and is focused on the cross of Christ. Further, this σοφία is the unique possession of the πνευματικοί; it cannot be comprehended by this world or by the rulers of this world. In this way, Paul employs an apocalyptic schema to exhort the Corinthians to unity in a hostile, unbelieving world. Thus, the Corinthians are to cease their divisive, this-worldly ways in order to reflect their proper status as the people of God. Paul's sarcastic argument in 3:1-4 serves to apply these ideas, first set forth in 2:6-16, directly to the Corinthian situation itself. Although the Corinthians are πνευματικοί, their factional behavior betrays the viewpoint of νήπιοι.

Finally, Paul describes the articulation of inspired knowledge to others within the community. Paul provides for a variety of inspired speech forms, and in 1 Corinthians, he consistently uses λαλέω to describe intra-Christian community speech in contrast to other speech. He distinguishes between his apostolic preaching and proclamation (usually designated by κηρύσσω or καταγγέλλω), which leads nonbelievers to conversion, and intracommunity speech. Inspired Christian speech includes not only prophecy and speaking in tongues but also prayer, teaching, singing, revelation, and simple confessions like those uttered at baptism. The discussions in 1 Corinthians 12 and 14 develop in considerable detail the communication of and by the inspired that is set forth in 2:6-16.

Thus, my reading of 1 Cor 2:6-16 emphasizes Paul's call for the end of factionalism using the fact that all Christians have access to the mind of God and to inspiration. Moreover, 1 Cor 2:6-16 lays the foundation for much of the letter to follow, particularly in 3:1-4 and chapters 12–14. Inspiration is part and parcel of Christian existence rather than grounds for human boasting. Inspiration in 1 Corinthians, then, has an important corporate dimension absent in most of the other ancient writers' texts examined here. Paul also differs from many of these other ancient writers since he provides for the validity of rational, nonecstatic inspiration, the priority of ἀγάπη and οἰκοδομή, and a missional aspect of corporate behavior. Paul simply insists that inspired manifestations of the

Spirit, including the variety of inspired speech forms, are to be exercised *in* and *for* the community.

God's Spirit alone searches the mind of God and reveals that mind to the believing community. This crucial role of the Spirit only serves to underscore how Paul takes a common ancient idea and modifies it to his purposes as he addresses a Christian community and seeks to modify its behavior. Other writers have no entity comparable to Paul's Spirit of God involved in their own descriptions of inspiration. Paul would say that this is the case because the Spirit is the sole possession of the believing, baptized πνευματικοί and τέλειοι.

These issues are important ones for the modern American church because much of what Paul says here has been lost with the rise to dominance of clericalism,[1] the exclusive claims of inspiration and access to the divine mind made by many pentecostal movements, and the general skepticism that pervades many mainline Protestant denominations when the subject of the activity of the Spirit arises. Paul's words remind the reader that all Christians possess the Spirit, and the Spirit alone searches and knows the mind of God. Such knowledge is the Spirit's to dispense. Likewise, the gifts of ministry(ies) are within the sole jurisdiction of the Spirit. Any exclusive claims to access to the Spirit and any hoarding of tasks or roles within the church are both countered in 1 Cor 2:6-16 and in the letter as a whole. "We have the mind of Christ," and "We speak a wisdom among the perfect," because *we all* have received the Spirit of God.

---

[1]For more on this idea, see David L. Bartlett, *Ministry in the New Testament*, Overtures to Biblical Theology (Minneapolis: Fortress, 1993). In his chapter 2, Bartlett looks at the Pauline view of ministry, particularly as it is expressed in the image of the body of Christ.

Bibliography

Reference Works

Bauer, W. A. *Greek-English Lexicon of the New Testament and Other Early Christian Literature.* Translated and revised by W. F. Arndt, F. W. Gingrich, and F. W. Danker. Second edition. Chicago: University of Chicago Press, 1979.

Blass, F. and A. Debrunner. *A Greek Gramar of the New Testament and Other Early Christian Literature.* Translated and revised by R. W. Funk. Chicago: University of Chicago Press, 1961.

Donlan, Walter. *The Classical World Bibliography of Philosophy, Religion, and Rhetoric.* New York: Garland, 1978.

Hammond, N. G. L. and H. H. Scullard. *The Oxford Classical Dictionary.* Oxford: Clarendon, 1970.

Kittel, G., editor *Theological Dictionary of the New Testament.* 10 volumes. Translated by G. W. Bromiley. Grand Rapids: Eerdmans, 1964–1976.

Lampe, G. W. H. *A Patristic Greek Lexicon.* Oxford: Clarendon Press, 1961.

Metzger, Bruce. *A Textual Commentary on the Greek New Testament.* London: United Bible Societies, 1971.

Smyth, H. W. *Greek Grammar.* Cambridge MA: Harvard University Press, 1920; reprint 1980.

Ancient Sources: Texts, Editions, and Translations

Aeschylus. 2 volumes. Translated by H. W. Smyth. LCL. Cambridge MA: Harvard University Press, 1922-26.

The Apostolic Fathers. 2 volumes. Translated by K. Lake. LCL. New York: Putnam, 1912–1913.

Aristides: Orations. Volume 1. Translated by C. A. Behr. LCL. Cambridge MA: Harvard University Press, 1973.

Aristotle. 23 volumes. Translated by H. P. Cooke, H. Tredenick, et al. LCL. Cambridge MA: Harvard University Press, 1938-1960.

"Ascension of Isaiah." Translated by Michael A. Knibb. In *The Old Testament Pseudepigrapha*. 2 volumes. Edited by James H. Charlesworth. Garden City NY: Doubleday & Company, Inc., 1985. 2:143-76.

Athenagoras: Legatio and De Resurrectione. Edited by William R. Schoedel. Oxford: Clarendon Press, 1972.

Attic Nights of Aulus Gellius. 3 volumes. Translated by John C. Rolfe. LCL. Cambridge MA: Harvard University Press, 1927.

"2 Baruch." Translated by A. F. J. Klijn. In *The Old Testament Pseudepigrapha*. 2 volumes. Edited by James H. Charlesworth. Garden City NY: Doubleday & Company, Inc., 1983. 1:615-52.

John Chrysostom. *Hom. I-XLIV in I Cor*. Migne, PG 61.9-382.

Cicero. 28 volumes. Translated by G. L. Hendrickson, H. M. Hubbell, *et al*. LCL. Cambridge MA: Harvard University Press, 1912–1972.

Clemens Alexandrinus. Edited by Otto Stählin, L. Früchtel, and U. Treu. Volume 2, third edition, and volume 3, second edition. GCS. Berlin: Akademie-Verlag 2: 1960; 3:1970.

_____. Translated by G. W. Butterworth. LCL. New York: Putnam, 1919.

_____. *Stromateis*. Migne, PG 8.685-1382.

The Cynic Epistles. Edited by Abraham J. Malherbe. SBLDS 12. Missoula MT: Scholars Press, 1977.

Cyril of Alexandria. *Explanatio in I Cor*. Migne, PG 74.855-916.

Dio Chrysostom. 5 volumes. Translated by J. W. Cohoon and H. L. Crosby. LCL. Cambridge MA: Harvard University Press, 1932-51.

Diogenes Laertius. 2 volumes. Translated by R. D. Hicks. LCL. Cambridge MA: Harvard University Press, 1925.

Dionysius of Halicarnassus: Roman Antiquities. 7 volumes. Translated by E. Cary, on the basis of E. Spelman's translation. LCL. Cambridge MA: Harvard University Press, 1937–1950.

"1 Enoch." Translated by E. Isaac. In *The Old Testament Pseudepigrapha*. 2 volumes. Edited by James H. Charlesworth. Garden City NY: Doubleday & Company, Inc., 1983. 1.5-90.

"2 Enoch." Translated by F. I. Andersen. In *The Old Testament Pseudepigrapha*. 2 volumes. Edited by James H. Charlesworth. Garden City NY: Doubleday & Company, Inc., 1983. 1. 91-222.

Epictetus. 2 volumes. Translated by W. A. Oldfather. Cambridge MA: Harvard University Press, 1925–1928.

Euripides. 4 volumes. Translated by A. S. Way. LCL. New York: Putnam, 1912.

4 Ezra. Translated by Michael Stone. Hermeneia. Minneapolis: Augsburg, 1990.

The Greek Magical Papyri in Translation. Edited by Hans Dieter Betz. Second edition. Chicago: University of Chicago Press, 1992.

Herodotus. 4 volumes. Translated by A. D. Godley. LCL. Cambridge MA: Harvard University Press, 1920.

The Hymns of Qumran: Translation and Commentary. Edited by Bonnie Pedrotti Kittel. SBLDS 50. Chico CA: Scholars Press, 1981.

Iamblichus. *On the Mysteries*. Translated by Thomas Taylor. Chiswick: C. Whittingham, 1821.

Iamblichus: On the Pythagorean Way of Life: Text, Translation, and Notes. Edited by John Dillon and Jackson Hershbell. Atlanta: Scholars Press, 1991.

Irenaeus. *Against Heresies*. ANF. 1.309-567.

Testament of Job. Translated by R. P. Spittler. in *OT Pseudepigrapha*. 1. 829-68.

Josephus. 9 volumes. Translated by H. St. J. Thackeray, R. Marcus, and L. Feldman. LCL. Cambridge MA: Harvard University Press, 1956–1965.

Julian. 3 volumes. Translated by W. C. Wright. LCL. Cambridge MA: Harvard University Press, 1913–1923.

Justin. *Apologies*. ANF. 1.159-93.

Livy. 14 volumes. Translated by B. D. Foster *et al*. LCL. Cambridge MA: Harvard University Press, 1919–1959.

"Longinus." *On the Sublime*. Edited by D. A. Russell. Oxford: Clarendon, 1964.

Lucan. *The Civil War*. Translated by J. D. Duff. LCL. Cambridge MA: Harvard University Press, 1928.

Lucian. 8 volumes. Translated by A. M. Harmon. K. Kilburn, and M. D. Macleod. LCL. Cambridge MA: Harvard University Press, 1913–1967.

The Communings with Himself of Marcus Aurelius Antoninus, Emperor of Rome. Translated by C. R. Haines. LCL. Cambridge MA: 1916.

Novum Testamentum Graece. 26th edition. Revised and edited by K. Aland et al. Stuttgart: Deutsche Bibelstiftung, 1979; 1983.

The Old Testament Pseudepigrapha. Edited by James H. Charlesworth. 2 volumes. Garden City, NY: Doubleday, 1983, 1985.

Origen. *Origène. Contre Celse*. Edited by M. Borret. SC 132, 136, 147, 150. Paris: Cerf, 1967–1969.

_____. *Fragmenta ex commentariis in 1 Cor.* Edited by Claude Jenkins. "Documents: Origen on 1 Corinthians." *JTS* 9 (1907–1908): 232-47, 353-72, 500-14; *JTS* 10 (1909–1910): 29-51.

_____. *The Philocalia of Origen.* Edited by J. Armitage Robinson. Cambridge: University Press, 1893.

Papyri Graecae Magicae. Edited by Karl Preisendanz. Second edition. 2 volumes. Stuttgart: Teubner, 1973–1974.

Philo. 12 volumes. Translated by F. H. Colson, G. H. Whitaker, *et al.* LCL. Cambridge MA: Harvard University Press, 1929–1953.

Pindar. Translated by Sir John Sandys. LCL. Cambridge MA: Harvard University Press, 1915.

Plato. 12 volumes. Translated by H. N. Fowler, W. R. M. Lamb, *et al.* LCL. Cambridge MA: Harvard University Press, 1914–1935.

Plutarch's Moralia. 15 volumes. Translated by F. C. Babbitt, W. Helmbold, et al. LCL. Cambridge MA: Harvard University Press, 1927–1969.

A Part of the Works of Porphyry. The Life of Pythagoras. Edited by Amos Hulen. Private, 1973.

Pseudo-Philo. Liber Antiquitatum Biblicarum. Edited by Guido Kisch. Publications in Medieval Studies 10. Notre Dame IN: Notre Dame Press, 1949.

Saloustios: Des Dieux et du Monde. Edited by Gabriel Rochefort. Paris: Société D'Édition (Les Belles Lettres), 1960.

Secundus the Silent Philosopher: The Greek Life of Secundus. Edited by Ben Edwin Perry. Philosophical Monographs 22. Ithaca, New York: Cornell University Press, 1964.

Seneca Epistulae Morales. 3 volumes. Translated by Richard M. Gummere. LCL. Cambridge MA: Harvard University Press, 1917–1925.

Septuaginta. Edited by Alfred Rahlfs. 2 volumes. Stuttgart: Würtembergische Bibelanstalt, 1935.

Sophocles. 2 volumes. Translated by F. Storr. Cambridge MA: Harvard University Press, 1912–1913.

Strabo: Geography. 8 volumes. Translated by H. L. Jones. Cambridge MA: Harvard University Press, 1917–1932.

Thucydides. 4 volumes. Translated by C. F. Smith. LCL. Cambridge MA: Harvard University Press, 1919–1923.

Xenophon. 7 volumes. Translated by C. L. Brownson, O. J. Todd, et al. LCL. Cambridge MA: Harvard University Press, 1918–1925.

Secondary Literature Cited

Allison, Dale. "The Pauline Epistles and the Synoptic Gospels: The Pattern of the Parallels." *NTS* 28 (1982): 1-32.

Allison, Robert W. "Let Women Be Silent in the Churches (1 Cor 14:33b-36): What Did Paul Really Say, and What Did It Mean?" *JSNT* 32 (1988): 27-60.

Armstrong, A. H. "The Way and the Ways: Religious Tolerance and Intolerance in the 4th Century A.D." *Vigiliae Christianae* 38 (1984): 1-17.

Athanassiadi-Fowden, Polymnia. *Julian and Hellenism: An Intellectual Biography*. Oxford: Clarendon Press, 1981.

Attridge, Harold W. *First Century Cynicism in the Epistles of Heraclitus*. Harvard Theological Studies 29. Missoula MT: Scholars Press, 1976.

Aune, David E. *Prophecy in Early Christianity and the Ancient Mediterranean World*. Grand Rapids: Eerdmans, 1983.

_____. "The Use of προφήτης in Josephus." *JBL* 101 (1982): 419-21.

Balch, David; Ferguson, Everett; and Meeks, Wayne, eds. *Greeks, Romans, and Christians: Essays in Honor of Abraham J. Malherbe*. Philadelphia: Fortress, 1991.

Barrett, C. K. *The First Epistle to the Corinthians*. HNTC. New York: Harper and Row, 1968.

Barrow, R. H. *Plutarch and His Times*. Bloomington IN: Indiana University Press, 1967.

Barth, Karl. *The Resurrection of the Dead*. Translated by H. J. Stenning. New York: Revell, 1933. Repr. New York: Arno, 1977.

Bartlett, David L. *Ministry in the New Testament*. Overtures to Biblical Theology. Mineapolis: Fortress, 1993.

Barton, John. *Oracles of God: Perceptions of Ancient Prophecy in Israel after the Exile*. London: Darton, Longman, and Todd, 1986.

Barton, Stephen C. "Paul's Sense of Place: An Anthropological Approach to Community Formation in Corinth." *NTS* 32 (1986): 225-46.

Bassler, Jouette M. "1 Cor 12:3: Curse and Confession in Context." *JBL* 101 (1982): 415-18.

Berger, Klaus. "Zur Diskussion über die Herkunft von 1 Kor 2:9." *NTS* 24 (1978): 270-83.

Betz, Hans Dieter, Edited by *Plutarch's Theological Writings and Early Christian Literature*. SCHNT 3. Leiden: Brill, 1975.

Billerbeck, Margarethe. *Epiktet: Vom Kynismus*. Leiden: Brill, 1978.

Bjerkelund, C. J., *Parakalô: Form, Funktion, und Sinn der parakalô- Sätze in den paulinischen Briefen*. Bibliotheca Theologica Norvegica 1. Oslo Universitetsforlaget, 1967.

Blenkinsopp, Joseph. "Prophecy and Priesthood in Josephus." *JJS* 25 (1974): 239-62.

Boas, George. "Ancient Testimony to Secret Doctrines." *Philosophical Review* 62 (1953): 79-92.

Bourguignon, Erika. "The Self, the Behavioral Environment, and the Theory of Spirit Possession." Edited by Melford E. Spiro. *Context and Meaning in Cultural Anthropology: In Honor of A. Irving Hallowell*. New York: Free Press, 1965. 39-60.

Bousset, Wilhelm. *Der Erste Brief an die Korinther*. Die Schrifte des Neuen Testaments 2, 3rd edition Edited by W. Bousset and W. Heitmüller. Göttingen: Vandenhoeck und Ruprecht, 1917.

Bowersock, Glen Warren. *Julian the Apostate*. Cambridge MA: Harvard University Press, 1978.

Brenk, Frederick E. "From Mysticism to Mysticism: The Religious Development of Plutarch of Chaironeia." *SBL Seminar Papers*. Volume 1. Edited by George MacRae. Missoula MT: Scholars Press, 1975. 193-98.

Browning, Robert. *The Emperor Julian*. London: Weidenfeld and Nicolson, 1975.

Buechner, W. "Über den Begriff der *Eironeia*." *Hermes* 76 (1941): 339-58.

Bultmann, Rudolf. *Faith and Understanding*. Volume 1. Translated by L. P. Smith. New York: Harper and Row, 1969.

Bünker, Michael. *Briefformular und rhetorische Disposition im 1. Korintherbrief*. Göttinger Theologische Arbeiten 28. Göttingen: Vandenhoeck und Ruprecht, 1983.

Callan, Terrence. "Prophecy and Ecstasy in Greco-Roman Religion and in 1 Corinthians." *NovT* 27 (1985): 125-40.

Canter, H. V. "Irony in the Orations of Cicero." *AJPh* 57 (1936): 457-64.

Clark-Wire, Antoinette. *The Corinthian Women Prophets: A Reconstruction through Paul's Rhetoric*. Minneapolis: Fortress, 1990.

Cohen, Shaye J. D. *Josephus in Galilee and Rome: His Vita and Development as a Historian*. Leiden: Brill, 1979.

Conzelmann, Hans. *1 Corinthians*. Hermeneia. Translated by J. W. Leitch. Philadelphia: Fortress, 1975.

Crone, Theodore M. *Early Christian Prophecy: A Study of its Origin and Function*. Baltimore: St. Mary's University Press, 1973.

Dahl, Nils A. "Paul and the Church at Corinth According to 1 Corinthians 1:10–4:21." *Studies in Paul*. Minneapolis: Augsburg, 1977. 40-61.

Daube, David. "Typology in Josephus." *JJS* 31 (1980): 18-36.

Dautzenberg, Gerhard. "Botschaft und Bedeutung der urchristlichen Prophetie nach dem ersten Korintherbrief (2:6-16; 12–14)." *Prophetic Vocation in New Testament and Today*. Edited by Johannes Panago-poulos. NovTSup 45. Leiden: Brill, 1977. 131-61.

_____. *Urchristliche Prophetie: Ihre Erforschung, ihre Voraussetzungen im Judentum und ihre Struktur im ersten Korintherbrief.* BWANT 104, Stuttgart: Kohlhammer, 1975.

Davis, James A. *Wisdom and Spirit: An Investigation of 1 Corinthians 1:18–3:20 Against the Background of Jewish Sapiential Traditions in the Greco-Roman Period*, Lanham, New York, and London: University Press of America, 1984 .

Deissner, Kurt. "Das Sendungsbewußtsein der Urchristenheit." *ZSTh* 7 (1930): 772-90.

Delling, Gerhard. "ἐρευνάω." *TDNT*, 10 volumes. Edited by Gerhard Kittel and Gerhard Friedrich. Translated and edited by Geoffrey W. Bromiley. Grand Rapids: Eerdmans, 1964–1976. 2:655-57.

Dillon, John. *The Middle Platonists: A Study of Platonism 80 BC–AD 220*. London: Duckworth, 1977.

Dodds, E. R. *The Greeks and the Irrational*. Berkeley CA: University of California Press, 1951.

Duke, Paul D. *Irony in the Fourth Gospel*. Atlanta: John Knox Press, 1985.

Dungan, David L. *The Sayings in the Churches of Paul: The Use of the Synoptic Tradition in the Regulation of Early Church Life*. Philadelphia: Fortress, 1971.

Dunn, James D. G. *Jesus and the Spirit*. London: SCM Press, 1975.

DuPlessis, Paul Johannes. *Teleios: The Idea of Perfection in the New Testament*. Kampen: J. H. Kok, 1959.

Fascher, Erich. Προφήτης: *Eine sprach- und religionsgeschichtliche Unter-suchung*. 1927.

Fee, Gordon. *The First Epistle to the Corinthians*. NIC. Grand Rapids: Eerdmans, 1987.

Feldman, Louis. *Josephus and Modern Scholarship (1937–1980)*. Berlin: DeGruyter, 1984.

_____. "Prophets and Prophecy in Josephus." *JTS* 41 (1990): 386-422.

Festugière, O.P., A. M. J. *La révélation d'Hermes Trismégiste, IV (Le Dieu inconnu et la gnose)*. Paris: Gabalda, 1954.

Fiore, Benjamin J. " 'Covert Allusion' in 1 Corinthians 1–4." *CBQ* 47 (1985): 85-102.

_____. *The Function of Personal Example in the Socratic and Pastoral Epistles*. Analecta Biblica 105. Rome: Biblical Institute, 1986.

_____. "Passion in Paul and Plutarch: 1 Corinthians 5–6 and the Polemic Against Epicureans." *Greeks, Romans, and Christians: Essays in Honor of Abraham J. Malherbe*. Edited by David Balch, Everett Ferguson, and Wayne Meeks. Philadelphia: Fortress, 1991. 135-43.

Fiorenza, Elisabeth Schüssler. *In Memory of Her: A Feminist Theological Reconstruction of Christian Origins*. New York: Crossroads, 1983.

Fitzgerald, John T. *Cracks in an Earthen Vessel: An Examination of the Catalogues of Hardships in the Corinthian Correspondence*. SBLDS 99. Atlanta: Scholars Press, 1988.

Fontenrose, Joseph E. *The Delphic Oracle, Its Responses, and Operations*. Berkeley: University of California Press, 1978.

_____. "Oracle." *Oxford Classical Dictionary*. Edited by H. H. Scullard and N. Hammond. Oxford: Clarendon Press, 1970. 754.

Forbes, Christopher. "Early Christian Inspired Speech and Hellenistic Popular Religion." *NovTest* 28 (1986): 257-70.

_____. "Comparison, Self-Praise, and Irony: Paul's Boasting and the Conventions of Hellenistic Rhetoric." *NTS* 32 (1986): 1-30.

Francis, James. " 'As Babes in Christ'—Some Proposals Regarding 1 Corinthians 3:1-3." *JSNT* 7 (1980): 41-60.

Funk, Robert W. "Word and Word in 1 Corinthians 2:6-16." *Language, Hermeneutic, and the Word of God: The Problem of Language in the New Testament and Contemporary Theology*. New York: Harper and Row, 1966. 275-305.

Georgi, Dieter. *The Opponents of Paul in 2nd Corinthians*. Philadelphia: Fortress, 1986.

Gillespie, Thomas W. "Interpreting the Keygma: Early Christian Prophecy According to 1 Corinthians 2:6-16." *Gospel Origins and Christian Beginnings: Essays in Honor of James M. Robinson*. Edited by J. Goehring, C. Hedrick, J. Sanders, H. Betz. Sonoma: Polebridge, 1990. 151-66.

_____. "A Pattern of Prophetic Speech in First Corinthians." *JBL* 7 (1985): 74-95.

Goodenough, Erwin R. *The Politics of Philo Judaeus: Practice and Theory*. New Haven: Yale, 1938.

Grant, Robert M. *The Letter and the Spirit*. London: SPCK, 1957.

Gray, Rebecca. *Prophetic Figures in Late 2nd Temple Jewish Palestine: The Evidence from Josephus*. New York: Oxford University Press, 1993.

Gregory, Timothy E. "Julian and the Last Oracle at Delphi." *Greek, Roman, and Byzantine Studies* 24 (1983): 355-66.

Grudem, Wayne. *The Gift of Prophecy in 1 Corinthians*. Washington: University Press of America, 1982.

Grundmann, Walter. "δέχομαι." *TDNT*, 10 volumes. Edited by Gerhard Kittel and Gerhard Friedrich. Translated and edited by Geoffrey W. Bromiley. Grand Rapids: Eerdmans, 1964–1976. 2:50-54.

Hauck, Robert J. *The More Divine Proof: Prophecy and Inspiration in Celsus and Origen*. AAR Series 69. Atlanta: Scholars Press, 1989.

Haury, Auguste. *L'ironie et l'humour chez Cicéron*. Leiden: Brill, 1955.

Hecht, Richard. "Scripture and Commentary in Philo." *SBL Seminar Papers 1981*. Edited by K. Richards. Chico CA: Scholars Press, 1981. 129-64.

Hill, David. "Christian Prophets as Teachers or Instructors in the Church." *Prophetic Vocation in New Testament and Today*. Edited by Johannes Panagopoulos. NovTSup 45, Leiden: Brill, 1977. 108-30.

_____. "On the Evidence for the Creative Role of Christian Prophets." *NTS* 20 (1974): 262-74.

Hofius, Ottfried. "Das Zitat 1 Kor 2:9 und das koptische Testament des Jakobs." *ZNW* 66 (1975): 140-42.

Holladay, Carl R. "1 Corinthians 13: Paul as Apostolic Paradigm." *Greeks, Romans, and Christians: Essays in Honor of Abraham J. Malherbe*. Edited by David L. Balch, Everett Ferguson, and Wayne Meeks. Minneapolis: Fortress, 1990. 80-98.

Horsley, Richard A. "'How Can Some of You Say That There Is No Resurrection of the Dead?' Spiritual Elitism in Corinth." *NovT* 20 (1978): 203-31.

_____. "Like One of the Prophets of Old: Two Types of Popular Prophets at the Time of Jesus." *CBQ* 47 (1985): 435-63.

_____. "Wisdom of Word and Words of Wisdom in Corinth." *CBQ* 39 (1977): 224-39.

Hurd, John C. *The Origin of First Corinthians*. Second edition. Macon GA: Mercer University Press, 1983.

Jeremias, Joachim. "Ὅμως (1 Cor 14,7; Gal 3,15)." *ZNW* 52 (1961): 127-28.

Jewett, Robert. *Paul's Anthropological Terms: A Study of Their Use in Conflict Settings*. AGJU 10. Leiden: Brill, 1971.

Johannson, Nils. "1 Cor 13 and 1 Cor 14." *NTS* 10 (1964): 383-92.

Johanson, B. C. "Tongues, A Sign for Unbelievers?: A Structural and Exegetical Study of 1 Corinthians 14:20-25." *NTS* 25 (1979): 180-203.

Johnson, Luke T. "Norms for True and False Prophecy." *American Benedictine Review* 22 (1971): 29-45.

Keck, Leander. "Images of Paul in the New Testament." *Interpretation* 43 (1989): 341-51.

Kelly, Robert A. "Luther's Use of 1 Corinthians 14." *Church Word and Spirit: Historical and Theological Essays in Honor of Geoffrey W. Bromiley*. Edited by James Bradley and Richard Muller. Grand Rapids: Eerdmans, 1987. 123-34.

Kennedy, George A. *The Art of Rhetoric in the Roman World: 300 BC–AD 300*. Princeton NJ: Princeton University Press, 1972.

Klein, Richard, editor *Julian Apostata*. Wege der Forschung; Bd 509. Darmstadt: Wissenschaftliche Buchgesellschaft, 1978.

Knox, Wilfred Lawrence. *St. Paul and the Church of the Gentiles*. Cambridge: Cambridge University Press, 1939.

Kovacs, Judith L. "The Archons, the Spirit, and the Death of Christ: Do We Need the Hypothesis of Gnostic Opponents to Explain 1 Corinthians 2:6-16?" *Apocalyptic and the New Testament*. Edited by J. Marcus and M. Soards. Sheffield: JSOT, 1989. 217-36.

Kuck, David W. *Judgment and Community Conflict: Paul's Use of Apocalyptic Judgment Language in 1 Corinthians 3:5-4:5*. Leiden: Brill, 1992.

Lewy, Hans. *Sobria Ebrietas: Untersuchungen zur Geschichte der Antiken Mystik*. BZNW 9. Giessen: Töpelmann, 1929.

Lindner, Helgo. *Die Geschichtsauffasung des Flavius Josephus in Bellum Judaicum: Gleichzeiting ein Beitrag zur Quellenfrage*. Leiden: Brill, 1972.

Lührmann, Dieter. *Das Offenbarungsvergsverständnis bei Paulus und in paulinischen Gemeinden*. WMANT 16. Neukirchen-Vluyn: Neukirchener Verlag des Erziehungsvereins, 1965.

Lyons, George. *Pauline Autobiography: Toward a New Understanding*. SBLDS. Atlanta: Scholars Press, 1985.

Mack, Burton L. "Under the Shadow of Moses: Authorship and Authority in Hellenistic Judaism." *SBL Seminar Papers, 1982*. Edited by Kent Richards. Chico CA: Scholars Press, 1982.

MacDonald, Dennis Ronald. *The Legend and the Apostle: The Battle for Paul in Story and Canon*. Philadelphia: Westminster, 1983.

Malherbe, Abraham J., editor *The Cynic Epistles: A Study Edition*. SBLSBS 12. Atlanta: Scholars Press 1977.

_____. "Cynics." *IDBS*. Nashville: Abingdon, 1976. 201-203.

_____. "Hellenistic Moralists and the New Testament." *ANRW*. 26.1. Edited by W. Haase. Berlin: DeGruyter, 1992. 267-333.

_____." 'Pastoral Care' in the Thessalonian Church." *NTS* 36 (1990): 375-91.

_____. *Paul and the Popular Philosophers*. Minneapolis: Augsburg, 1989.

Martin, Dale B. *Slavery as Salvation*. New Haven: Yale, 1990.

_____. "Tongues of Angels and Other Status Indicators." *JAAR* 59 (1991): 547-89.

McKim, Donald K., editor *The Authoritative Word: Essays on the Nature of Scripture*. Grand Rapids: Eerdmans, 1983.

Meeks, Wayne A. *The First Urban Christians: The Social World of the Apostle Paul*. New Haven: Yale, 1983.

_____. "The Image of the Androgyne: Some Uses of a Symbol in Earliest Christianity." *History of Religions* 13 (1973): 165-208.

_____. *The Origins of Christian Morality*. New Haven: Yale, 1993.

_____. "The Social Functions of Apocalyptic Language in Pauline Christianity." in *Apocalypticism in the Mediterranean World and the Near East: Proceedings of the International Colloquium on Apocalypticism, Uppsala, August 12–17, 1979* . Tübingen: J. C. B. Mohr, 1982. 687-705

Mitchell, Margaret M. *Paul and the Rhetoric of Reconciliation: An Exegetical Investigation of the Language and Composition of 1 Corinthians*. Tübingen: J. C. B. Mohr, 1991.

Moles, John. "The Career and Conversion of Dio Chrysostom." *Journal of Hellenic Studies* 98 (1978): 79-100.

Munck, Johannes. *Paul and the Salvation of Mankind*. Translated by F. Clarke. Atlanta: John Knox, 1959.

Munro, Winsome. *Authority in Paul and Peter: The Identification of a Pastoral Stratum in the Pauline Corpus and 1 Peter*. NTSMS 45. Cambridge; Cambridge University Press, 1983.

_____. "Women, Text, and the Canon: The Strange Case of 1 Corinthians 14:33-35." *BTB* 18 (1988): 26-31.

Murphy-O'Connor, Jerome. "Interpolations in 1 Corinthians." *CBQ* 48 (1986): 81-94.

Nikiprowetzky, Valentin. *Le commentaire de l'écriture chez Philon d'Alexandrie: son caractère et sa portée*. Leiden: Brill, 1977.

Odell-Scott, David W. "Let the Women Speak in Church: An Egalitarian Interpretation of 1 Cor 14:33b-36." *BTB* 13 (1983): 90-93.

Paige, Terence. "1 Corinthians 12.2: A Pagan *Pompe?*" *JSNT* 44 (1991): 57-65.

Parke, H. W. and Wormell, D. E. W. *The Delphic Oracle.* Oxford: Blackwell, 1956.

Pearson, Birger A. *The Pneumatikos-Psychikos Terminology in 1 Corinthians: A Study in the Theology of the Corinthian Opponents of Paul and Its Relation to Gnosticism.* SBLDS 12. Missoula MT: Scholars Press, 1973.

Pogoloff, Stephen M. *Logos and Sophia: The Rhetorical Situation of 1 Corinthians.* SBLDS 134. Atlanta: Scholars Press, 1992.

Ponsot, H. "D'Isaie 64:3 a la 1 Corinthiens 2:9." *RB* 90 (1983): 229-42.

Prigent, Pierre. "Ce que l'oeil n'a pas vue, 1 Kor 2:9." *ThZ* 14 (1958): 416-29.

Rajak, Tessa. *Josephus: The Historian and His Society.* London: Duckworth, 1983.

Reiling, Jannes. *Hermas and Christian Prophecy: A Study of the 11th Mandate.* NovTSup 37. Leiden: Brill, 1973.

_____. "Prophecy, the Spirit, and the Church." *Prophetic Vocation in the New Testament and Today.* Edited by Johannes Panagopoulos. NovTSupp 45. Leiden: Brill, 1977. 58-76.

_____. "Wisdom and the Spirit: An Exegesis of 1 Corinthians 2, 6-16." In *Text and Testimony: Essays in Honor of A. F. J. Klijn.* Edited by T. Baarda, A. Hilhorst, G. P. Luttikhuizer, A. S. Van der Woude. Kampen: Vitgeuers-Maatschappij J. H. Kok, 1988. 200-11.

Reitzenstein, Richard. *Hellenistic Mystery Religions: Their Basic Ideas and Significance.* Translated by J. E. Steely. Pittsburgh Theological Monographs 15. Pittsburgh: Pickwick, 1978.

Richardson, Peter and Gooch, Peter. "Logia of Jesus in 1 Corinthians." *Gospel Perspectives: The Jesus Tradition Outside the Gospel.* Edited by David Wenham. Volume 5. Sheffield: JSOT Press, 1985. 39-62.

Rogers, E. R. "Ἐποτίσθημεν Again." *NTS* (1983): 139-41.

Runia, David T. and Radice, Roberto. *Philo of Alexandria: An Annotated Bibliography 1937-86.* Leiden: Brill, 1988.

_____. *Philo of Alexandria and the Timaeus of Plato.* Leiden: Brill, 1986.

Sandnes, Karl Olav. *Paul—One of the Prophets?: A Contribution to the Apostle's Self-Understanding.* Wissenschaftliche Untersuchungen zum Neuen Testament: 2 Reihe 43. Tübingen: Mohr, 1991.

Schmithals, Walter. *Gnosticism in Corinth: An Investigation of the Letter to the Corinthians*. Translated by John Steely. Nashville: Abingdon, 1971.

Schübert, Paul. *Form and Function of the Pauline Thanksgivings*. BZNW 20. Berlin: Töpelmann, 1939.

_____. "Rhetorical Situation and Historical Reconstruction in 1 Corinthians." *NTS* 33 (1987): 386-403.

Schütz, John Howard. *Paul and the Anatomy of Apostolic Authority*. Cambridge: University Press, 1975.

Scroggs, Robin A. "Paul: Σοφὸς καὶ πνευματικός." *NTS* 14 (1967–1968): 33-55.

Senft, Christophe. *La Première Épitre de Saint-Paul aux Corinthiens*. CNT 2/7. Neuchâtel/Paris: Delachaux & Niestlé, 1979.

Stone, Michael. *4 Ezra*. Hermeneia. Minneapolis: Augsburg, 1990

Stuhlmacher, Peter. *Biblische Theologie des Neuen Testaments*. Göttingen: Vandenhoeck und Ruprecht, 1: 1992; 2: forthcoming.

_____. "The Hermeneutical Significance of 1 Cor 2:6-16." Translated by Colin Brown. *Tradition and Interpretation in the New Testament: Essays in Honor of E. E. Ellis*. Edited by Gerald F. Hawthorne and Hans Dieter Betz. Grand Rapids: Eerdmans, 1987. 328-47.

Swain, Simon. "Plutarch: Chance, Providence and History." *American Journal of Philology* 110 (1989): 272-302.

Sykutris, Johannes. *Die Briefe des Sokrates und der Sokratiker*. Studien zur Geschichte und Kultur des Altertums. Paderborn: Schöningh, 1933.

Talbert, Charles H. "Paul's Understanding of the Holy Spirit: The Evidence of 1 Corinthians 12–14." *Perspectives in Religious Studies* 11 (1984): 95-108.

Theissen, Gerd. *The Social Setting of Pauline Christianity: Essays on Corinth*. Translated by J. H. Schütz. Philadelphia: Fortress, 1982.

Vanhoye, Albert, S. J. "Nécessité de la diversité dans l'unité selon 1 Co 12 et Rom 12." Edited by Henri Cazelles, *Unité et diversité dans l'église*. Vatican City: Libreria Editrice Vaticana, 1989. 143-56

Von Nordheim, E. "Das Zitat des Paulus in 1 Kor 2:9 und seine Beziehung zum koptischen Testament Jakobs." *ZNW* 65 (1974): 112-20.

Von Rad, Gerhard. *Old Testament Theology*. 2 volumes. Translated by D. M. G. Stalker. London: Oliver and Boyd, 1962.

Weiss, Johannes. *Der Erste Korintherbrief*. MeyerK 5:9. Göttingen: Vandenhoeck und Ruprecht, 1910. Reprint 1970.

Welborn, Laurence L. "A Conciliatory Principle in 1 Cor 4:6," *NovT* 29 (1987): 320-46.

_____. "On the Discord in Corinth: 1 Corinthians 1-4 and Ancient Politics." *JBL* 106 (1987): 85-111.

Widmann, Martin. "1 Kor. 2:6-16: Ein Einspruch gegen Paulus." *ZNW* 70 (1979): 44-53.

Wilckens, Ulrich. *Weisheit und Torheit: Eine exegetische-religionsgeschichtliche Untersuchung zu 1 Kor. 1 und 2.* BHTh 26. Tübingen: Mohr, 1959.

_____. "Zu 1 Kor 2: 6-16." *Theologia Crucis–Signum Crucis, Festschrift für Erich Dinkler zum 70. Geburtstag.* Edited by Carl Andresen and Günter Klein. Tübingen: Mohr, 1979. 501-37.

Wilken, Robert L. "The Jews and Christian Apologetics after Theodosius I *Cunctos populos.* " *HTR* 73 (1980): 451-71.

Willis, Wendell. "The 'Mind of Christ' in 1 Corinthians 2,16." *Biblica* 70 (1989): 110-22.

Wilson, Robert R. "Prophecy and Ecstasy: A Reexamination." *JBL* 98 (1979): 321-37.

_____. *Prophecy and Society in Ancient Israel.* Philadelphia: Fortress, 1980.

Winston, David. *Logos and Mystical Theology in Philo of Alexandria.* Cincinnati: Hebrew Union Press, 1985.

_____. "Philo and the Contemplative Life." *Jewish Spirituality.* Edited by Arthur Green. New York: Crossroad, 1987. 198-232

_____. "Two Types of Mosaic Prophecy According to Philo." *SBL Papers 1988.* Edited by David Lull. Atlanta: Scholars Press. 442-55.

Winter, Martin. *Pneumatiker und Psychiker in Korinth: Zum religionsgeschichtlichen Hintergrund von 1 Kor 2:6–3:4.* Marburger Theologische Studien 12. Marburg: N. G. Elwert, 1975.

Wolfson, Harry A. *Philo: Foundations of Religious Philosophy in Judaism, Christianity, and Islam.* Cambridge: Harvard, 1947.

Wuellner, Wilhelm. "Paul as Pastor: The Function of Rhetorical Questions in 1 Corinthians." *L' Apôtre Paul: Personnalité, Style et Conception du Ministére.* BETL 73. Edited by Albert Vanhoye. Leuven: Leuven University Press, 1986. 46-77.

Index of Scripture Cited

Index of Subjects

wisdom (see also σοφία) 3, 4, 7,
    9, 16, 17, 19, 22, 27, 31, 33, 37,
    45, 49, 56, 63, 64, 66, 67, 69,
    75-79, 81, 82, 85, 86, 88, 91,
    93, 104, 108, 110, 111, 115,
    143-45
zeal (see also ζῆλος) 121, 140,
    144
ζῆλος (see also zeal) 13, 93, 95,
    97, 120-122, 125, 141
ζητέω (seek) 26, 27, 31, 32, 34,
    37, 39, 40, 42, 49, 59, 66, 120,
    125